KENT SERIES IN MANAGEMENT

Barnett/Wilsted, *Cases for Strategic Management*

Barnett/Wilsted, *Strategic Management: Concepts and Cases*

Barnett/Wilsted, *Strategic Management: Texts and Concepts*

Berkman/Neider, *The Human Relations of Organizations*

Carland/Carland, *Small Business Management: Tools for Success*

Crane, *Personnel: The Management of Human Resources*, Fourth Edition

Davis/Cosenza, *Business Research for Decision Making*, Second Edition

Finley, *Entrepreneurial Strategies: Text and Cases*

Kemper/Yehudai, *Experiencing Operations Management: A Walk-Through*

Kirkpatrick, *Supervision: A Situational Approach*

Mitchell, *Human Resource Management: An Economic Approach*

Nkomo/Fottler/McAfee, *Applications in Personnel/Human Resource Management: Cases, Exercises, and Skill Builders*

Plunkett/Attner, *Introduction to Management*, Third Edition

Punnett, *Experiencing International Management*

Scarpello/Ledvinka, *Personnel/Human Resource Management: Environments and Functions*

Singer, *Human Resource Management*

Starling, *The Changing Environment of Business*, Third Edition

Steers, Ungson, Mowday, *Managing Effective Organizations: An Introduction*

KENT INTERNATIONAL DIMENSIONS OF BUSINESS SERIES

Series Consulting Editor, David A. Ricks

Adler, *International Dimensions of Organizational Behavior*, Second Edition

AlHashim/Arpan, *International Dimensions of Accounting*, Second Edition

Dowling/Schuler, *International Dimensions of Human Resource Management*

Folks/Aggarwal, *International Dimensions of Financial Management*

Garland/Farmer, *International Dimensions of Business Policy and Strategy*, Second Edition

Litka, *International Dimensions of the Legal Environment of Bu:* ~~Edition~~

Phatak, *International Dimensions of Management*, Second Edi

Terpstra, *International Dimensions of Marketing*, Second Edit

KENT SERIES IN HUMAN RESOURCE MANAGEMENT

Series Consulting Editor, Richard W. Beatty

Bernardin/Kane, *Performance Appraisal*, Second Edition

Cascio, *Costing Human Resources: The Financial Impact of Behavior in Organizations*, Second Edition

Kavanagh/Gueutal/Tannenbaum, *Human Resource Information Systems: Development and Application*

Ledvinka/Scarpello, *Federal Regulation of Personnel and Human Resource Management*, Second Edition

McCaffery, *Employee Benefit Programs: A Total Compensation Perspective*

Wallace/Fay, *Compensation Theory and Practice*, Second Edition

EXPERIENCING OPERATIONS MANAGEMENT   A WALK-THROUGH

ROBERT E. KEMPER
NORTHERN ARIZONA UNIVERSITY

JOSEPH YEHUDAI
YEHUDAI CONSULTING COMPANY

PWS-KENT PUBLISHING COMPANY, BOSTON

This text recognizes a dedicated accounting professor
who taught meritiously in Northern Arizona University's
College of Business Administration for nearly 25 years.
His outstanding teaching performance is widely and
enthusiastically acclaimed among students, faculty, staff, and
administrators. Accordingly, this publication is respectfully
dedicated to the fond memory of
Larry D. Gardner.

PWS–KENT
Publishing Company

Managing Editor	Rolf A. Janke
Production Editor	Eve B. Mendelsohn
Cover Designer	Eve B. Mendelsohn
Manufacturing Coordinator	Peter Leatherwood
Text Preparation	Robert E. Kemper
Text and Cover Printer	Edwards Brothers

PWS-KENT PUBLISHING COMPANY IS A DIVISION OF WADSWORTH, INC.

Printed in the United States of America
1 2 3 4 5 6 7—94 93 92 91 90

ISBN: 0-534-92245-7

PREFACE

We wrote this book to stimulate your interest in your first course in production and operations management (OM). OM is usually a required course for the undergraduate business student that assumes a basic knowledge of principles of management (planning, organizing, leading [facilitating], and controlling), college algebra, basic business statistics, and principles of financial and managerial accounting. While this book is designed for use in all business-oriented programs, it satisfies the production and operations requirements of the AACSB (American Assembly of Collegiate Schools of Business). This book also meets the requirements of corporate training programs requiring basic knowledge in OM.

The typical introductory course in OM consists of readings from a selected textbook and associated lectures that contain the information necessary for the study of production and operations management and for the development of the functional skill base needed for a successful career in business. However, this approach provides little direct experience in operations management and allows only for passive observation of OM events.

We believe OM is best learned by active participation in the process. There must be a link between theory and practice, and the case approach found in many textbooks does not demonstrate adequately the relationships among the situation (the competitive time frame), management, and human resources.

This book contains a variety of experiences. Some are designed for the individual and some require group effort. The experiences include those that may be completed in class, those that involve limited outside work, and some that may be assigned as homework. Some experiences may be used as examinations. The instructor may choose to use all the experiences or only those that are most appropriate for a particular course and a particular group of students.

Experiencing Operations Management is different from previous OM textbooks in that it provides a framework for examining crisis-ridden U.S. industries and offers opportunities for interpretive analysis and decision making. The pedagogical structure of this book is based on the eighteen learning objectives outlined in the Instructor's Manual.

This book may be used with any current OM textbook although it is textbook-specific to six production and operations management titles. It stimulates interest in the subject by using a "real" corporation scenario. Sixteen OM tool-related chapters will enable you to understand, formulate, apply, control, and implement operations management concepts and processes. This experiential "walk through" will allow you to participate in operations management and gain an understanding of the implicit and explicit usefulness of the many OM tools that are applied in a job situation.

This approach will show you how to think about operations as a value-adding component of an organization. You will learn to consider the impact of global and international issues, competition, and ethical and human resource concerns. (Indeed, while human resource considerations are essential to effective operations management, they are often slighted in other OM textbooks.)

When you complete the operations management course, we want you to have gained the ability to organize and evaluate facts. While other textbooks often assume that OM tools are of use only to operations managers, the quantitative skills presented in this book are also needed by managers of marketing, finance, accounting, human resources, and computer information.

Finally, our book is designed to be user-friendly. With few exceptions, it can be used in conjunction with most production and operations management textbooks. We have attempted to present operations management concepts and procedures in a clear and concise way so that they may be grasped easily and quickly. Our experiential approach should help even a nontechnical reader to understand the subject. This book is organized to help you attain learning goals. The exercises follow the same structure throughout the book and their clear directions are designed to enable you to perform consistently. It is our hope that the user-friendly experiential approach provided in this book will enhance your mastery of operations management skills and prepare you to work in the multinational business environment of the future.

Robert E. Kemper
Joseph Yehudai
March 30, 1990

Acknowledgments

The key to the successful completion of any creative endeavor is good people. We surrounded ourselves with good people--family, friends, teachers, and trusted colleagues.

To the right our gracious, trusting, and devoted family members: Joyce, Daniele, Michele, Hagit, Ohad, and Tal. To the left an inspired group of colleagues that provided perspective, expertise, and technical assistance: Finn Agenbroad, Mac Bosse, Jack Dustman, Eugene Grape, Hank Hassell, Christine Hutchens, Maureen McAuliffe, Michael Todd Madrid, Mike Morano, and Michael Wunsch.

To the rear the committed people at PWS-KENT: Maureen Brooks, Anne Fitzpatrick, Rolf Janke, Peter Leatherwood, Eve Mendelsohn, Laura Mosberg, and Wanda Wilking. To the front the people who were particularly generous with their comments on and contributions to various parts of the book: Oscar Fowler (University of Tennessee), Benjamin Harrison (Salisbury State University), Bob Mingus (International Brotherhood of Electrical Workers), Rhonda Rhodes (California State Polytechnic University, Pomona), and Joel Stinson (Syracuse University).

Contents

SECTION **I**
INTRODUCTION 1

CHAPTER **1.** **Introduction to Operations Management 3**
   What Is Management? 3
   What Is Strategy? 4
   What Is a System and a Process? 4
   The OM Tool Kit 5
   An OM Model 5
    Tactical Core Operations Activities 5
    Tactical Support Operations Activities 5
    Functional Activities 5
    Strategic Activities 7
    External Environment 7
   The State of Automation 7
   Manufacturing in the United States 8
   Addressing Operations Management Decisions 8
    The Consumer Electronics Domain 9
    The ABZ Story 9
    ABZ's Plight 10

SECTION **II**
STRATEGIC ACTIVITIES 13

CHAPTER **2.** **Welcome to ABZ's New Employee Orientation 15**
   An Overview of ABZ 15
    History of ABZ Electronics 16

Mission of ABZ 16
Organizational Components 16
Plants, People, and Sales 17
Culture and Values 17
The Personal Values of CEO Kemper 19
An ABZ SWOT Analysis 19
Strengths 22
Weaknesses 22
Opportunities 22
Threats 22
Financial Analysis 22

CHAPTER **3.** **More ABZ Orientation 25**
ABZ's Competitive Environment 26
The Microcomputer Industry 26
The Consumer Electronics Industry 27
Financial Analysis of ABZ's Consumer Electronics
Competition 28
ABZ's Strategies 29
1978 29
1979 30
1980 30
1981 31
1982 32
1983 33
1984 34
1985 34
1986 35
1987 36
1988 36
Now What? 37

CHAPTER **4.** **ABZ and the International Consumer
Electronics Union (ICEU) 39**
ABZ and the Clarkstown Plant 39
Industry Changes 39
Plant Relocation 40
More Job Losses 40
The International Consumer Electronics
Union and ABZ 40
Recognition 41
Management Rights 41
Productivity and Efficiency 42
Technological Progress 42
Failure to Meet Production Standards 42
No Strike-No Lockout Guarantee 42
Five-Year Plant Operations Guarantee 42
The ICEU-ABZ Challenge 42

SECTION III
FUNCTIONAL OPERATIONS ACTIVITIES 45

CHAPTER **5.** **Functional Management Activities 47**
 Functional Management 47
 Levels of Strategy 48
  Strategic Level Strategy 48
  Functional Level Strategy 49
  Tactical Level Strategy 49
 A Functional Strategy Situation at ABZ 49
 Ethical and Cultural Considerations 51
 Listing and Description of Appropriate OM Tools 51
  Experiences 53

CHAPTER **6.** **Capacity Strategy Activities 61**
 Listing and Description of Appropriate OM Tools 62
  Financial Investment Evaluation Methods 62
  Waiting Lines 62
  Decision Trees 62
  Payoff Tables 62
  Forecasting Methods 63
  Break-Even Analysis 63
  Make-or-Buy Analysis 63
 The Functional Operations Situation at ABZ 63
  Experiences 65

CHAPTER **7.** **Location Strategy Activities 77**
 Ethical and Cultural Considerations 78
 Listing and Description of Appropriate OM Tools 79
  Forecasting 79
  Linear Programming 80
  Center of Gravity Method 80
  Factor Rating 80
  Cost Comparisons 80
  Break-Even Analysis 80
 Review of the Operations Situation at ABZ Electronics 81
  Experiences 83

CHAPTER **8.** **Product Strategy Activities 95**
 Listing and Description of Appropriate OM Tools 96
  Linear Programming 96
  Break-Even Analysis 96
  Decision Trees 96
  Payoff Tables 97
  Make-or-Buy Analysis 97
  Experiences 98

CHAPTER **9.** **Process Strategy Activities** **111**

Listing and Description of Appropriate OM Tools **112**

Financial Investment Evaluation Methods *112*
Break-Even Analysis *112*
Payoff Tables *112*
Decision Trees *112*
Process Planning Charts *113*
Experiences *114*

CHAPTER **10.** **Layout Strategy Activities** **129**

Listing and Description of Appropriate OM Tools **130**

Process Layout Analysis Techniques *130*
Systematic Layout Planning *130*
Assembly Line Balancing Heuristics *130*
Waiting Lines *131*
Experiences *131*

CHAPTER **11.** **Human Resource Strategy Activities** **147**

Ethical and Cultural Considerations **148**

The Role of Top Management *148*
Importance of a "Code" *149*
Making Ethics Work *150*
Involvement and Commitment of Personnel at All Levels *151*
Measuring Results *151*
Self-Interest, Survival, and Achievement *152*

Listing and Description of Appropriate OM Tools **152**

Work Methods Analysis *152*
Work Measurement Methods *153*
Behavioral Job Design Methods *153*
Compensation Methods *153*
Learning Curves *154*
Linear Programming *154*
Experiences *155*

SECTION **IV**
TACTICAL SUPPORT ACTIVITIES **167**

CHAPTER **12.** **Quality Assurance Activities** **169**

Listing and Description of Appropriate OM Tools **170**

Acceptance Sampling *170*
Process Control *171*
Experiences *171*

CHAPTER **13.** **Maintenance Activities 179**
　　　　　Listing and Description of Appropriate OM Tools 180
　　　　　　　Simulation 180
　　　　　　　Waiting Lines 180
　　　　　　　Financial Investment Evaluation Methods 181
　　　　　　　Preventive Maintenance Versus Breakdown Policy 181
　　　　　　　Payoff Tables 181
　　　　　　　　　Experiences 182

CHAPTER **14.** **Cost Control Activities 195**
　　　　　Listing and Description of Appropriate OM Tools 196
　　　　　　　Cost Standards 196
　　　　　　　Cost-Variance Analysis 196
　　　　　　　Value Analysis 197
　　　　　　　Standardization 197
　　　　　　　Learning Curves 197
　　　　　　　　　Experiences 198

CHAPTER **15.** **Materials Management Activities 209**
　　　　　Listing and Description of Appropriate OM Tools 210
　　　　　　　Vendor Selection Systems 210
　　　　　　　Marginal Analysis (Single-Period Inventory) 210
　　　　　　　Distribution Requirements Planning (DRP) 210
　　　　　　　Payoff Tables 211
　　　　　　　Make-or-Buy Analysis 211
　　　　　　　Linear Programming 211
　　　　　　　　　Experiences 212

CHAPTER **16.** **Advanced Manufacturing Support Activities 225**
　　　　　Listing and Description of CIM Systems and OM Tools 226
　　　　　　　Computer-Aided Design (CAD) and Computer-Aided
　　　　　　　　　Manufacturing (CAM) 226
　　　　　　　Flexible Manufacturing Systems 226
　　　　　　　Manufacturing Resource Planning (MRPII) 226
　　　　　　　Just-in-Time (JIT) Production System 227
　　　　　　　Financial Investment Evaluation Methods 227
　　　　　　　Cost-Benefit Analysis 227
　　　　　　　　　Experiences 228

CHAPTER **17.** **Project Planning and Control Activities 241**
　　　　　Listing and Description of Appropriate OM Tools 242
　　　　　　　Program Evaluation and Review Technique (PERT) 242
　　　　　　　Critical Path Method (CPM) 242
　　　　　　　　　Experiences 243

SECTION **V**
TACTICAL CORE ACTIVITIES 259

CHAPTER **18. Aggregate Planning and Master Scheduling 261**
Listing and Description of Appropriate OM Tools 262
Aggregate Planning—Trial and Error 262
Aggregate Planning—Mathematical Models 262
Rough-Cut Capacity Planning 262
Master Scheduling 263
Experiences 263

CHAPTER **19. Inventory Control/Independent Demand Activities 277**
Listing and Description of Appropriate OM Tools 278
Lot-Sizing Technique 279
Order Point, Safety Stock, and Service Level 279
Simulation 279
Experiences 280

CHAPTER **20. Resource Requirements Planning Activities 289**
Listing and Description of Appropriate OM Tools 290
Materials Requirements Planning (MRP) 290
Capacity Requirements Planning (CRP) 290
Experiences 291

CHAPTER **21. Shop Floor Control Activities 303**
Listing and Description of Appropriate OM Tools 304
Sequencing 304
Linear Programming 304
Line of Balance (LOB) 304
Input/Output Control 305
Experiences 305

SECTION **VI**
EPILOGUE 321

CHAPTER **22. An Exit Interview 323**
Experiences 324

References and Suggested Readings 335

Index 357

SECTION I

INTRODUCTION

Operation management is best learned through the practical application of theory to real-life problems in order to obtain desired results. This book's experiential activities are designed to lead you step-by-step through the operations management process and to provide opportunities to interpret and apply OM theory in the context of a realistic business situation based on an actual U.S. consumer electronics company. Experiences are structured dynamically to help you quickly learn the operations management process through the practical application of OM tools and theory. The hands-on method of problem solving should make it easier for you to understand the theories and theoretical application skills and retain them for future on-the-job use.

While working to achieve the course goals, you will become adept at applying theory to obtain the desired results. This ability is the cornerstone of a successful business career and is the link between knowledge gained in a classroom setting and the practical skills of operations management that you as a future employee will use on the job.

You will work in a simulated competitive business environment both individually and in groups of your peers toward one goal: to save the ABZ Electronics Corporation's consumer electronics division. As noted at the beginning of this section, ABZ is based on an actual company that is the last major U.S. manufacturer of television sets and equipment. Because you will apply your unique skills and knowledge to the simulation project, you will learn how to become a self-starter and a leader in the area of operations management. At the same time, you will learn how to work effectively in a group toward a common goal.

We have created a fictional company for our experiential activities. ABZ cannot be depicted as the real company on which it is based because, although most of the information you will use in the activities is real data derived from the company's public statements, all companies must and do have secrets. You, however, must have full access to and use of the full range of capabilities and options of a particular system presented in a way that can be easily understood by a nontechnical user. The concepts and procedures must be clear and concise to facilitate quick learning. Therefore, so that you may perform consistently with unambiguous directions and complete information, we have filled the gaps in the data from the real company and put you to work for the ABZ Electronics Corporation. As a result, our book is user-friendly--easy to use, easy to learn from, helpful in attaining goals, and so forth.

Yes, you can still actively solve real business problems with this structure, even though ABZ is not a real company. Only the names and some procedures have been changed. We hope that this method will keep your interest high as you proceed through the experiences in this book. Not only first-year OM students and business instructors, but lay readers of business literature, self-taught students of operations management, and any reader seeking perspectives on global competition will find *Experiencing Operations Management* a fascinating and insightful study.

The first chapter of the book introduces the discipline of operations management--the systematic direction (strategy) and control of the processes that transform resources into finished goods and services. The chapter discusses the overall role and significance of operations management; explains how operations management relates to management, systems, processes, and strategy; and introduces an operations management model.

The OM model illustrates what operations managers do and what issues are important. It shows how operations activities fit together with and among the other functions of management. It clarifies the logic behind the organization of this and other production and operations management books.

Chapter 1 also includes an extensive list of operations management tools and a discussion of levels of automation. Finally, the chapter explains how this book addresses the teaching of operations management decision making. The plight of ABZ Electronics in the global consumer electronics industry is introduced as a simulated real-life setting for operations management.

Introduction to Operations Management

Operations is a function that is vital to all business and government organizations. In America it is the foundation of the profit system. It is through the productivity of American workers and machines that a satisfactory Gross National Product (GNP)--the sum total of all tangible goods and services produced during a given period of time--is achieved. An effective and efficient operations manager is skilled in management, service, production, systems, processes, control, strategy, models, and OM tools. The narrative that follows introduces the scope and nature of operations management.

What Is Management?

Management is the process of planning, organizing, coordinating (leading), and controlling a business's financial, physical, human, ideational, and information resources in order to achieve its goals.

Production and operations management is a concept that has undergone a change in definition and meaning. Production used to refer to goods (merchandise), while operations denoted the service side of the business. Today we use the term *operations* to include both goods and services.

According to the new and expanded definition, operations management is the systematic direction (strategy) and control of the processes that transform resources into finished goods and services. Operations managers are those managers who are responsible for controlling operations, inventory, and the quality of a firm's products and services.

A *product* is a good, service, or idea that satisfies buyers' needs and demands.

Operations control is the monitoring of a firm's operations activities, comparing actual performance with planned performance, and taking corrective action where needed to bring actual and planned performance into accord.

What Is Strategy?

A *strategy* is a plan of action. We use the term *grand strategy* only when we refer to a firm that consists of several business units. These units may be divisions of the parent company or they may be self-contained business units or subsidiaries; e.g., Case International is a unit of Tenneco. A grand strategy for Tenneco would include plans of action for all units of Tenneco. It is a comprehensive, general plan of major actions that a firm implements to achieve its long-term objectives for all of its business units.

Corporate strategy is the pattern of decisions regarding the types of businesses in which a firm should be involved. It permits the flow of financial and other resources to and from its divisions. It facilitates the relationship of the corporation to key groups in its environment and defines the ways in which a corporation can increase its return on investment.

A *business strategy* is a plan of action at the divisional or single business-unit level. It emphasizes improvement of the competitive position of a corporation's products or services in the specific industry or market segment served by the unit.

Functional strategy is a set of strategic plans of action (operations, marketing, finance, research and development, and so forth) that seeks to make optimal use of company resources.

What Is a System and a Process?

A *system* is a particular linking of components that facilitates carrying out a process. The word *particular* signifies that there is more than one system that could be used to produce an item and that these systems can be different in some respects. For example, System A (the production of a Sony television set) may be different in some respects from System B (the production of a Zenith television set), although both contribute to the carrying out of similar process--producing a television set. The components of a system are its mission, goals, objectives, strategies, policies, plan, programs, procedures, rules, schedules, people, machines, and raw materials. Facilitate means that the system evolves as a way of carrying out processes. *Carrying out* means unfolding or progressive development (French, pp. 44-46).

A *process* is a flow of interrelated events moving toward a goal, purpose, or end. *Flow* is movement through time and in the direction of a consequence. *Interrelated* implies interaction among the events, which are highly relevant to one another. An *event* is a change or happening that occurs at one point in time; events may include any number or type of phenomena. A *goal* is a human objective, while *purpose* suggests either human objectives or objectives in a theoretical sense. *End* implies some conclusion or consequence that may not necessarily be sought or planned by people. Thus, a process may lead to unintended consequences (French, pp. 43-44).

The OM Tool Kit

Good managers use a variety of analytical tools. The OM tool kit includes acceptance sampling, aggregate planning, assembly line balancing, behavior job-design methods, break-even analysis, capacity requirements planning (CRP), center of gravity method, compensation methods, computer-aided design (CAD), control charts, critical path method (CPM), cost-benefit analysis, cost comparisons, cost standards, decision trees, distribution requirements planning, factor rating, financial investment evaluation methods, flexible manufacturing systems, forecasting, input/output control, layout analysis, just-in-time (JIT), learning curves load leveling, line of balance, linear programming, lot-sizing techniques, make-or-buy analysis, master scheduling, material requirements planning (MRP), MRPII, payoff tables, process layout analysis techniques, process planning charts, project evaluation and review technique (PERT), rough-cut capacity planning, simplex, simulation, waiting lines, and vendor selection systems.

Not every manager uses every tool named. Each tool, as will be explained later, is suited for a particular situation at a particular time.

Of all the tools in the manager's tool kit, the most important on any given day is the human being. The challenge for the good manager is to select the right tool at the right time in the right place.

An OM Model

Exhibit 1.1 presents a model of the major components of the operations (production) management system that is part of an overall management process/system model. The model depicts what operations managers do and what issues are important, shows how operations activities fit together among the other functions of management, and clarifies the logic behind the organization of this and other production and operations management books. In the following discussion of the model, the numbers in parentheses refer to the relevant chapters in this book.

Tactical Core Operations Activities

The inner layer of the model includes the tactical core operations activities: aggregate planning and master scheduling (18), inventory control--independent demand (19), resource requirements planning (MRP, CRP) (20), and shop and service floor control (21).

Tactical Support Operations Activities

The next layer of activities involves tactical support operations activities: quality assurance (12), maintenance (13), cost control (14), material management (15), advanced manufacturing support (16), and project planning and control (17).

Functional Activities

Marketing, finance, and operations are functional management activities. In this book we focus and provide details on operations. A marketing book would focus and provide details on marketing.

EXHIBIT 1.1 Operations Management System

Suppliers • Market • Competitors • Regulators Associations • Labor Unions • Politics • Technology Economy • Public Attitudes • Demographics • Prices

EXTERNAL ENVIRONMENT

GRAND STRATEGY

CORPORATE STRATEGY

BUSINESS STRATEGY

STRATEGIC ACTIVITIES

MARKETING • OPERATIONS • FINANCE

Capacity Strategy
Location Strategy
Product Strategy
Process Strategy
Layout Strategy
Human Resources Strategy

FUNCTIONAL ACTIVITIES

Quality Assurance   Maintenance
Material Management
Cost Control   Advanced Manufacturing Support
Project Planning & Control

TACTICAL SUPPORT ACTIVITIES

AGGREGATE PLANNING & MASTER SCHEDULING
INVENTORY CONTROL - INDEPENDENT DEMAND
RESOURCE REQUIREMENTS PLANNING (MRP - CRP)
SHOP FLOOR CONTROL

TACTICAL CORE ACTIVITIES

Operations Management System

The third layer of the model includes the functional operations activities (5): capacity strategy (6), location strategy (7), product strategy (8), process strategy (9), layout strategy (10), and human resource strategy (11).

Strategic Activities

The next layer of organizational activities involves strategic management (2, 3, and 4). The firm first determines its *mission* (what it wants to achieve), *goals* (what must be done in order to achieve the mission), and *objectives* (specific targets that state when goals are to be accomplished). Then, *strategies* (patterns that integrate the organization's major goals, policies, and action sequences into a cohesive whole), *policies* (major guidelines that express the limits within which action should occur), and *programs* (major step-by-step sequences of actions necessary to achieve major objectives) are developed.

Once the mission and related activities are determined, the firm establishes a set of hierarchial strategies--grand, corporate, and business.

External Environment

Finally, the outer layer of the model represents the *external environment*, which consists of all outside influences on the organization: suppliers, markets, competitors, regulators, associations, labor unions, public attitudes, technology, economic conditions, politics, demographics, and prices. These influences are discussed throughout the book.

The State of Automation

There are five levels of automation found in existing business firms (Port, pp. 142-148).

Level 1. Firms attempt to make optimal use of company resources without additional or updated automation. They do this by simplifying manufacturing procedures and reorganizing the shop or service floor. Asian countries generally excel at this level. Companies in the United States have adopted such techniques but have had difficulty with implementation. Western European companies lag behind both Asian and U.S. companies.

Level 2. Firms at the second level use robots, computers, OM tools, advanced shop-floor systems, and flexible manufacturing processes to perform repetitive, menial work in specific areas. These resources are used widely in Japan and the United States. The Japanese companies are the leaders. European countries lag far behind the United States and Japan.

Level 3. Firms at the third level use shared hierarchical or object-oriented computer data bases to link specific automated areas to one another and to computer-aided design techniques. Many U.S. manufacturers have implemented this automation step, but these techniques have been most widely adopted by non-unionized smaller companies. Japanese companies are slightly ahead of U.S. companies at this level, while the European companies lag far behind.

Level 4. Firms automate the complex steps of production scheduling and diagnostics through the use of artificial computer intelligence, computer-aided design, and object-oriented computer software. U.S. companies are the most progressive in implementing these techniques. Few Japanese companies have adopted these techniques, but those that have are more effective than the U.S. companies.

Level 5. Firms create a computer-integrated enterprise where everything from product planning to customer service is determined by expanded artificial intelligence (AI) and object-oriented techniques. This factory of the future remains beyond the capabilities of most companies, but consultants paint a rosy picture of an environment where new computer-designed products zip from computer terminal to machines on the factory floor and production lines switch at a moment's notice from making television sets to making personal computers.

The goals of new automation are reduced inventories, higher productivity, and faster billing and product distribution cycles. The Asian countries appear to be doing the best job of making optimal use of company resources through automation.

Manufacturing in the United States

How are U.S. manufacturers coping given the nature of today's influences from suppliers, markets, competition, regulations, associations, labor unions, public attitudes, technology, economics, politics, culture, ethics, demographics, and prices?

The position of the United States in the world economy is weakening. U.S. manufacturers no longer dominate domestic and international markets, and America can no longer rest comfortably in the belief that it will continue to be the leading economic power in the world. Business organizations need to have a global perspective if they are to survive.

Manufacturing productivity in the United States is no longer soaring. The quality of U.S. manufactured products is being matched by Asian and European manufacturers. U.S. products do not get to market quickly and new technologies have not cut costs dramatically. As a result, U.S. manufacturers have been priced out of most markets. At the same time, there has been a decrease in the availability of individuals with expertise in operations management.

Addressing Operations Management Decisions

Universities have responded to the manufacturing situation in the U.S. by emphasizing the service sector of the economy through classroom lectures. When the operations side is addressed, it is often difficult for business students to appreciate the practical implications of operations management decisions in the classroom. The purpose of this book is to give students an opportunity to address operations management decisions in a simulated real-life setting. Additionally, to make sure that the practical implications of operations management are appreciated, we will examine the consumer electronics industry, which has been particularly challenged by the developments noted previously.

The Consumer Electronics Domain

The impact that Japanese and European electronics companies have had on U.S. electronics manufacturers has been substantial. Japanese and European electronic giants now own such venerable American brand names as RCA, GE, Philco, Quasar, and Magnavox, among others. These foreign companies also have distribution channels and high-volume plants that will allow them to gear up for the advent of high-definition television (HDTV), a configuration of sophisticated video and audio technologies that results in a significantly upgraded wide-aspect television picture and much improved sound quality. This technological advance may be as sweeping for the world of video as the replacement of propeller-driven aircraft was for aviation.

The ABZ Story

As noted earlier, the simulation in this book involving the ABZ Electronics Corporation is based on an actual U.S. electronics company. The information in this section is real data; however, we shall refer to the company as ABZ for the sake of clarity.

ABZ remains the only world-class U.S.-owned television producer, although many of its sets are made in Mexico. The company has been under pressure from its major stockholders to sell off its television business, which the stockholders insist has soaked up profits over the past five years.

ABZ wants to become a major player in HDTV--the biggest thing since color. According to *Fortune* (October 24, 1988, p. 161), HDTV could become a $145 billion business over the next twenty years. ABZ sees HDTV as an economic opportunity of almost unparalleled proportions and forecasts likely replacement of 160 million American television receivers and videocassette recorders. However, ABZ can only participate if its commercial television division survives.

The challenge for ABZ is twofold: (1) to gain and maintain exports to other nations, and (2) to defend domestic markets against imported goods. ABZ cannot afford to ignore the presence of international competition. If it does, it may be vulnerable in the future. For example, ABZ is now the only major American company producing televisions, and yet it made just 2 million units in 1986. Japanese firms made 18 million units and European firms made 15 million units.

ABZ's market share dropped from 20.5 percent in 1982 to 14.5 percent in 1987. While industry color television unit sales to dealers were at a record high for the eighth consecutive year, up 6 percent over 1986, ABZ's color television sales declined modestly. This was principally due to lower unit sales volume as a result of continued price-cutting by competitors at a time when ABZ briefly held its selling prices in an attempt to encourage industry stability.

Price reductions--far in excess of significant cost reductions--have been the main deterrent to achieving reasonable profitability in color television. Long-anticipated industry price stability never materialized because of continued dumping of television sets below costs by Far Eastern suppliers, ineffective antidumping law enforcement by the U.S. government, and the failure of Korea and other newly industrialized Far East countries to revalue their currencies. European-controlled companies, pushing for market share, also cut prices.

ABZ has encouraged the U.S. government to enforce more effectively existing antidumping laws and to enact trade legislation to close loopholes that have been abused by Far East television manufacturers. Recognizing that unrealistically low industry pricing would very likely continue to be a problem, ABZ implemented restructuring programs in late 1987 to reduce operating costs. Staffing reductions and other changes were implemented in an attempt to reduce ongoing corporate operating costs by more than $20 million in 1988.

Industry-wide videocassette recorder (VCR) and camcorder unit sales to dealers increased one percent in 1987. But following a significant increase in 1986, ABZ unit sales declined in 1987, as many new competitors introduced compact VHS camcorders and as VCR decks from Korea became a major factor in the market.

ABZ's video products operating results were down considerably for 1987 and sales margins for its video products shrank severely. The introduction of video products with new performance features, combined with recently improved industry inventory levels, improved in 1988, but a strong yen put severe cost pressures on profit margins.

ABZ's Plight

What should ABZ be doing if it is to survive as America's only world-class producer of television sets? To fully appreciate ABZ's plight, you will be given the opportunity to be its savior via appropriate operations management techniques and activities. The exercises and projects included in the remainder of this book encompass many of the major management processes in operations management and include decisions that relate to the various business functions. They are intended to give you an appreciation of decision making in the complex operations management environment.

EXHIBIT II.1 Operations Management System

SECTION II

STRATEGIC ACTIVITIES

You have just been hired by ABZ Electronics as an operations specialist. You were hired by Joseph Yehudai, Operations Group Manager of the Consumer Electronics Division. Your name is Pat Hancock. Hancock! How American can you get? Pat! Patricia or Patrick, you make the choice. For group experiences, you may be Leslie or even Kelly.

You will know when you are in the role-playing mode (orientation and experiences) when the material is printed in **bold letters**.

The layers outlined in the operations model (Exhibit 1.1) illustrate the components of the material presented in the next three chapters. The analysis is guided by the interplay of the ABZ environment, leadership, and organization; the pattern of strategic change; and the processes by which strategies form.

Our "operations management walk through" consists of sixteen phases, a step-by-step application of operations management tools and knowledge to a U.S. corporation that competes in the global consumer electronics industry. You will contend with the issues that plague the U.S. consumer electronics industry: foreign competition, product dumping, new technology, offshore suppliers, regulators, associations, labor unions, public attitudes, technology, politics, demographics, economics, and prices.

Our operations management walk through draws extensively from experience, current business periodicals, company and labor union interviews and materials, OM research, *Compact Disclosure*, *Electronics Digest*, and other available information.

Effective operations strategies require a synthesis of the future, present, and past. Henry Mintzberg ("Crafting Strategy," *Harvard Business Review*, July/August 1987, p. 75) echoes this sentiment when he states, "Organizations must make sense of the past if they hope to manage the future. Only by coming to understand the patterns that form in their own behavior do they get to know their capabilities and their potential." To make sure that you have sufficient information to properly manage the future, a rather detailed case study of ABZ Electronics is presented in Chapters 2, 3, and 4.

In Chapters 2, 3, and 4, you participate in "ABZ and You," a new-employee orientation program. Please note the **bold print**. As is true of most orientation programs, you are presented with more information than you can possibly digest in one, two, three, or even four days. However, you also know that decisions are not made in a vacuum and that it is important that you know as much about your company as possible. You take notes and you make points of reference so that you can recall information that may be critical to a particular operations decision.

Chapter 2 presents an overview of ABZ. ABZ's mission, organizational structure, plants, people, and sales are highlighted. A situational analysis of ABZ is presented, as is financial data.

Chapter 3 finds you back in orientation with ABZ's Vice President of Marketing. ABZ's competitive environment is discussed. You become involved in tracking ABZ's grand, corporate, and business strategies on a year-by-year basis to achieve that synthesis of the future, present, and past mentioned earlier.

A number of specific agreements between the International Consumer Electronics Union and ABZ Electronics Corporation are presented in Chapter 4. This information follows a brief history of the Clarkstown plant, a look at the ICEU situation at the plant, and a look at the future of ABZ-ICEU relations.

CHAPTER **2**

Welcome to ABZ's New Employee Orientation

**Jack R. Dustman
Director,
Human Resources**

Welcome to ABZ. My name is Jack Dustman, Director of Human Resources. You have joined a company where each person is an important part of a team. ABZ is nothing more than a combination of talented people working together to produce our total product line. We are a well-established company whose products have high inherent value and a reputation for excellence throughout the entire world. We are proud to be an all-American company that has been around since 1918 and plans to stay around for a long time.

Today you are participating in your orientation program, called "ABZ and You." You started this program this morning by having breakfast with various ABZ supervisors. Ms. Rosemary Anderson, one of our Human Resources Department staff specialists, has given you a copy of our *Employee Handbook*. This handbook describes key policies, procedures, and employee benefits.

Tomorrow morning, we will meet for breakfast at the company cafeteria located in this building. We are proud of our cafeterias for they offer quality food at reasonable prices. Immediately after breakfast you will be given a tour of ABZ headquarters. Later, you will meet with Todd Madrid, our union business agent. He will explain the benefits of our union. We consider the union to be an integral part of our company team.

Tomorrow--breakfast, a tour, and some union talk! Today--all about ABZ.

An Overview of ABZ

I plan to give you an overview of your company--its history, mission, culture, values, strengths, weaknesses, opportunities, and challenges. I will describe the values of your CEO so that you will have an understanding of the basis for decision making here at ABZ. This afternoon, Gene Grape, Vice

President for Marketing, will discuss our competition and the various strategies that we use to maintain market shares and profits.

The ABZ Electronics Corporation is chartered in the state of Delaware. Delaware enacted antitakeover legislation in February 1988. ABZ does not have an antitakeover policy. However, the corporation has studied the possibility of drafting one.

I hear you Pat. *Why should you care where ABZ is chartered? Why should you care if ABZ has a takeover policy?* Good questions. The point I wish to make is that although ABZ has been a target for a hostile takeover, such a takeover has not happened and management has done everything possible to make sure that it won't happen. I want you to know that you do not need to fear losing your new job because of a takeover. ABZ is a strong company, it has a strong management team, and we expect to be in business for a very long time.

History of ABZ Electronics

ABZ Electronics began operations in 1918 manufacturing amateur radio equipment. We incorporated under the name ABZ Radio Corporation in 1923 and kept that name until 1983, when our name was changed to ABZ Electronics Corporation. ABZ stuck to manufacturing radios and televisions until early 1978. In late 1978, ABZ began diversifying into cable television and computers, including peripherals, systems, and components. We will talk about that later.

Mission of ABZ

Let me quote the ABZ mission. Note that I do this in just one breath. "ABZ's mission is based on the essentials of successful manufacturing and service: (1) care and concern for stake holders; (2) the highest quality television and related consumer electronics products and services; (3) the highest quality microcomputers and high-technology electronic subsystems and components and services; and (4) true leadership in the development of the employees of a growth-oriented, innovative, and profitable electronics company."

ABZ seeks to:

1.   Always provide a totally satisfying business experience for each customer and to maintain customer satisfaction as our highest priority.
2.   Always maintain a dynamic spirit of unity and pride of craft among all employees to demonstrate sincerity, caring, and encouragement of continuous career development for each individual employee.
3.   Always seek improvement in our business and financial skills, assuring reasonable profit and return on investment.
4.   Always encourage new and creative ideas for the purpose of maintaining ABZ as one of the most successful electronics corporations in the world.

Organizational Components

Just how big is ABZ? Well, we are big, but not so big that we cannot pay attention to every employee. We are divided into several smaller units via a subsidiary system. ABZ operates the following subsidiaries: Cableproductos de Chihuahua, S.A. de C.V.; Electro Partes de Matamoros, S.A. de C.V.; Microcom Company; Interocean Advertising Corporation; Interocean Advertising Corporation of California; Interocean Advertising Corporation of Illinois; Productos Magneticos de Chihuahua, S.A. de C.V.; Partes de Television de Reynosa, S.A. de C.V.; S.A. ABZ Data Systems N.V.; ABZ Teleson de Mexico, S.A. de C.V.; Great Technology Electronics Corporation; ZCO de Chihuahua, S.A. de C.V.; ABZ Data Systems Corporation; ABZ Data Systems GMBH; ABZ Data Systems Ltd; ABZ Data

Systems, S.A.; ABZ Distributing Corporation of Illinois; ABZ Distributing Corporation - Midstates; ABZ Distributing Corporation of New York; ABZ Distributing Corporation of Northern California; ABZ Distributing Corporation of Southern California; ABZ Distributing (Ireland) Limited; ABZ Electronics Corporation of Arizona; ABZ Electronics Corporation of Indiana; ABZ Electronics Corporation of Pennsylvania; ABZ Electronics Corporation of Texas; ABZ Electronics (Ireland) Limited; ABZ Electronics Holdings Limited; ABZ Electronics (Pacific) Ltd.; ABZ Electronics Pty. Ltd.; ABZ Foreign Sales Corporation; ABZ/Inteq Inc.; ABZ International Inc.; ABZ International Sales Corporation; ABZ Microcircuits Corporation; ABZ Radio Canada Ltd../ABZ Radio Canada LTEE; ABZ Taiwan Corporation; ABZ Video Products Corporation; ABZ Video Tech Corporation; Ztrans Inc.; Ztrans Brokerage Inc.; Ztrans Maintenance Inc.; Z Sub, Inc.; and Z Tac, Inc.

Plants, People, and Sales

In 1978, ABZ employed approximately 18,000 people. Employee costs accounted for 15 percent of sales. Research and development accounted for 3 percent.

One year later, ABZ employed approximately 22,700 people. This figure grew to 24,000 in 1980. Most of the growth was a result of the Microcom Company acquisition, which we will discuss later when we talk about strategies. In 1981, ABZ used approximately 10.1 million square feet of space for manufacturing, warehousing, engineering developments, administration, and distribution, and employed approximately 25,000 people. Employee costs accounted for 20 percent of sales; research and development 4 percent; and depreciation 5.7 percent. Estimated plant age at the time was nine years.

In 1982, employee costs again accounted for 20 percent of sales. Research and development was 4 percent of sales. A depreciation rate of 5.8 percent was also charged to sales. Twenty-eight thousand employees worked for ABZ.

Color television sales accounted for 50 percent of 1983 revenues. Research and development accounted for 5.1 percent of sales. There were 30,000 ABZ employees.

Employees numbered 29,000 by December 31, 1984. One year later, the number of persons employed by the ABZ was approximately 33,000.

ABZ currently owns thirty-two manufacturing plants that produce and service its television and computer products. Nineteen of the plants are located in Mexico and other countries. The current manufacturing and service capacity of the plants is approximately three million square feet.

Culture and Values

ABZ's motto is "Quality with a view!" This indicates that quality is a cornerstone value of the firm. This fact was confirmed in the October 24, 1988, issue of *Television Digest With Consumer Electronics* (Volume 28, Number 43, page 16) when it cited an American Video Association (AVA) report on television servicing. The AVA survey asked 487 service centers whether any one brand of television *seems to require more service than another.* "Affirmative responses showed that Emerson was cited 35.5 percent, Fisher 33.9 percent, Goldstar 23.7 percent, Samsung 19.4 percent, Sharp 12.4 percent, Sanyo 6.5 percent, Symphonic 3.2 percent, Toshiba 3.2 percent, "Korean brands in general" 2.7 percent, Mitsubishi 2.7 percent, RCA 2.7 percent, Multi-Tech 2.2 percent, NEC 2.2 percent, Lloyds 1.6 percent, and TMK 1.1 percent. ABZ was not cited!

Not only do we promote quality products, but we reward employees who excel by promoting them to more responsible positions. Our CEO, Robert Kemper, joined ABZ in 1971. He became head of the computer division when it was first formed. He became CEO in 1983 because his computer division had grown enormously and had become very profitable. Even though he was a young man in his early 40s, ABZ promoted him to CEO based on his track record.

We place a very high value on the "work ethic." Kemper expects his officers to put in sixty to seventy fun-hour work weeks. Working hard and making money can be fun!

We believe in getting the job done—implementing! To quote the CEO, "Everyone else is planning to death, but we're out there implementing."

We vigorously support tariffs on Japanese electronic products, so that value-added American jobs may be saved. I hear you. *"What about our nineteen plants located in Mexico and other countries? What about the cabinet manufacturing plant that was moved from Illinois to Juarez, Mexico?"*

We did this to cut labor costs. We traded 265 American jobs for lower manufacturing costs. This permitted us to compete in the very competitive consumer electronics industry. These were not highly technical jobs and they required very few skills. It was our excellent training that made our new employees productive. We moved a type of job that was not a high priority among American workers.

What did we accomplish by such a move? We kept an American television brand name under American ownership! We did not follow other American consumer electronics firms that have sold American brand names and American divisions to foreign competitors. When GE sold its television component to a French firm, ABZ became the last American-owned consumer electronics company in the global market.

We are proud to be the last major American television and television component manufacturer. Furthermore, we disapprove of any manufacturer who dumps products in America at costs far below what it costs to produce them. We believe in fighting for American rights. We pursued Japanese

Robert E. Kemper
CEO and President

Michael R. Wunsch
Group President

Rudiger B. Wysk
Group President

Charles W. Baldwin
Group President

Maureen McAuliffe
Vice President

Christine Hutchens
Controller

firms all the way to the U.S. Supreme Court for dumping consumer electronics products on the American market. ABZ lost the suit, which was time-consuming and expensive, but we believe ABZ made a statement in standing up to the Japanese. We believe it was worth it. CEO Kemper is quoted as saying, "Undercut us with illegal pricing and we will sue like hell."

One final value—we believe that the American consumer is knowledgeable and prefers a quality product at a higher price than a mediocre product at a low price. The proof is in our advertisements. Check out one of our ads. You will get the picture.

The Personal Values of CEO Kemper

I told you the name of the CEO—Robert E. Kemper. Mr. Kemper obtained his BA, with a major in business, from Western State College in Gunnison, Colorado. He received an MA from Denver University in 1963. The University of Washington at Seattle awarded Mr. Kemper a Ph.D. in 1967. He has been with ABZ for the past seventeen years, and has been the CEO for five years. Last year's annual compensation was $435,000. This figure included profit-sharing income, as well as stock options. Mr. Kemper owns 51,195 shares of voting common stock.

Why is this important? It is important to know that your management has a large stake in the company. It is important to know that ABZ is a very important part of every ABZ manager's life.

Mr. Kemper is an American! He drives an American-made car. He uses an American-made computer in his home. He wears American-made clothes. He buys American!

Mr. Kemper possesses an overall focus on ABZ Electronics. He is aware of the strengths and weaknesses of the corporation's divisions. He knows what actions are necessary in each division to achieve profitability.

Mr. Kemper values the family. Before he came to ABZ, he was offered a promotion by another firm. However, he would have had to move out of the Chicago area. He refused to move, because he did not want to move away from his relatives.

He is quite a fighter. He believes in getting what he wants. When he graduated from college he interviewed with thirty-five firms and received thirty-four offers. He wanted the offer he did not receive. He did not quit. He pursued the company until he secured the job. This quality is evident in the Japanese dumping suit pursued by ABZ.

Mr. Kemper is involved in community activities. He has served on the local police committee, the board of trustees of a local youth organization, and a parish council within his church. He has also coached little league baseball in his hometown of Eugene.

A work-hard/play-hard attitude dominates Mr. Kemper's value system. He works sixty to seventy hours Monday through Friday. He spends his weekends boating and water skiing.

Mr. Kemper once wanted to own his own company. However, he now prefers working for a large firm because he is challenged by the competition and the variety of products, distribution channels, and markets that are in place. He feels that these attributes are not available in the small business environment.

An ABZ SWOT Analysis

So how is ABZ doing? Let us now talk about the significant corporate issues challenging ABZ. I will show you several exhibits concerning the financial condition of ABZ. Exhibit 2.1 shows ABZ's five-year sales, net income, and earnings per share data. In Exhibit 2.2, you see a listing of ABZ's annual assets for the period 1985 through 1988. Exhibit 2.3 provides you with a listing of annual liabilities for 1985 through 1988. Annual income for the years 1985, 1986, 1987, and 1988 is provided in Exhibit 2.4.

EXHIBIT 2.1
ABZ Electronics Corporation
Five-YearSummary
Sales, Net Income, And Earning Per Share

YEAR	SALES (000$)	NET INCOME	EPS
1988	2,685,700	5,300	0.002
1987	2,362,700	(19,100)	(0.007)
1986	1,892,100	(10,000)	(0.004)
1985	1,623,700	(7,700)	(0.003)
1984	1,716,000	63,600	2.88
1983	1,361,300	46,300	2.26
GROWTH RATE	18.4	(35.3)	(25.1)

Source: Compact Disclosure

EXHIBIT 2.2
ABZ Electronics Corporation
Annual Assets (000$)

FISCAL YEAR ENDING	12/31/88	12/31/87	12/31/86	12/31/85
CASH	17,400	19,500	1,100	6,800
MARKETABLE SECURITIES	8,900	NA	1,800	300
RECEIVABLES	488,400	417,700	378,200	283,200
INVENTORIES	579,200	583,600	502,800	332,100
OTHER CURRENT ASSETS	73,700	68,700	82,500	64,900
TOTAL CURRENT ASSETS	1,167,600	1,089,500	966,400	687,300
PROPERTY, PLANT, AND EQUIPMENT	660,900	633,300	592,500	536,600
ACCUMULATED DEPRECIATION	406,600	366,500	336,000	298,400
NET PROPERTY AND EQUIPMENT	254,300	266,800	256,500	238,200
OTHER NON-CURRENT ASSETS	5,600	16,700	12,100	NA
DEPOSITS AND OTHER ASSETS	NA	NA	NA	1,800
TOTAL ASSETS	1,427,500	1,373,000	1,235,000	927,300

Source: Compact Disclosure

EXHIBIT 2.3
ABZ Electronics Corporation
Annual Liabilities

FISCAL YEAR ENDING	12/31/88	12/31/87	12/31/86	12/31/85
NOTES PAYABLE	100,000	113,000	95,000	19,000
ACCOUNTS PAYABLE	273,200	220,500	199,000	84,000
CURRENT LONG-TERM DEBT	6,900	6,900	6,900	6,900
ACCRUED EXPENSES	127,700	126,100	103,900	97,000
INCOME TAXES	7,800	2,300	7,400	7,400
OTHER CURRENT LIABILITIES	69,300	79,300	78,800	76,900
TOTAL CURRENT LIABILITIES	584,900	548,100	491,000	291,200
DEFERRED CHARGES	30,800	31,300	40,000	33,800
LONG-TERM DEBT	308,600	315,400	272,400	165,100
TOTAL LIABILITIES	924,300	894,800	803,400	490,100
PREFERRED STOCK	NA	NA	NA	NA
COMMON STOCK NET	26,700	25,900	23,300	23,100
CAPITAL SURPLUS	145,300	132,800	69,700	65,500
RETAINED EARNINGS	331,200	319,500	338,600	348,600
TREASURY STOCK	NA	NA	NA	NA
SHAREHOLDER EQUITY	503,200	478,200	431,600	437,200
TOTAL LIABILITIES AND NET WORTH	1,427,500	1,373,000	1,235,000	927,300

Source: Compact Disclosure

EXHIBIT 2.4
ABZ Electronics Corporation
Annual Income (000$)

FISCAL YEAR ENDING	12/31/88	12/31/87	12/31/86	12/31/85
NET SALES	2,685,700	2,362,700	1,892,100	1,623,700
COST OF GOODS	2,252,800	2,017,900	1,588,400	1,363,300
GROSS PROFIT	432,900	344,800	303,700	260,400
RESEARCH AND DEVELOPMENT	100,600	103,400	99,700	96,000
SELLING, GENERAL AND ADMINISTRATIVE EXPENDITURES	278,100	239,300	202,700	187,400
INCOME, BENEFITS, DEPRECIATION AND AMORTIZATION	54,200	2,100	1,300	(23,000)
NON-OPERATING INCOME	12,100	14,700	8,100	25,500
INTEREST EXPENSE	51,200	45,700	29,600	23,400
INCOME BEFORE TAX	15,100	(28,900)	(20,200)	(20,900)
PROVISIONS FOR INCOME TAXES	9,800	(9,800)	(10,200)	(13,200)
NET INCOME	5,300	(19,100)	(10,000)	(7,700)
OUTSTANDING SHARES	26,708,475	25,920,280	NA	NA

Source: Compact Disclosure

Strengths

The establishment of a global image has played a role in ABZ's continued success. ABZ is currently among the largest sellers of color televisions. ABZ is also the largest seller of personal computers to the United States military. These contracts with the military have opened the door to potential revenues from future sales. ABZ has been able to capitalize on IBM's marketing superiority by being the second-largest manufacturer of IBM compatibles.

ABZ is highly regarded in the United States personal computer market, especially for laptop computers. Among ABZ's innovations in this field is a new screen, called the flat tension mask. This screen is used for television and computer monitors and has exceptional clarity and high definition.

One of ABZ's strengths is our high market share in the television and computer industries. Gross sales have increased over the past five years (see Exhibit 2.1). Government defense contracts have provided some of this growth. In 1988, ABZ experienced gross sales of $2,685,700,000.

Weaknesses

Most of ABZ's weaknesses seem to center around the consumer electronics division where pricing is a major issue. In 1988, manufacturing and distribution costs increased the cost of goods sold by 11.64 percent. This resulted in a lower gross profit margin. Another weakness was the decline in net income over the last five-year period (see Exhibit 2.1).

Opportunities

A research and development budget of $100,600,000 in 1988 (see Exhibit 2.4) was designed to allow ABZ to capitalize on a continually changing and innovative computer industry. ABZ spent $99,700,000 in 1986 and $96,000,000 in 1985 on research and development. Since the average age of a computer is four to five years, new innovations in computer systems are necessary to maintain ABZ's personal-computer market share.

ABZ needs to take advantage of opportunities to penetrate the corporate market for personal computers. The corporate market has twice the pre-tax profit margin that the highly competitive educational and governmental computer markets have.

Threats

The clone computer industry is booming. New manufacturers enter the market each year, which makes ABZ vulnerable to price cutting and reduced profits. ABZ is also vulnerable to reductions in defense spending by the U.S. government. This threat is a result of ABZ's reliance on U.S. military computer contracts. The other major threat to ABZ is new electronics technology. For example, one change in a computer chip or a change in monitor technology by IBM could leave ABZ and other IBM personal-computer clone competitors with obsolete products.

Financial Analysis

ABZ has been losing money for three of the past four years because of strong competition in the television and videocassette recorder markets. Competition from foreign firms that manufacture U.S. brand names (e.g., General Electric, RCA, Philco) as well as from foreign firms that market their own brands have resulted in price wars. ABZ has been selling its products below cost for the past three years in order to maintain market share.

ABZ has had an increase in sales from $1,361.3 million to $2,685.7 million (Exhibit 2.1) in the past six years. At the same time, our net income decreased from $46.3 million in 1983 to $11.7 million in 1988. At the end of 1987, we had $113 million in notes payable. A year later, our notes payable was reduced to $100 million. ABZ's earning per share was below zero from 1985 through 1987 (Exhibit 2.1). By the end of 1988, the earning per share was a positive .45.

Several weaknesses can be observed when ABZ is compared with other firms in the same industry. ABZ's ratios, taken from SEC 10-K reports, for the past four years can be found in Exhibit 2.5. Exhibit 2.6 compares ABZ's financial ratios with other firms in the electronics industry. The profitability ratio (profit as a percentage of sales) indicates that ABZ, with .81 percent, falls toward the bottom when compared to the overall industry ratio of 3.8 percent.

Return on equity figures are also low. ABZ's ratio is 1.00 percent compared to the industry's lowest of 2.60 percent. These figures indicate that investors prefer short-term benefits rather than long-term benefits.

Activity ratios indicate how well we are employing our assets. The industry average of total asset turnover is 2.11 compared to ABZ's 1.88. This indicates that ABZ may need to either increase its sales or reduce capital expenditures.

The average collection period for an average firm in the industry is 45.59 days, while ABZ's is 65.47 days. This is one reason why ABZ has to use additional capital. Customers are not paying their bills as quickly as they should. ABZ can reduce its interest burden by collecting receivables earlier.

The industry average for the annual inventory turnover ratio is 4.71, while ABZ's is 3.45. Although this ratio has improved over the previous year, it is still not in line with the industry. ABZ must reduce its inventory considerably.

The fixed asset ratio in industry is 13.05, while ABZ's is 10.56. This shows that ABZ is not utilizing its plant and equipment to their full capacities and capabilities. A low activity ratio indicates that ABZ is being run inefficiently. ABZ could have uncollectible accounts receivable, obsolete inventory, or obsolete equipment on its books.

Leverage ratios measure the relationship of funds supplied by creditors to the funds supplied by the owners. The use of borrowed funds should improve the return on equity. However, it also increases risk, and if used in excessive amounts, can result in financial embarrassment. Debt ratio measures the total funds provided by the creditors as a percentage of total assets. The industry ratio is 46.0 percent. ABZ's debt ratio is 65.17 percent. This indicates that ABZ is relying too heavily on borrowed funds.

The accounts payable industry ratio is 8.90 percent while ABZ's is 10.17 percent. This shows that ABZ is more dependent on its suppliers for financing than are the majority of its competitors.

Finally, liquidity ratios measure the ability of a firm to meet its financial obligations as they become current. The current ratio for the industry at the middle quarter is 2.60, while ABZ's is 2.0. This shows that ABZ is below the industry average when it comes to converting its liquid assets to cash within a one-year period. The quick ratio, or the acid-test ratio, excludes inventory from current assets. Inventory is more difficult to convert to cash in times of adversity. ABZ's acid-test ratio of .88 compares to an industry average of 1.10. Having the acid-test ratio below one increases risk.

ABZ's financial picture has deteriorated over past years because ABZ has relied more on borrowing than on raising money through equity.

Hey, I see young Pat Hancock struggling to stay awake so let's call it a morning and get some lunch. When we come back, Gene Grape will take over and give you some insight to our competitive market and our strategies for survival.

EXHIBIT 2.5
ABZ Electronics Corporation
Key Annual Financial Ratios

FISCAL YEAR ENDING	12/31/88	12/31/87	12/31/86	12/31/85
QUICK RATIO	0.88	0.80	0.78	1.00
CURRENT RATIO	2.00	1.99	1.97	2.36
SALES/CASH	102.12	121.16	652.45	228.69
SG & A/SALES	0.10	0.10	0.11	0.12
RECEIVABLES TURNOVER	5.50	5.66	5.00	5.73
RECEIVABLES DAYS SALES	65.47	63.64	71.96	62.79
INVENTORIES TURNOVER	4.64	4.05	3.76	4.89
INVENTORIES DAYS SALES	77.64	88.92	95.67	73.63
NET SALES/WORKING CAPITAL	4.61	4.36	3.98	4.10
NET SALES/PLANT & EQUIPMENT	10.56	8.86	7.38	6.82
NET SALES/CURRENT ASSETS	2.30	2.17	1.96	2.36
NET SALES/TOTAL ASSETS	1.88	1.72	1.53	1.75
NET SALES/EMPLOYEES	74,603.00	67,506.00	51,138.00	49,203.00
TOTAL LIABILITIES /TOTAL ASSETS	0.65	0.65	0.65	0.53
TOTAL LIABILITIES /INVESTED CAPITAL	1.14	1.13	1.14	0.81
TOTAL LIABILITIES /COMMON EQUITY	1.84	1.87	1.86	1.12
TIMES INTEREST EARNED	1.29	0.37	0.32	0.11
CURRENT DEBT/EQUITY	0.01	0.01	0.02	0.02
LONG-TERM DEBT/EQUITY	0.61	0.66	0.63	0.38
TOTAL DEBT EQUITY	0.63	0.67	0.65	0.39
TOTAL ASSETS/EQUITY	2.84	2.87	2.86	2.12
PRETAX INCOME/NET SALES	0.01	(0.01)	(0.01)	(0.01)
PRETAX INCOME/TOTAL ASSETS	0.01	(0.02)	(0.02)	(0.02)
PRETAX INCOME/ INVESTED CAPITAL	0.02	(0.04)	(0.03)	(0.03)
PRETAX INCOME/COMMON EQUITY	0.03	(0.06)	(0.05)	(0.05)
NET INCOME/NET SALES	0.00	(0.01)	(0.01)	0.00
NET INCOME/TOTAL ASSETS	0.00	(0.01)	(0.01)	(0.01)
NET INCOME/INVESTED CAPITAL	0.01	(0.02)	(0.01)	(0.01)
NET INCOME/COMMON EQUITY	0.01	(0.04)	(0.02)	(0.02)

Source: Compact Disclosure

EXHIBIT 2.6
ABZ Electronics Corporation
Key Industry Financial Ratios, 1988

	ABZ RATIO	INDUSTRY RATIO		
		UQ	MED	LQ
QUICK RATIO	0.88	2.10	1.10	0.70
CURRENT RATIO	2.00	4.90	2.60	1.60
RECEIVABLES DAYS SALES	65.47		42.59	
NET SALES/WORKING CAPITAL	4.61		5.26	
NET SALES/CURRENT ASSETS	2.30		2.95	
NET SALES/TOTAL ASSETS	1.88		2.11	
TOTAL LIAB/TOTAL ASSETS	0.65		0.46	
NET INCOME/NET SALES	0.00	8.90	4.70	1.60
NET INCOME/TOTAL ASSETS(ROA)	0.00	13.80	6.20	1.40
NET INCOME/COM. EQUITY(ROE)	0.01	28.20	12.20	2.60
NET SALES/PLANT & EQUIPMENT	10.56		13.05	
ACCOUNT PAYABLE/SALES %	10.17	2.10	5.00	8.90

Source: Compact Disclosure

CHAPTER 3

More ABZ Orientation

Eugene F. Grape
Director,
Marketing

Good afternoon, fellow managers and supervisors. My name is Gene Grape. It is indeed a pleasure to greet you people today and to talk about ABZ's competitive marketing environment. In the process of doing this, you will note that I will mention a number of important business and marketing concepts that highlight the role and operation of marketing in our organization. These concepts are marketing, global competition, grand strategy, corporate strategy, business strategy, and marketing strategy.

Our marketing strategy includes five important concepts: (1) market measurement and forecasting, (2) market segmentation, (3) market targeting, (4) market positioning, and (5) marketing mix.

We use market measurement and forecasting to estimate the current and future size of the market and its segments, competitive products, and probabilities for successful entry.

Categorizing customers according to different needs, characteristics, and behaviors in order to assess their relative size and potential is the purpose of market segmentation.

Market targeting is used to select one or more market segments to enter based on ABZ's size, potential, competition, company resources, and objectives.

We use the concept of market positioning to decide on the position ABZ wants to project to its target customers relative to our competition. At this point, considerable attention is given to the notion of differential advantage, wherein the company can successfully distinguish its product from the competition's.

The controllable factors of product, price, promotion, and place (the four P's) and the relative strategies by which a company seeks to achieve its marketing objectives are referred to as marketing mix.

ABZ's Competitive Environment

ABZ is a diversified corporation doing business in the consumer electronics industry and the microcomputer industry. Both industries are characterized by fierce global competition. The microcomputer market (computers selling for less than $12,000) is the growing segment of the computer industry. Manufacturers in the minicomputer market (computers in the $12,000-$700,000 price range) and the main frame market (computers selling for more than $700,000) are not experiencing the same growth as the microcomputer market. In 1987, the main competitors in the microcomputer industry were IBM (36.3% market share), Apple (16.9% market share), Compaq (8.6% market share), ABZ (5.8% market share), and all others (32.4%).

The Microcomputer Industry

The microcomputer industry is divided into two markets, IBM compatibles and non-IBM compatibles. The significant manufacturer in the non-compatible industry is Apple, which has developed its own system. The rest of the market consists of IBM and IBM compatibles (clones). This is where ABZ competes.

Where does ABZ receive its strongest competition? There are many companies competing in this market. Let us look at a few that we feel are significant.

Tandy. The Tandy Corporation poses a threat to ABZ because

> 1. They have been well established in the computer industry for over ten years.
> 2. They have the widest range of personal computer systems in the microcomputer industry.
> 3. They distribute their products through 6,879 Radio Shack outlets.
> 4. They have the ability to service their consumers through the Radio Shack network.

Because of these strengths, Tandy has increased its foothold in the corporate and government markets. This places competitive pressure on ABZ.

Compaq. The Compaq Corporation may be the fastest growing company in history. In 1987, it had a turnover of $1.2 billion and an 8.6 percent microcomputer market share. Their competitive motto is, "Find out who to compete against and then cooperate with everyone else."

Compaq poses a threat to ABZ, because of these strengths:

> 1. From design to market, they excel in turn-around time.
> 2. They maintain tight control over research, meaning that managers keep engineers working on what customers might want to buy rather than what the engineers want to invent.
> 3. They concentrate on the IBM standard that helps establish most technical specifications for any new machine.
> 4. They use hardware designed for IBM computers by other companies.
> 5. They refuse to compete with dealers, while most computer manufacturers sell large orders directly to buyers. Dealers respond by giving Compaq's computers priority shelf space.
> 6. Internally, they encourage everybody to voice an opinion on products and plans regardless of whether the individual is a member of the particular unit working on a product or idea.

Compaq is the fastest growing company pursuing more by experience than by luck. Each of its original twenty employees had worked with computers for between fifteen and twenty years. All workers feel they have a stake in the company and they are concerned as to how their money is spent.

IBM. The International Business Machines Corporation is the largest supplier of information processing equipment, systems, services, and program products. IBM is the current leader in the micro, or personal computer market. IBM poses a threat to ABZ because of these strengths:

1. They underwent major restructuring in February 1988 in order to make the company more competitive and responsive to customer needs. This included the creation of a new division called IBM United States that will be responsible for profits and revenues in this country and oversee the new lines of business. IBM has also created five new organizations, each responsible for its own business line, and all to be overseen in their day-to-day operations by IBM United States. By implementing this program, IBM will be able to speed technological innovations and move products to the marketplace more quickly and efficiently.
2. IBM's service has long been the cornerstone of customer satisfaction and loyalty.
3. Shipments of the IBM Personal System/2, announced in April 1987, reached one million units in seven months. This new product line spurred new market growth for personal computing applications.
4. The American Society for Quality Control surveyed more than 600 senior executives last year, and the results showed that IBM is considered the leader in quality control.
5. IBM sells software that includes applications that are easy to install and use. They develop software products to help customers design their own applications more quickly.
6. They are building a strong foundation to help customers connect systems, networks, and organizations. Around the world, more than 30,000 networks are based on IBM's System Network Architecture; these connect from a few to as many as 100,000 elements.

IBM continues to surpass others involved in the computer industry with their effective management teams, innovation, and increased market growth.

The Consumer Electronics Industry

The consumer electronics industry includes televisions, VCRs (videocassette recorders), and camcorders. ABZ has been involved in price wars with other manufacturers. This fierce competition and price cutting by foreign competitors has caused ABZ to show a negative profit for the past few years. ABZ is the largest and only American manufacturer of consumer electronics. Other American companies have either sold their consumer electronics divisions to foreign companies or have eliminated them altogether.

Television Digest With Consumer Electronics reported on July 25, 1988, that in 1988 ABZ ranked second in market share in U.S. color televisions sold to dealers. In 1982, ABZ held 19.4 percent of the market, but we held only 12.75 percent of the market in 1988.

According to the April 3, 1989, issue of *Television Digest With Consumer Electronics*, ABZ ranked tenth among camcorder manufacturers with a 3 percent market share. This was a 3 percent decrease in market share from 1986. In the same issue, *Television Digest With Consumer Electronics* placed ABZ eighth, with a 4.45 percent market share, for home VCR and VCP decks. This was a slight increase from 1982.

The industry now has turned its attention to HDTV (high definition television). The HDTV picture has the quality of a 35 mm camera. Forecasts indicate that HDTV may be a $15 billion industry. The problem with this new technology is that there are no specification standards in the a United States. Additionally, U.S. technology is far behind that of foreign competitors.

Sanyo and Sony are among the foreign consumer electronic firms that compete with ABZ. Profiles of these companies are presented here to show the nature of the ABZ's competition.

Sony Corporation. Sony Corporation is a leading maker of consumer and industrial electronic products. Sony is famous for familiar trade names, including Betamax, Trinitron, Walkman, and Video 8.

Sony's market percentages of sales by product are: video, 31 percent; audio, 28 percent; television, 22 percent; and others for the remainder.

Sony has over four and a half times the net sales of ABZ Electronics and Sony has shown continual profitability. Sony poses a threat to ABZ because of these strengths:

1. It returns 8 to 10 percent of its revenues to research and development.
2. It is recognized as an expert in the audio, video, and miniaturization fields.
3. Its sales in the United States account for 30 percent of total sales.
4. It plans to expand into the VHS market.

These are major strengths, but Sony also faces major challenges. For example, the decline of the U.S. dollar has lowered the profit contribution of goods sold in the United States.

Sony is looking to introduce VHS systems in the videocassette industry with a unit manufactured for Sony under contract with Hitachi and retail salespeople expect Sony to jump immediately to number two behind Mitsubishi because of its strong reputation for quality. Sony could have capitalized much earlier in the VCR industry if it had pioneered VHS systems as it did the Beta system thirteen years ago.

Sanyo. The Sanyo Manufacturing Corporation experienced a net loss of $118.9 million for the year ending November 30, 1987. This loss was due primarily to such continued competitive pressures as price reductions of color television and microwave ovens.

Sanyo poses a threat to ABZ because of these strengths:

1. It opened a plant in Mexico to keep costs down.
2. It increased product values by offering consistent prices.

The big loss came from the cost of products sold in 1986, which had been affected unfavorably by higher material cost caused by the strength of the Japanese yen against the U.S. dollar and high overhead costs due to under-used plant capacity.

Financial Analysis of ABZ's Consumer Electronics Competition

Twenty companies manufacture television sets, tubes, and related equipment. These twenty companies employ 32,695 operations personnel in thirty-five plants located in the United States. These plants produce 16,482,500 color sets annually.

Profitability ratios are used to compare the profits of the firm to activities in the firm. Profit as a percentage of sales is the measure of net profits when compared to sales. Both ABZ and Sanyo show negative profit balances while Sony shows a profit.

Leverage ratios measure the relationship of funds supplied by creditors and the funds supplied by the owners. The use of borrowed funds by profitable companies will improve the return on equity, but it also increases risk.

The debt ratio measures the total funds provided by creditors as a percentage of total assets. The times interest earned ratio recognizes that lease payments under long-term contracts are usually as mandatory as interest and principal payments on debt. Relating accounts payable to cost of goods sold can show whether a company is dependent on its suppliers for financing. All three ratios seem to be in line with the industry ratio, with the exception of Sanyo's times interest earned ratio. Sanyo has been losing money for a number of years and its interest payment is tremendous, due mainly to the devaluation of the United States dollar relative to the Japanese yen.

Finally, the liquidity ratios measure a company's ability to meet financial obligations as they become current. Current ratio and the acid-test ratio are liquidity ratios. There were no data available for Sanyo, but ABZ's and Sony's ratios are about the same.

The major challenge for ABZ is its excessive debt. ABZ also faces heavy competition in its consumer electronics division due to price cutting by foreign firms. The consumer electronics division is where ABZ is losing money, and price competition is the culprit.

ABZ's Strategies

So how did we get to where we are? Let's take a chronological look at the selected emergent grand, corporate, business, and functional strategies implemented by ABZ since 1978. Please note that our highest strategy level until 1980 was corporate. Once we added Microcom to our structure, we began developing a grand strategy.

1978

Corporate Strategies. ABZ achieved the reductions in overhead costs targeted in 1977 to produce significant cost savings. The company continued to pursue antitrust and antidumping laws through Congress and the courts. Television sales accounted for about 80 percent of total revenues. Color television sales amounted to more than 70 percent. RCA was ABZ's main competitor for the top spot in color television sales.

Another ABZ corporate strategy was to modernize and recover from past stagnation in product introduction. Corporate leaders wanted to rely on engineering to provide products that matched or exceeded competitive standards in performance, reliability, and innovation.

Business Strategies. ABZ moved some operations activities to Taiwan and Mexico. This sharply lowered overhead and manufacturing costs and resulted in improved profitability. The company implemented a two-tier product line.

In May, ABZ unveiled "System 3," a line of high-priced color television sets that competed directly with RCA's "Colortrak" line. ABZ kicked off the "System 3" with a massive advertising campaign. System 3 sets used ABZ's new 100-degree tri-focus picture tube, which improved picture sharpness and detail. A new modular chassis design reduced the number of chassis parts. Innovative electrical and mechanical connections provided for greater reliability and easier servicing—important selling features.

The 1978 pricing pressure, oddly enough, was initiated by ABZ and RCA. Both companies sought to take advantage of price increases by Japanese manufacturers, who were victims of a falling U.S. dollar against the yen. ABZ lowered its cost of operations substantially and dropped prices from 2 to 3 percent while increasing profitability.

1979

Corporate Strategies. ABZ firmly pursued its longstanding goals of technical excellence and product quality and reliability. The company was dedicated to preserving its most valuable asset, quality.

ABZ entered the computer industry by purchasing Microcom from Schlumberger Limited on October 1, 1979. Microcom produced and marketed electronic kit products for communications, testing, and so forth. The purchase price of $64.5 million was financed by borrowing $60 million from the Prudential Insurance Company. The merger gave ABZ a toehold in the small-computer market which was forecasted to be the fastest growing electronic product area in the 1980s.

ABZ's long-term growth prospects hinged on diversification. The domestic television market had become saturated and was not expanding, while imports, particularly from Japan, were encroaching on ABZ's market. ABZ looked especially vulnerable to lost market share and lost profits because we were basically a one-business company—television sets accounted for 80 percent of sales.

In 1979, ABZ Data Systems was formed to produce the ABZ brand of fully assembled microcomputer products and systems for business and home use.

Business Strategies. ABZ maintained market strength through product development and the introduction of new models. In February, ABZ introduced the 17-inch "System 3" models as well as the modified "System 3" models with a unique modular chassis. ABZ also developed a line of cable television converters and decoders for use on over-the-air subscription television.

1980

Grand Strategies. ABZ increased its manufacturing efficiency by making more of its own components in lower cost foreign facilities, which resulted in a dramatic increase in earnings compared to 1979. ABZ also automated and mechanized its plants. The company budgeted capital spending of over $30 million and increased outlays to over $60 million. In addition, ABZ jumped on the videodisc bandwagon by joining with rival RCA to sell a videodisc player using RCA's technology.

The recession hampered profit growth in the second half. Television sales were soft and business was not expected to increase until the economy improved. Price competition among the industry leaders showed no signs of abating. ABZ was not able to raise prices enough to cover labor and material costs that were rising with inflation.

Corporate Strategies. ABZ developed space phone color television, an application of "state of the art" video advertising communication technology in ABZ computer space receivers. The space phone enabled a remote-control television set to be used as an extension of a telephone receiver and was an example of the emergence of the television set as an active electronics device in the home.

Management's efforts to institute operations efficiency began to affect profits positively. In addition, ABZ invested in more automated equipment that held the promise of lower manufacturing costs.

Business Strategies. The color television market continued to be strengthened by replacement demand and by new technological developments. ABZ believed that it would be able to participate profitably in broadening opportunities in video technology.

Videodisc development continued, and ABZ made it available to consumers in the fall of 1980. ABZ began the manufacture and shipment of subscription television decoders to five U.S. metropolitan areas for over-the-air pay television systems.

ABZ kept ahead of its competitors in color television. The company's 1981 product line included several new features that were not available from anyone else. "Space Phone," for example, was an extra on several remote-control color television models.

The company found new markets for its basic products. It manufactured and sold black and white televisions for use in computer terminal displays.

Although ABZ's computer business was only two years old, ABZ computer systems were being used by over forty large and small terminal manufacturers. Additionally, the profit margin was greater than for consumer television products.

1981

Grand Strategies. ABZ offset the effect of inflation and competitive industry pricing by developing and implementing cost-control programs through design and productivity improvements.

ABZ's board reduced the dividend payment from $.15 to $.075 per share in an attempt to provide additional cash to support productivity, product quality, and working capital requirements for new products and businesses.

ABZ continued to pursue its private lawsuit charging a number of Japanese television manufacturers and others with violation of antitrust and antidumping laws.

Diversification steps at ABZ included new video products—videodiscs and videocassette recorders—to serve as a long-range buffer to diminishing color television sales. Color television sales accounted for about 65 percent of ABZ's total revenues, a decrease of 5 percent since 1979.

Corporate Strategies. Even as ABZ pursued diversification, it remained committed to sustaining its key position in consumer electronics by emphasizing quality, reliability, and innovation. While the recession reduced consumer spending for home electronics products in the latter part of 1981, ABZ continued to make progress in developing new products and new businesses and in further improving its competitive cost position.

Business Strategies. ABZ developed a projection color television for the home featuring a unique 45-inch diagonal hide-away screen.

Pricing problems haunted ABZ. Earnings per share plummeted 50 percent compared to 1980. In addition, ABZ lost some market share.

Television receivers, videocassette recorders, videodisc players, radio receivers, console and modular stereos, stereo component parts and accessories, and color television picture tubes were sold to wholesale distributors and to manufacturers in the United States, Canada, and other foreign countries. Seventy distributor operations in the United States were independently owned and operated.

ABZ had four wholly owned distributors in Secaucus, New Jersey; Lenexa, Kansas; San Francisco, California; and Northlake, Illinois. In Canada, ABZ's products were sold through two wholesale distributors, one that was independently owned, and one that was a company-owned subsidiary with branches in Toronto, Montreal, Winnipeg, and Vancouver. The distributors sold to retail dealers who then sold to the consumers.

Consumer electronics products were exported to more than fifty foreign countries. In a number of foreign countries, ABZ's products were manufactured and sold by licensees. The company had a minority interest in one of these licensees.

Other ABZ products included microcomputer systems, video display terminals and components, cable and subscription television, and videotext products.

There were seven ABZ facilities in the Chicago area, used primarily for television set assembly, cathode ray tube production, and related marketing, engineering, development, and administration.

In Clarkstown, Missouri, ABZ assembled color television sets and produced portable color television cabinets. This facility included a 700,000 square foot plant leased from the city of Clarkstown. This capitalized lease, signed in 1968, was for a period of twenty years. ABZ had an option to purchase the facility at any time during the term of the lease for an amount sufficient to redeem the full principal and interest of the landlord's outstanding bonds.

Lewiston, Pennsylvania, was the location of audio instrument production activities. Two plants were located in Petersburg, Indiana, for the manufacture of television cabinets. In Paris, Illinois, the repair of electronic assemblies was performed.

Taiwan was the site of a black and white television and electronic component assembly plant. In Mexico, three manufacturing plants and one warehouse were operated by ABZ. These were used to manufacture electronic components and to assemble television chassis.

In Canada, ABZ had four locations for the purpose of distributing consumer electronic products. Eleven ABZ facilities were located in Europe to handle Microcom product sales, support, and services.

1982

Grand Strategies. Operating results were very disappointing, primarily due to severe competitive pricing conditions in the industry and the delayed national economic recovery. ABZ continued to emphasize engineering and design for innovation and uniqueness and lower product cost in all business areas. ABZ's undiminished goal was to maintain a leadership role in improving products, developing new products and features, and designing to increase quality and reliability.

The board suspended dividend payments in the third quarter of 1982, citing the operating loss and the need to conserve cash for capital spending programs and to provide working capital for ABZ's expanding new businesses.

Corporate Strategies. ABZ continued to make excellent progress in reducing the cost of producing television products. Improvements in design and manufacturing efficiencies, including the consolidation of color television final assembly operations, were implemented.

Product quality continued to represent a prime manufacturing and engineering objective of the company. The company continued to pursue efforts designed to reduce unfair competition from television imports.

ABZ expanded and automated the operations facilities in Mexico. In addition, ABZ reevaluated its staffing requirements and implemented programs in all operations to eliminate a number of salaried positions. Management also imposed further operating cost controls, including a six-month freeze on the salaries of all U.S. personnel.

Business Strategies. ABZ lowered its price on color televisions by 3 percent in order to compete with low-priced imports from the Far East. ABZ expanded its television decoder business through the introduction of videotext products, addressable converter/decoders, and related products for cable television. Eight-bit and sixteen-bit Z-100 desktop computer systems were introduced by the computer division.

Three warehouses were located at Brownsville and McAllen, Texas. A fourth warehouse was located in Douglas, Arizona. In St. Joseph, Michigan, a plant, a warehouse, and a store facility were used for Microcom computer products. There were sixty-three retail outlets for Microcom products in 1982, located throughout the world. Color television sales accounted for approximately 62 percent of total revenues, and RCA remained ABZ's main competitor for the top spot in color television sales. ABZ continued to be plagued by inflation, which had hurt it for years by driving up costs faster than prices could rise to meet them.

New products continued to cushion ABZ's financial slide. The first-half volume gains were primarily attributable to improved small-computer sales and continuing success in the marketing of cable television decoders. ABZ's tiered addressable cable television, introduced in 1981, was well received, which lifted decoder bottom-line contributions, but hefty product and marketing expenses curtailed computer profit advances.

Second-half results were better. In March, ABZ completed the consolidation of its television assembly operations into its Clarkstown plant. Efficiency gains that had begun in the June period accelerated along with seasonal volume increases in the second half. Earnings also got a boost via small price hikes. In addition, the beginnings of a modest economic recovery provided a lift.

1983

Grand Strategies. Consistent with the diversification changes that had taken place, the board recommended to the stockholders that the company change its names from "ABZ Radio Corporation" to "ABZ Electronics Corporation." ABZ believed that the new name would enable it to address the broader product areas of the four ABZ business groups.

Margin expansion continued to be the key to profits. Gross margin widened 50 percent in one quarter. Two factors accounted for that surge: cost reduction programs and "new" wider margin products. The success of new products started to transform the company.

In December 1983, the U.S. Court of Appeals (Third Circuit) reinstated ABZ's private damage claims against Japanese television manufacturers and their co-conspirators and remanded the case to a lower court for trial. The alleged violations were being argued under the Antidumping Act of 1916 and the Sherman Antitrust Act.

Corporate Strategies. ABZ Data Systems made substantial progress during 1983 in establishing a noteworthy market position with educational institutions, large businesses, and government organizations. ABZ implemented a strategy to reduce inventory levels. The combined demand for ABZ's products increased earnings over those recorded in 1982. ABZ introduced programs to increase capacity for power supplies and other components in Mexico, Ireland, and Taiwan.

The near-term prospects in each of ABZ's business areas were excellent. ABZ was committed to sustaining those characteristics that had always been synonymous with ABZ products—quality, reliability, value, and serviceability. ABZ's organizational strategy to decentralize decision making. Each unit pursued ABZ's grand strategy, but was free to determine appropriate corporate, business, and functional strategies.

Business Strategies. ABZ developed a multichannel television stereo sound transmission system. An all-new VCR product line was introduced that included state-of-the-art VCRs and video cameras. ABZ also developed an impulse pay-per-view decoder module in the cable product line. The Z-100 family of microcomputers was broadened considerably with the introduction of a new desktop personal computer and a new portable personal computer.

ABZ increased the number of facilities in Mexico from four to seven. The facilities were used to manufacture and warehouse electronic components, chassis assemblies, and color television cabinets. ABZ added a facility in Ireland for the marketing of electronic components.

1984

Grand Strategies. The company's grand strategy was geared to maintaining ABZ's established position of strength in the design, low-cost manufacture, and marketing of high-volume, quality electronics products in all business groups.

The company had no unique or unusual practices related to working capital items. No part of the business was dependent on a single customer or a few customers.

In 1984, the company continued to pursue efforts designed to reduce unfair competition from television imports. The estimated dollar expenditure for engineering and research related to new and improved products and services was $86.9 million. The amounts expended in 1983 and 1982 were $67.3 million and $64.3 million, respectively.

Corporate Strategies. ABZ continued to capitalize on its established market position with the U.S. military, educational institutions, and large businesses. The company targeted Mexico and Ireland for automated component manufacturing.

Revenue and profit advances would have been greater had it not been for the highly competitive television pricing. Color television unit sales were running at a record clip, yet prices were off 5 percent from 1983. The pricing climate was nothing new and it had been the basis of corporate planning for years. ABZ combated the effects of pricing by continuing to automate plants, increasing offshore operations, emphasizing higher end products, and introducing new television and computer products.

Business Strategies. ABZ lowered its color television prices in order to compete with the rest of the industry. It improved its operating margin in 1985 by introducing new features and stereo models of color televisions. ABZ's multichannel television and stereo sound transmission system was accepted uniformly by the industry. ABZ maintained its leadership in the cable industry through the development of product technology and its superior manufacturing cost positioning. In December, ABZ introduced a new line of lower-cost decoders that was still fully addressable and offered baseband scrambling.

1985

Grand Strategies. ABZ was determined to stay at the forefront of innovation in the electronics and computer marketplace. It made its mark with personal computers against formidable competition. There were many materials, such as copper, plastic, steel, wood, glass, aluminum, and zinc, that were essential to the business and these were available from many sources.

During 1985, the company continued to pursue efforts designed to reduce unfair competition from television imports.

The estimated dollar expenditure for engineering and research relating to new products and services and to improvement of existing products and services amounted to $96.0 million. The amount expended in 1984 had been $86.9 million.

Corporate Strategies. ABZ examined all options and made appropriate investments to assure their established position in the design and production of quality electronics products.

ABZ began developing a flat tension mask for television monitors. Five IBM-compatible computer models were introduced.

The number of ABZ plants located in Mexico numbered fifteen, including facilities for the manufacture of electronic components, assembly of television set chassis, the manufacture of color television cabinets, and the assembly of color television sets and cable television products. All of ABZ's product areas became dependent on the continued availability of components from its Mexican operations facilities.

Three distribution centers for consumer electronic products were established in Canada. There were now seven locations where Microcom computer products were retailed.

Business Strategies. Early in 1985, impulse pay-per-view television programming was launched in several U.S. cities. The system was composed of ABZ electronic products.

ABZ improved its profits in color television by strategically pricing its high-end models and by lowering costs through staff reductions.

Due to a slowdown in the cable product industry, ABZ initiated programs in the fourth quarter that would reduce manufacturing and support costs.

ABZ committed substantial resources to develop the flat tension mask that delivered high-resolution color displays on a perfectly flat surface. This new development was designed to keep increases in the price of television monitors to a minimum and was a unique feature in the industry.

Battered by falling prices for color televisions and videocassette recorders, ABZ turned in a June-quarter loss of $.20 a share. Fierce competition from foreign manufacturing continued to depress revenues and squeeze profits. In the second quarter alone, ABZ's pretax earnings for color television sales were $15 million lower than they would have been at price levels of a year earlier. Sales of videocassette recorders were satisfactory, but competition from offshore firms and softer pricing were increasingly evident.

Shipments of Z-150 microcomputers under a five-year contract with the Pentagon were delayed due to the need for final approvals and other red tape. The units were adapted to meet high-security "Tempest" specifications using a technology developed by Intel that ABZ had just acquired. The company hoped that eventual revenues from the deal would be $100 million.

On other fronts, sales of fully assembled computer products to government departments, schools and universities, and corporations were up 12 percent in the first half, bucking the industry trend. Sales of components to original equipment manufacturers (OEMs), on the other hand, declined in line with the industry-wide slowdown.

1986

Grand Strategies. ABZ continued to seek improvements in profits by emphasizing product and operating controls. It invested in new products to strengthen the product mix and increase sales. The company also continued to pursue efforts designed to reduce unfair competition from television imports.

The estimated dollar expenditure for engineering and research related to new products and services, improvement of existing products and services, and company-sponsored operations activities amounted to $99 million. The amount expended in 1985 had been $96.0 million.

Corporate Strategies. ABZ was convinced that long-term profitability in its television business could only be assured through product innovation and quality as well as through continued improved efficiency.

ABZ maintained its position in the United States and European markets by beginning shipments of a new line of more powerful desktop computers. ABZ also tried to improve the profitability of its computer line through cost reductions, especially in its systems and components division.

The flat tension mask was not only offered in ABZ's computer monitors and television screens, but also was offered to other manufacturers.

Business Strategies. Early in 1986, ABZ implemented a new low-cost television chassis design. ABZ produced the first U.S. designed and manufactured digital and large-screen televisions with high-performance stereo sound. ABZ also introduced several new models such as the popular nine-inch screen.

ABZ introduced the highly popular laptop computer model. The high-resolution flat tension mask completed in 1986 was scheduled for production.

1987

Grand Strategies. ABZ continued to encourage the government to enforce antidumping laws, but it recognized that low industry pricing in consumer electronics would likely continue. To remain competitive against low pricing, ABZ implemented new restructuring programs in late 1987 to reduce operating costs. Staff reductions and other changes were planned in an effort to reduce operating costs by more than $20 million.

Corporate Strategies. ABZ was well positioned to respond to market opportunities after several years of significant investments in research and development. All options to restore overall corporate profitability were examined. ABZ continued to introduce new computer and television products.

Business Strategies. The computer division grew by 20 percent because of penetration into the European markets as well as domestic contracts with the defense department, educational institutions, and larger corporations. ABZ desktop and laptop computers increased distribution through five of the nation's leading retail chains.

ABZ introduced new product features on many of its video products in order to improve its product mix.

The first shipments of the flat technology monitor began in August of 1987. Volume build-up was much slower than planned, but production delays were overcome by the end of the year.

In October 1987, the U.S. Court of Appeals (Third Circuit) heard arguments in ABZ's consolidated appeals from a lower court decision. The lower court had dismissed ABZ's private damage claims against Japanese and other television manufacturers.

1988

Grand Strategies. ABZ continued its grand strategy of making significant investments in research and development in order to place the company in a strong position to respond to new market demands for a broad array of advanced television and computer products.

ABZ planned to maintain its position as a leading designer and supplier of high-performance television, video, and cable products. It also planned to maintain its market position in computer systems, components, and products.

Corporate Strategies. The primary corporate strategies for ABZ in 1988 were to retain the consumer electronics division and to return the company to profitability. The strategy to provide working capital requirements in lieu of dividends was continued.

Business Strategies. ABZ continued to encourage the government to enforce effectively the existing antidumping laws and to enact legislation to close loopholes that have been abused by Far East television manufacturers.

Additional cost reductions were targeted for implementation. A renewed marketing and distribution effort to promote the flat technology monitor was undertaken.

Now What?

Well, Jack and I have given you a brief view of your company. I have told you of the role that marketing plays in our organization. Recall that other ABZ managers and I believe that marketing must work hand-in-hand with operations and other departments. Achieving grand, corporate, and business strategies requires a team effort.

So, consider yourself a part of the ABZ team. Feel free to ask your supervisor anything that will help you adjust to your new work environment. Feel free to visit my office, and Jack's, at any time if you have questions. Thank you for your attention. Have a good day and enjoy your orientation program—"ABZ and You."

CHAPTER **4**

ABZ and the International Consumer Electronics Union (ICEU)

Good morning! Yesterday you began your orientation program called "ABZ and You." We gave you a history of ABZ. We talked about mission, plants, people, sales, and competition. This morning we had breakfast in our cafeteria.

ABZ and the Clarkstown Plant

We have just completed a tour of the Clarkstown plant. You found that this facility has two functions: it supports the manufacture of color television sets with screen sizes nineteen inches to fifty-four inches, and it supports the production of plastic cabinets and parts for all plastic-encased color television units.

We are proud of this plant. You found a factory as big as an auto plant where American workers put American television sets together. You found American managers calling the shots.

This 1.7 million square foot plant is the only domestically owned television assembly plant in the United States. Right here on the flats north of the green Ozark hills is the last outpost of America's consumer electronics industry.

Industry Changes

When this assembly plant was constructed in 1967, it was anticipated that 4,000 persons would be employed here. Television assembly was highly labor intensive then because the tube sets were all hand assembled.

The industry changed in the late 1960s and early 1970s. The Japanese began introducing low-cost "tubeless" television sets filled with inexpensive and reliable circuitry. The sets were produced at a fraction of our labor costs, yet they used American technology.

Whereas the tube television sets were labor intensive, requiring 120 to 130 people per line, the new circuit boards need only 50 or 60 people per line. Even with ABZ's new technology, the tough competition from the Far East required that ABZ cut 1,000 workers at this plant.

Plant Relocation

Later, nearly 4,000 jobs were moved from American ABZ plants to Mexico and Taiwan. ABZ moved the lower skilled, labor-intensive jobs from Clarkstown. Soon, even more operations crossed the border. Now, Mexico is the site of nineteen ABZ manufacturing and warehouse facilities. Television chassis are assembled in the plants and stored in the warehouses. Then they are shipped back to the United States where final assembly is accomplished.

Other foreign plants support the manufacture of television and computer components. Some assemble television sets sold in the United States. Taiwan became the site of two video display, microcomputer, and electronic component manufacturing facilities.

These cost-cutting, offshore moves kept ABZ competitive through the 1970s and early 1980s. Despite these measures, however, profits remained difficult to achieve because of price cutting, which has made today's color television sets cheaper than those of a decade ago.

More Job Losses

ABZ anticipated these job losses. In 1987 we announced plans to move 650 more jobs to Mexico. The only thing that kept us from going through with it was an offer of concessions from the ICEU. In exchange for those concessions, ABZ promised that it would do its best not to move more jobs out during the life of the new 1987-1992 contract. The ICEU knew that if 650 jobs were to move out of this plant, it would not be long before the rest of the Clarkstown operations moved to Mexico.

Despite these difficulties, ABZ is still in Clarkstown. We will continue to operate five of seven production lines. Eventually, we hope to win our fight against dumping by foreign competitors. If ABZ were able to raise its television prices by 3 percent to 5 percent, we could make money. So far that has not happened.

The International Consumer Electronics Union and ABZ

M. Todd Madrid
President/Business
Manager, ICEU

The ICEU is still here and we are glad they are. So now let me introduce you to Todd Madrid, President-Business Manager of union local.

Thank you on behalf of the 1,750 hourly workers and approximately 400 salaried workers in our three-shift operation. I am pleased to be here. I am reminded that the workers and management at this plant have forged a significant agreement. It serves as a model throughout American industry in this time of intense pressure from low-wage foreign competition.

ICEU workers recently agreed to an 8.1 percent pay cut and a two-year wage freeze. ABZ managers agreed to similar trimmings in their own salaries and also agreed to refrain from transferring vital Clarkstown production to Mexico.

Our current five-year contract is disappointing to our workers because each faces a shrinking paycheck. However, we have the comforting assurance of job security until 1992 and ABZ now has a new economic edge—lower labor costs. We hope to use these lower wages to battle domestic and foreign competitors. Clarkstown and the Ozarks have every reason to believe that southwest Missouri will prosper and continue to contribute to the betterment of the region.

ABZ and ICEU executives fought for this innovative and equitable agreement, and they should be applauded. Perhaps other industries that are struggling against foreign competition and racked by labor unrest can imitate our agreement.

The ICEU has some visions and dreams we live by. I think politicians are going to start scratching their heads to figure out how to salvage what's going on. I have some ideas for a turn-around. It might involve "foreign trade becoming fair trade." Maybe something can be done to require companies to stay home. We have five years to change labor laws. If those dreams come true, I think we have a shot at becoming more stable in our incomes and fringe benefits.

I mention all of this to impress upon you the idea that "ABZ and You" includes the ICEU. This is our future. Enough of history, it is the future that is important. What I want to do today is make you aware of ICEU's role here in Clarkstown. I gave you a copy of the agreement between ABZ's Clarkstown Division and the local ICEU. Today I want to note a few critical features of our contract.

Recognition

ABZ recognizes the Union as the sole and exclusive collective bargaining agent for all production, maintenance, and custodial employees at the Clarkstown, Missouri, plants of ABZ—Clarkstown Division. This incudes truck drivers, delivery men, and quality-control technicians. This excludes training center instructors, printing division employees, production clerks, confidential employees, office clerical employees, professional employees, guards, and supervisors. We and ABZ agree that the signal-deck control technicians shall be included in the bargaining unit.

Management Rights

Management determines operating policies and manages the business in the light of experience, business judgment, and changing conditions. Management has the right to direct the work force, including the right to hire, retire, assign, layoff, transfer, and promote. Management maintains the discipline and efficiency of its employees; may relieve employees from duty due to lack of work or other legitimate reasons; and may schedule and re-schedule work, hours, shifts, and work assignments. Further, management has the right to assign employees to shifts and the right to assign employees to particular jobs or pieces of equipment.

Management can determine the work to be done and the manner in which it shall be done by its employees. Management has the right to determine the number of employees it shall employ in any classification, department, or subdivision of the plant, at any time.

Management has the right to introduce new or improved products, production methods, processes, or equipment, to determine maintenance, service, and distribution methods, and to determine the scheduling of production, the method of training employees, the design and engineering of products, and the control of raw and finished materials.

Management has the right to assign work to outside contractors; to eliminate, change, or consolidate jobs and operations; to decide the number and location of plants; and to transfer work from one plant of the company to another.

Management determines financial policy, accounting procedures, and the prices of goods or services rendered or supplied. Management has the right to establish quality, quantity, and job standards, and to establish job evaluation procedures and job content. Management has the right to terminate, merge, or sell the business, or any part thereof. Management has the right to make and enforce reasonable work, conduct, health, and safety rules.

Productivity and Efficiency

It is the intent of ABZ and the ICEU to secure and sustain a high level of productivity per employee. Consistent with the principle of a fair day's work for a fair day's pay, the Union and the employees it represents agree with the objectives of achieving and maintaining a high level of employee performance and efficiency. The union, its agents, and its members agree that they will not take, authorize, or condone any action that interferes with the attainment of such objectives.

Technological Progress

The union and ABZ recognize that the wages and other benefits established for the employees depend to a great extent on technological progress. Technological progress requires better tools, methods, processes, and equipment. A cooperative spirit on the part of the ICEU and ABZ is vital. The union recognizes that such progress is bound to occur.

Failure to Meet Production Standards

ABZ employees are required to meet established quality and production standards. Any written reprimand issued to an employee for failure to satisfy a production standard must be countersigned by a member of the Manufacturing Engineering Department. This helps verify whether the production rate in question is correct. If the employee who has been disciplined contends that his standard is incorrect, the union, at its discretion, may introduce the Union Time Study Steward into the investigation of the grievance or dispute as the first step of the grievance procedure outlined in Article 7.2.1 of the contract.

No Strike-No Lockout Guarantee

ABZ has agreed that there will be no lockout during the life of our 1987-1992 contract. The union has agreed that neither it nor the employees will engage in a strike. The union will not interrupt or interfere with work. We will do this even though it is alleged that the basis for the action taken is an unfair labor practice within the meaning of the National Labor Relations Act.

Five-Year Plant Operations Guarantee

Finally, ABZ has agreed that the final assembly of all color television sets with screen sizes ten inches and over will be performed at its Clarkstown plant for the duration of the union agreement. This assumes that the Clarkstown plant has the capacity to produce the cabinets and color television sets as required to support ABZ's manufacturing and inventory requirements. Final assembly is defined as the installation of the picture tube and the succeeding steps necessary to complete the product.

The ICEU-ABZ Challenge

Folks, I probably am not the first to tell you that the ICEU-ABZ agreement is not all sweetness and light. We have had a number of problems. ICEU workers are glad they have jobs, but sometimes we are not happy about management and working conditions. We think our differences are solvable. Contractually, both ABZ and the ICEU have lived up to what each said it would do.

Yes, we squabbled about a proposal to contract janitorial work to outsiders. We argued about a decision to move parking for plastic workers to the west lot. Management's fifteen-minute change in shift times created baby-sitting problems—many problems. Management's policy of inspecting purses and any large bags carried in and out of the plant seemed to be an infringement on the women's civil rights, but through an attorney we found out it isn't.

Union members cheered when President Reagan let the controversial plant-closing bill stand. We felt this was legislation that was needed. ABZ's management just didn't think it was fair to require sixty-day notices to workers if a plant is planning a shutdown or a layoff affecting one-third of the work force. It became law and we are glad—management has to live with it.

The bottom line is that we are all in this together. Neither management nor the union can survive alone. We are as unhappy with the Japanese as management is. If something doesn't happen to level up the playing field, ICEU and ABZ may not survive. We can't get in the Japanese market. You couldn't find twenty ABZ televisions in Japan, but you find millions of theirs in the United States. *Is that fair?*

We are the people who decided that the only way to reverse the trade deficit, save the economy, and preserve jobs—including those at ABZ—was to get Americans to buy American-made products. This was the impetus behind our forming the Americans for America Committee.

You can help. Buy American! I'm not saying we are going to check the parking lot to see if you drive an American car. However, we will be disappointed if you are not doing your share to help save American jobs everywhere.

I guess that does it for me. Remember, I'm Todd Madrid. When you can't find me in the plant, I'll be at my office downtown. I can be reached by telephone—we are in the book!

Thank you.

Thank you Todd. That does it for "You and ABZ."

EXHIBIT III.1 Operations Management System

SECTION III

FUNCTIONAL OPERATIONS ACTIVITIES

The seven chapters in this section comprise our discussion of *functional operations management*, to which this entire book is keyed. Collectively, Chapters 5 through 11 represent functional operations strategy. Specifically, Chapter 5 is concerned with broad functional management concepts and the intralocking role of strategy. A discussion of the three levels of strategy--strategic, functional, and tactical--is presented.

Chapter 6 focuses on capacity strategy. *Capacity strategy* provides an organization with the right amount of capacity at the right time. If you concentrate on this chapter, you should be able to apply financial investment evaluation methods, waiting-line techniques, decision-tree analysis, payoff-table techniques, forecasting methods, break-even analysis, and make-or-buy analysis to achieve the right amount of capacity for a particular company.

Location strategy is the subject of Chapter 7. Location strategy provides an organization with a competitive location for its headquarters, manufacturing, service, and distribution activities. A location decision requires a company to consider long-range ethical and cultural factors and these factors receive special attention in this chapter. After completing Chapter 7, you should be able to implement a location strategy that benefits the company, the employees, and the community.

Chapter 8 examines *product strategy*. Once you have studied the chapter, you should be able to apply linear programming, break-even, decision-tree, payoff-table, and make-or-buy analysis to product considerations.

Chapter 9 discusses *process strategy*–the means and methods used to transform resources into goods and services. When you finish this chapter, you should be able to develop a successful process strategy with the aid of financial investment evaluation methods, break-even analysis, payoff tables, decision trees, and process planning charts.

Layout strategy is the focus of Chapter 10. You will be concerned with the location and flow of organizational resources around, into, and within an organization's production and service facilities. When you finish this chapter, you should be able to complete a process layout analysis, develop a systematic layout plan, develop a product or assembly line layout, and complete a measurement of service demand and service capacity for an existing facility.

Human resource strategy is presented in Chapter 11. Human resource strategy is concerned with employees, ethics, and culture. Discussions center around the role of top management, the importance of a code of ethical conduct, the involvement of personnel in ethical considerations, the measurement of effective corporate ethics, and corporate self-interest, survival, and achievement. The OM tools presented in Chapter 11 will give you the skills you need to deal with human resource matters.

A thoughtful analysis of each of the operations chapters in this section requires, to a varying extent, that the following items be presented: general background information; description of the appropriate OM Tools; suggested readings (these are located in the *References and Suggested Readings* section at the end of the book); operations situations at ABZ; ethical and cultural considerations; individual experiences; and group experiences. To avoid redundancy, however, some sections are eliminated when they have been adequately covered elsewhere in the book.

The first three items listed focus on the knowledge that is necessary for the study of particular operations components. The four following items emphasize participation in operations management and are intended to take you beyond the formal requirements of items one through three.

Each chapter contains one individual experience and two group experiences. Your instructor will determine which experience to use depending on the size of the class and nature of the instruction. Of the three experiences, the individual experience is the least complex. The final experience is designed to be more complex and more difficult.

The experiences generally begin with the introduction of an operations challenge. Activities one and two instruct you to apply a particular OM tool or to choose from among a number of OM tools. Activity three is designed to demonstrate the impact of ethics and culture on the situation. The fourth activity requires you to go beyond the immediate problem-solving situation by seeking additional factors and information.

CHAPTER 5

Functional Management Activities

Effective management is essential if an organization is to accomplish its mission. The role of management is to plan, control, organize, and facilitate the use of the *natural* (property), *material* (facilities, equipment, inventories), *financial* (securities, receivables, income, stock, equity) and *human* (employees) *resources*. Planning, controlling, organizing, and coordinating are the same four management processes required for any successful organization--business, government, educational, or social. These management processes are necessary regardless of the function being performed--operations (production), marketing, engineering, research and development, or finance.

Functional Management

Functional management conveys three key concepts. First, functional management involves managers, people who get things done by working with or through other people.

Second, functional management takes place within the context of objectives and policies that drive the organization's grand, corporate, business, and functional strategies.

Third, the criteria relevant for judging the actions taken as a result of functional management are standards for effectiveness and efficiency. *Effectiveness* is the ability to determine appropriate objectives: "doing the right things." *Efficiency* is the ability to minimize the use of resources in achieving organizational objectives: "doing things right." A review of performance based on these standards (feedback) is essential.

To understand the intra-locking role of strategy, five factors must be considered. First, *organizational planning* must be comprehensive. It should cover all aspects of the organizational structure. It should relate one intra-organizational strategy to another, and corporate, business, and functional aspects to the external environment.

Second, *operations strategy* should be functionally related to all top-level strategies. For example, an operations strategy should reflect marketing strategies that in turn should affect the financial strategies.

Third, *corporate planning* should designate responsibility for the development and implementation of all strategies. Each organizational component should be expected to accomplish a goal. Each component should be responsible for its own strategy and its own detailed plan. Each component's plans must fit with the plans of other units and reflect a grand, corporate, or business strategy. Responsibility for planning must be assigned to every organizational component that is responsible for achieving a strategy.

Fourth, the *strategy system* must be dynamic. Not only must effectiveness and efficiency of operation be achieved, but new operations and the improvement of current operations activities must be developed as a result of new environmental pressures.

Fifth, the *functional strategies* should provide criteria by which to measure the qualitative and quantitative output of the various operations units. Objectives in the form of standards must serve as yardsticks against which to measure the output of the organizational unit.

Levels of Strategy

There are three levels of strategy in any business unit: (1) the strategic, (2) the functional, and (3) the tactical.

Strategic Level Strategy

Strategic plans of action involve deciding on the mission, goals, objectives, and programs of the business unit. They involve changes in the mission, goals, objectives, and programs, and they involve the resources used to attain them. Finally, they involve the policies that are to govern the acquisition, use, and disposition of these resources.

An organization may have several business components, each having its own set of *business strategies*. The strategy used to simultaneously manage several intra-organizational businesses combined into a whole is called the *corporate strategy*. Corporate strategy is determined by the types of businesses the organization is in and how it conducts itself in those businesses.

The comprehensive, general plan of major actions by which a firm intends to achieve its collective strategic mission, goals, objectives, policies, and programs is called *grand strategy*.

Functional Level Strategy

The second level of strategy consists of detailed, uniform, and comparatively complete set of strategies. Here you will find marketing, financial, operations, and research and development strategies. Collectively, we refer to these plans of action as *functional strategies*. They describe how the organization will support its business strategies and are associated with the on-going manufacture and service aspects of the organization. Functional strategies focus on effective and efficient use of resources.

In this book we focus and provide details on the functional operations activities (5). (The numbers in parentheses refer to chapters in this book.) A marketing book would focus and provide details on the functional marketing activities.

Operations strategies--capacity (6), location (7), product (8), process (9), layout (10), and human resource (11)--are designed to assure that resources are obtained and used effectively and efficiently. An *operational strategy* is implemented by people who get things done with and through people. It is achieved in a context of objectives and policies derived from the organization's grand, corporate, and business strategies.

Once a decision is made to design an operational plan of action, resource allocations are considered. After the functional operations strategy has been determined using marketing and financial plans of action, specific tasks to accomplish the functional objectives are considered. This is known as tactical programming.

Tactical Level Strategy

Tactical programming specifies the activities to be carried out. Tactical strategy includes quality assurance (12), maintenance control (13), cost control (14), material management (15), advanced manufacturing support (16), and project planning and control (17). We refer to these as tactical support activities. Tactical programming also includes aggregate planning and master scheduling (18), inventory control--independent demand (19), resource requirements planning (MRP, CRP) (20), and shop floor control (21). We refer to these as *tactical core activities*.

A Functional Strategy Situation at ABZ

There are a number of functional strategies in effect at ABZ, one of which is the operations strategy practiced by the consumer electronics division. In the following memorandum you will find information pertinent to an operations strategy for the consumer electronics division of ABZ.

**Joseph Yehudai
Group Manager,
Operations**

ABZ Electronics
"Quality With A View!"

MEMORANDUM

From the Desk of Bob Kemper

Joe:

By now you have hired the several consumer electronics operations specialists you felt you needed. I assume that they have completed the payroll activities, have attended one of Jack Dustman's orientation sessions, and are now ready to help us save our market share in the consumer electronics industry.

Before you assign these new people to specific duties, let's make sure they understand the ABZ challenge, the ABZ plan to stay in the consumer electronics business, and the desire of ABZ to maintain current market shares in the consumer electronics industry, and that they are given an opportunity to express some opinions or recommendations about our functional strategies. Let them concentrate on the television, videocassette, and camcorder aspects of ABZ. Let's see what they really know and if they are ready to apply some of their business school knowledge.

Hope things are going well. I saw your office light on last Friday night. Didn't want to disturb you.

ABZ Electronics
"Quality With A View!"

MEMORANDUM

From the Desk of Joe Yehudai
Group Manager, Operations
Consumer Electronics Division

TO: Pat Hancock

Jack Dustman tells me that you have completed the basic ABZ orientation session and that you may be ready to do some thinking about functional operations strategy. So, I plan to pick your brains during the next week or so, before you get settled into the ABZ way of thinking. I want practical ideas about our functional operations strategy. Perhaps you already have some thoughts about:

1. whether ABZ should stay in the consumer electronics business;
2. what we can do to further reduce our television, VCR, and camcorder production costs;
3. whether we need to relocate any of our plants;
4. whether we can lower our labor costs and still satisfy our union members.

Happy thinking!

Ethical and Cultural Considerations

No matter what level the strategy, functional managers must be aware of the ethical and cultural ramifications of decisions. These ethical and cultural considerations are a reflection of the entire corporate culture.

ABZ Electronics
"Quality With A View!"

M E M O R A N D U M

From the Desk of Joe Yehudai
Group Manager, Operations
Consumer Electronics Division

TO: New Operations Specialists

Previously I sent you a memorandum asking you to think about our functional strategies. At ABZ we believe that any functional operations strategy should address the following ethical topics:

1. fundamental honesty and adherence to U.S. law;
2. product safety and quality;
3. health and safety in the workplace;
4. conflicts of interest;
5. fairness in selling and marketing practices;
6. financial reporting;
7. supplier relationships;
8. pricing, billing, and contracting;
9. payments to obtain business;
10. protection of the environment; and
11. intellectual property and proprietary information.

In short, ABZ believes that a strong ethical corporate culture is crucial key to survival and profitability in a highly competitive era. Please keep these factors in mind when choosing among alternative strategies.

Listing and Description of Appropriate OM Tools

A functional operations (production) strategy implemented by any division of a business must be linked to grand, corporate, business, and functional strategies. Functional operations strategy does not operate in a vacuum. This is true at ABZ, as illustrated in the following memoranda.

ABZ Electronics
"Quality With A View!"

MEMORANDUM

From the Desk of Joe Yehudai
Group Manager, Operations
Consumer Electronics Division

TO: Operations Specialists

To prevent ABZ's operations strategies from existing in a vacuum (independent from the remainder of the organization), the ABZ Operations Group has listed in priority order the factors that form the basis for an operations strategy.

1. **Quality.** This refers to the customers' perception of the degrees of excellence exhibited by our products and service. These perceptions include product appearance, product reliability, service acceptability, and product functioning.

2. **Production cost.** This refers to the unit cost of each product. It includes labor, material, transportation, and factory overhead costs. ABZ lowered its operations costs by the in-house design of products, investment in the most efficient operations processes, and in-house engineering studies and equipment modifications aimed at cost reductions. No rejects!

3. **Product availability.** This refers to the degree to which customers may expect immediate delivery (30 days maximum) of products after they are ordered. The secret of quick delivery is the finished goods inventory that awaits customers' demands.

4. **Dependability.** This refers to the ability to deliver products to customers when they are promised. The key variables are the size of the contract order and the time of the delivery.

5. **Flexibility.** This refers to the ability to promptly change production to other product and service designs and to other production volumes. Process designs must be kept simple so that they may be easily modified.

Individual Experience 5-1
Market Share Analysis

Review the information covered in Chapters 2 through 4. Review the information you may have read from the suggested readings and other information concerning the consumer electronics industry. Be prepared to respond to any or all memoranda directed to you from ABZ personnel. Immediately following any ABZ memoranda, appropriate space is provided so that you may list answers and other information prior to issuing an official response to your supervisor.

ABZ Electronics
"Quality With A View!"

M E M O R A N D U M

From the Desk of Joe Yehudai
Group Manager, Operations
Consumer Electronics Division

TO: Pat Hancock

As the newest employee in the department, would you please provide a position memo on the strengths, weaknesses, opportunities, and threats of our current operations strategy? Take a few minutes within the next day or two for this task. Consider ABZ's position in the consumer electronics industry. One or two pages will be great!

Once you have accomplished this, would you also list four or five strategies that may result in an increase of our market share? Please consider our television, videocassette recorder, and camcorder markets.

Activity 5-1-1   Strengths

Activity 5-1-2   Weaknesses

Activity 5-1-3   Opportunities

Activity 5-1-4   Threats

Activity 5-1-5   Recommendations for Market Share Increase

Individual Experience 5-2
Bringing the ABZ Story Up To Date

Review the information covered in Chapters 2 through 4. Review the notes you may have taken when you read additional information about the consumer electronics industry. Be prepared to respond to any or all memoranda directed to you from ABZ personnel.

ABZ Electronics
"Quality With A View!"

M E M O R A N D U M

From the Desk of Joe Yehudai
Group Manager, Operations
Consumer Electronics Division

TO: Pat Hancock

Using, but not limiting yourself to, *Compact Disclosure*, *Television Digest*, and *Value Line*, bring up to date this ABZ orientation presentation. Your final report, in memorandum form please, should be similar to the ABZ orientation presentation. Please include exhibits and headings.
I need this yesterday!

Group Experience 5-1-1G
Strategy Analysis of ABZ

Review the information covered in Chapters 2 through 4; the information you may have read from the suggested readings; and any other information concerning the consumer electronics industry. Be prepared to respond to any or all memoranda directed to you from ABZ personnel. Immediately following any ABZ memoranda, appropriate space is provided so that you may compile notes and data and other information prior to issuing an official response to your supervisor.

ABZ Electronics
"Quality With A View!"

M E M O R A N D U M

From the Desk of Joe Yehudai
Group Manager, Operations
Consumer Electronics Division

TO: Operations Specialists

Could you please send me a 1 to 4 page report that tells me what you think drives ABZ's grand, corporate, and business strategies in the consumer electronics market? Is it price? Is it competition in general? Is it foreign competition? Is it market share or profits? Is it survival?

Hey, let's hear what you have to say!

Grand Strategy

Corporate Strategy

Business Strategy

CHAPTER 6

Capacity Strategy Activities

Capacity strategy is a plan of action aimed at providing the organization with the right amount of capacity at the right time. The output capacity of the organization determines its ability to meet future demands for goods and services. *Insufficient capacity* results in loss of sales that in turn affects profits. *Excess capacity* results in higher production costs. The *optimal capacity strategy*, where quantity and timing are in balance, provides an excellent basis for minimizing operating costs and maximizing profits.

Capacity flexibility enables the company to deliver its goods and services to its customers in a shorter time than its competitors. Capacity flexibility is part of capacity strategy and includes having flexible plants and processes, broadly trained employees, and easy and economical access to external capacity such as subcontractors.

Targeting a 100 percent capacity utilization sounds and looks good in the short term. However, as a long-term strategy, 100 percent capacity is not sound practice. When a plant operates at or close to capacity, longer delivery times, increased back orders, and dissatisfied customers result over the long term. Such a practice also increases the risk of machine breakdown.

Management uses capacity strategy to balance the costs of overcapacity and undercapacity. The inability to accurately forecast long-term demand makes the balancing task difficult and risky. Modifying long-range capacity decisions while in production is difficult and costly. In a highly competitive environment, construction of a new high-tech facility might take longer than the life cycle of the product. In the case of overcapacity, closing a plant saddles management with a high economic cost and an even higher social cost. Closing a plant is a tremendous burden on employees and the community in which the plant operates. These high social costs will have an adverse effect on the firm.

Traditionally, the concept of economies of scale has lead to large plants that tried to do everything. More recently, the concept of the focused facility has suggested that better performance can be achieved if the plant is more specialized, concentrates on fewer tasks, and is therefore smaller.

A five-step process can aid management in making sound strategic capacity decisions: measure the capacity of currently available facilities, estimate future capacity needs based on demand forecasts, compare future capacity needs and available capacity to determine whether capacity must be increased or decreased, identify ways to accommodate long-range capacity changes (expansion or reduction), and select the best alternative based on a quantitative and qualitative evaluation.

Listing and Description of the Appropriate OM Tools

There are a number of quantitative operations tools available to the operations manager. Among the ones to be discussed in this chapter are financial investment evaluation methods, waiting lines, decision trees, payoff tables, forecasting, break-even analysis, and make-or-buy analysis.

Financial Investment Evaluation Methods

The traditional methods of net present value, payback period, internal rate of return, and profitability index can be used in a variety of long-range capacity decisions. The most common situation involves a choice between two or more processes and the evaluation of equipment replacement.

Waiting Lines

Waiting-line models are best used for capacity planning of services. These models aid in the measurement of service capacity and the identification of expanded or reduced capacity needs.

Decision Trees

Decision-tree analysis is a statistical and graphical multi-phased decision-making technique. Decision trees allow a decision maker to deal with uncertain events by determining the relative expected-value of each alternative course of action. The probabilities of different possible events are known as are the monetary payoffs that result from a particular alternative and a particular event. Decision trees are best used where capacity decisions involve several capacity expansion alternatives and where the selection of the alternative with the highest expected profit or the lowest expected cost is necessary.

Payoff Tables

A payoff table is a statistical, single-phase decision-making technique. A decision is made in an environment of risk. The probabilities of different possible events are known as are the monetary payoffs that result from a particular alternative and a particular event. The expected-value concept is used to find the best alternative. Payoff tables are best used where capacity decisions involve several capacity expansion alternatives and where the selection of the alternative with the highest expected profit or the lowest expected cost is necessary.

Forecasting Methods

The basic methods of forecasting are time series, linear regression, exponential smoothing, and moving average. These methods assist in forecasting future capacity needs for the purpose of deciding on the quantity and timing of capacity expansion or reduction.

Break-Even Analysis

Break-even analysis can be used to compare the costs of two or more facilities. When annual production volumes are known, break-even analysis can identify the least-cost alternative. It can also identify the annual production volumes that represent points of indifference among different facilities.

Make-or-Buy Analysis

This technique is used in capacity planning to evaluate the economic consequences of switching from a make-it-yourself strategy to a buy-it-from-someone-else strategy (or vice versa). The focus of the make-or-buy analysis is to determine whether expansion or reduction of capacity is needed.

The Functional Operations Situation at ABZ

Ladies and gentlemen, may I get your attention please? Please! Thank you! As you know, our television tube plant in Melrose Park, Illinois, has a work force of 2,500 to 3,000 people who make most of the television tubes for ABZ. In addition, the Melrose people produce approximately 500,000 television tubes annually for other television manufacturers and as ABZ replacements.

The Melrose plant has been running three shifts, seven days a week for the past year. Our situation at ABZ is the same as at other television tube manufacturers, including the Japanese companies with U.S. plants. There is a shortage of television tubes.

Additionally, ladies and gentlemen, HDTV is on the horizon. So, we need to consider both short- and long-range alternatives for increased production capacity of television tube production.

Plus--and do not forget this--or marketing department wants to increase our market share.

No Pat. Our strategy does not need to be limited to expanding the Melrose plant. We should consider all alternatives and perhaps all locations when we do our capacity strategy.

Now here is what I need at this time. I want us to look at the capacity aspects. Later I will get you information for a location strategy. Right now I want you to concentrate on capacity planning. Think about subcontracting with other companies; about acquiring other company's available facilities; about developing other sites; about developing other buildings; about buying new equipment; about expanding, updating, or modifying existing facilities; about reactivating facilities on standby status; and about the possibility of combining television picture tube production with computer monitor tube production.

We need more capacity now. We will need more capacity in the future. I want you to draw on all your knowledge, all your experience, and all of the various OM tools available. In fact, what I would like to do is to split you into ad hoc groups that each might use certain tools--financial investment evaluation methods, waiting lines, decision trees, payoff tables, forecasting methods, break-even analysis, and make-or-buy analysis.

Now there is no emergency here, but do realize that all our competitors are involved in the same planning situation. In fact, we understand that Matushita plans to increase capacity at Troy, Ohio, and Philips plans to increase production at Ottawa, Ohio, and Emporium, Pennsylvania. Toshiba plans to increase production at its Horseheads, New York, plant from 1 million tubes to 1.5 to 2 million tubes.

Hold it! Hold it! Remember ladies and gentlemen, you are doing capacity planning for factories that employ people—human beings, union folks, Americans. You are dealing with people's livelihood. Should expansion be accomplished in Juarez, Tijuana, or Matamoros rather than Melrose and Clarkstown? Is it right to move low-skilled jobs to other countries?

Hey, this is important! You hold those labor costs down. Remember, the picture tube and cabinet together make up about 60.5 percent of the factory costs, or about 32.2 percent of the retail price. The picture tube alone is about 50 percent of the factory cost of a television set. Think in terms of value added. Television manufacturers and associated trade groups are responsible for about 65 percent of value added and nearly 70 percent of the employment contributions of television manufacturing.

So, I will get back to you with some group and individual assignments. Be ready to go within the week. Thank you.

Individual Experience 6-1
When to Expand?

ABZ Electronics
"Quality With A View!"

MEMORANDUM

From: Joe Yehudai

To: Operations Specialists

RE: Flat-Tension Television Tube

ABZ Electronics has lost market share in the domestic color television market. On a company-wide scale, ABZ plans to regain market share. This increase will be 0.5 percent per year starting with 1989. In the following chart you will find statistics on ABZ's color television market share and total color television units sold in the U.S. during the years 1982-1988.

Year	Total Color TV Sales (Units)	ABZ's Share (%)
1988	19,328,374	12.75
1987	18,859,559	14.50
1986	17,317,478	15.75
1985	16,180,402	16.50
1984	15,196,870	17.50
1983	12,232,935	18.50
1982	11,236,621	19.40

In 1988 ABZ utilized 75 percent of its three-shift assembly capacity in its Clarkstown plant and 60 percent of its three-shift color picture tube manufacturing capacity at Melrose Park. We supplied all the picture tubes for our color sets. We sold an additional 500,000 color picture tubes to other television manufacturers and as ABZ tube replacements. The company policy is to expand capacity when the utilization rate exceeds 95 percent.

Here are a number of activities I would like you to undertake. I have provided space within this memo for your recommendations.

Activity 6-1-1 Use a time series to determine the year that additional assembly capacity will be needed.

Activity 6-1-2 ABZ would like to maintain color picture tube sales to other manufacturers and for ABZ replacement tubes at 1988 levels. Use a time series to determine the year that additional color picture tube manufacturing capacity will be needed.

Activity 6-1-3 What ethical and cultural factors should be considered in the decision? Explain.

Activity 6-1-4 Upon the completion of activities 1 and 2, what additional factors should be incorporated into the final decision-making process? What additional information will be needed to make a good decision? Explain.

Group Experience 6-1
Constructing a New Plant

ABZ Electronics
"Quality With A View!"
M E M O R A N D U M

From: Joe Yehudai

To: Operations Specialists

RE: New Plant Construction

     Television manufacturers around the world are experiencing a shortage of color picture tubes, especially large tubes. ABZ's management is considering the construction of a new plant that will manufacture color picture tubes that are 30 inches and larger. Competition in this capital-intensive picture tube manufacturing market dictates that the plant be located in the U.S. The location has not yet been determined. Preliminary data has been gathered so that a recommendation may be made in regard to the initial plant size and possible future expansion.

     Please keep in mind that the level of demand at a new facility will be affected by global economic conditions. These conditions are described as moderate, good, or excellent, with probabilities .15, .40, and .45 respectively. In the following chart, you will find some financial estimates expressed in present-value terms.

Facility	Demand Level	Profit/Loss	Expansion Cost
Large	moderate	(5,000,000)	
	good	10,000,000	
	excellent	17,500,000	
	+ small expansion		
	excellent	21,000,000*	3,000,000
Medium	moderate	(2,000,000)	
	good	11,000,000	
	excellent	12,000,000	
	+ moderate expansion		
	excellent	16,500,000*	4,000,000
Small	moderate	1,500,000	
	good	6,000,000	
	+ moderate expansion		
	good	9,000,000*	4,000,000
	excellent	6,000,000	
	+ moderate expansion		
	excellent	9,000,000*	4,000,000
	+ large expansion		
	excellent	16,000,000	6,000,000

* before the cost of expansion is deducted

Here is what I need from you as soon as possible.

Activity 6-1-1G Construct a decision tree. Make a recommendation as to the size of a plant that meets our initial needs and the possibility of future expansion.

Activity 6-1-2G Now that you have made your recommendation, management thinks that your economic forecast regarding projected demand levels was too optimistic. Revise your analysis using new probabilities for the demand levels. For the moderate, good, and excellent demand levels, use .40, .45, and .15 respectively.

Activity 6-1-3G What ethical and cultural factors should be considered in the decision? Explain.

Activity 6-1-4G Upon the completion of activities 1 and 2, what additional factors should be incorporated into the final decision-making process? What additional information will be needed? Explain.

Group Experience 6-2
Equipment Replacement

ABZ Electronics
"Quality With A View!"

M E M O R A N D U M

From: Joe Yehudai

To: Operations Specialists

RE: Equipment Replacement

   Melrose Park's management wants to consider replacing an old machine that is part of the color picture tube manufacturing process. Because the machine continues to produce at a low output rate and because the machine experiences frequent breakdowns, management considers the machine to be a bottleneck that is restricting the output capacity of the production line. The result? Maintenance and overtime costs have skyrocketed!

   A new machine with a higher output rate will cost approximately $750,000. It will save $150,000 a year. The old machine cannot be sold but common replacement parts valued at $40,000 can be salvaged and used for future maintenance. The new machine is expected to have an economic life of eight years and falls into the five-year IRS depreciation category. It will have a salvage value of $100,000. A 10 percent cutoff is used by ABZ for evaluating financial investments. The corporate tax rate is 45 percent.

   Given this scenario, please complete the following activities. I need your data and analysis as soon as possible.

Activity 6-2-1G Based on a net-present-value analysis, do you recommend the purchase of the new machine? Explain.

Activity 6-2-2G If a 15 percent cutoff rate were to be targeted by management, will you need to revise your recommendation? Explain.

Activity 6-2-3G What ethical and cultural factors should be considered in the decision? Explain.

Activity 6-2-4G Given the scenario in activities 1 and 2, are there any additional factors that should be incorporated into the final decision-making process? Explain. Will any additional information be needed? Explain.

CHAPTER 7

Location Strategy Activities

"My company is operating its manufacturing plant at 95 percent capacity and the demand for its product is increasing at the rate of 8 percent per year."

"My company has determined that the plant that it built nine years ago no longer allows us to compete effectively in our market because our potential new vendors and our only other available vendors have relocated, our labor costs have soared, our plant cannot accommodate new robotics, and our transportation and utility costs are eroding our profit margins."

"I am a partner in a new company that is going to manufacture high-definition television sets and we are going to need a plant that will allow us to produce them. The sales from this production will net us a minimum of 15 percent return on equity."

Each of these statements represents a need for a location strategy. Considerable experience, factual data, and location principles could be cited to support one plant location over another. *How important is a location strategy?*

The location of a major manufacturing plant in a community results in an augmented tax base to support municipal services. It creates opportunities for the unemployed and for entrants into the work force. It creates opportunities for local entrepreneurs to expand markets for goods and services, and provides additional sources of support for civic and charitable endeavors. It challenges educators to provide education and training. The relocation of a major manufacturing plant from a community in which the company has operated for many years will result in economic hardships for people. The loss of the company will be a shock to a community's economic vitality and perhaps to its fiscal stability as well. People will be hurt, some will endure actual hardship, while others will find their future expectations diminished to the point of despair.

In deciding to locate a manufacturing operation, a company has long-term moral obligations to its employees and to the community in which the operation is located. As a result, location strategy is of vital importance to the company, to its investors, to its employees, to future employees, to the country.

Location strategy is a plan of action that provides the organization with a competitive location for its headquarters, manufacturing, service, and distribution activities. A competitive location results in lower transportation and communication costs among the various facilities, costs that may run as high as 20 to 30 percent of a product's selling price. These costs greatly affect the volume of sales and amount of profit generated by a particular product. Additionally, many other quantitative and qualitative factors are important when formulating location strategy.

Change in facility location may be very costly. The facility location should only be changed, when product cost considerations have been studied.

A successful location strategy requires a company to consider the following major location factors in its location study: the nearness to market and distribution centers; the nearness to vendors and resources; the requirements of federal, state, and local governments; the character of direct competition; the degree of interaction with the rest of the corporation; the quality and quantity of labor pools; the environmental attractiveness of the area; the requirements of taxes and financing; the kinds of existing and potential transportation; and the quality of utilities and services. The dynamic nature of these factors could make what is a competitive location today an undesirable location in five years.

Ethical and Cultural Considerations

Prudent use of resources, particularly scarce resources, favors the use of capital in one location over another; e.g., a television assembly plant in Clarkstown, Missouri, as opposed to a television assembly plant in Horseheads, New York, or Scranton, Pennsylvania, or Marion, Indiana, or Troy, Ohio, or Juarez, Mexico. Effective location strategy has required management to weigh economic factors very carefully before making a decision about where to locate or relocate a plant. Management has considered whether or not the location of a plant in a particular community would effect production, sales, public relations, and profit. On the basis of reasonable assumptions, management has projected these factors into anticipated outcomes for a number of options under consideration.

Management has not been as effective when it has come to making long-range projections about the impact on employees and on the community. Implementing a location strategy without the benefit of long-range employee and community impact statements has raised a number of questions that deserve answers.

Is a company morally free to ignore the impact that a relocation of an existing plant will have on employees and members of the community? Are employees and members of the community mere factors in economic calculus, or are they people whom the company has an obligation not to harm?

If a company takes the obligation to the community and employees seriously, where does location strategy start and end? Is it reasonable to require a company to avoid a move if possible? Is it reasonable to require a company to notify affected parties as soon as possible if the decision is to make a move? Is it reasonable to require a company to take positive measures to help employees and the community?

Locating and operating a manufacturing plant in a community produces certain externalities that affect both workers and the community. Externalities are unintended side effects, some are good and some are bad. Externalities are produced by a manufacturing and service operation right along with its intended product.

The reduced quality of local air and water is one of the most obvious examples of an externality produced by today's manufacturing plants. The company does not produce these products intentionally, but in doing what it does intend to do, it also, perforce, produces unwanted products--polluted air and water.

A company provides an employee life style that contributes to the accomplishment of its work. A community network of services supports the life style of employees, community members, and the manufacturing company. A company provides the environment in which a symbiotic relationship develops among the plant, its workers, and the community. When a major plant operates in a community, it has an unintended influence on employees and the community. Businesses dependent on the company feel its impact. The municipality and its taxpayers may develop an infrastructure that they may not need were it not for the company. Schools, churches, and private associations become dependent on the company for support.

There is nothing extraordinary about external environment forces. These social relationships that the employees, the community, and the company become involved in are legitimate expectations that are often left unstated in the agreement a company makes when it locates in a community. Fairness requires that a company make an ethical commitment to a community so as to avoid long-term hardship to workers and the community should a decision be made to move or close a plant.

So, a successful location strategy and an effective location study require that a company not only consider the major location factors listed earlier, but also long-range ethical and cultural factors as well.

Listing and Description of Appropriate OM Tools

A proper location strategy will be aided by the use of the following OM tools: forecasting, linear programming, center of gravity method, factor rating, cost comparisons, and break-even analysis.

Forecasting

Forecasting is an attempt, using specific techniques, to predict outcomes and project future trends. The basic OM methods of forecasting are time series, linear regression, exponential smoothing, and moving average. A location decision is long range in nature. These methods assist in forecasting future values of variables that are included in a location decision.

Linear Programming

Linear programming is a mathematical technique that can be used when the relationship between the variables in a problem is linear. It can assist in identifying the optimal solution of a host of different problems. For example, different proposed locations of plants and warehouses can be compared based on the total shipping costs between them. The optimal locations that minimize the total shipping cost can then be selected. Linear programming could be used graphically or with the aid of a computation method such as Simplex. There is also a modified method for the transportation problem described here. This method is known as the *transportation method of linear programming*.

Center of Gravity Method

The *center of gravity method* is used to locate a single distribution facility. It can be used to locate a new facility or to relocate an existing one so that shipping costs are at least reduced if not minimized. It also can be used to identify low-cost shipping routes. It considers distance, volume, and cost.

Factor Rating

Factor rating is a multi-criteria method that can be used to compare two or more locations for a manufacturing plant of any type. It can identify the location that is superior according to the criteria used. It can combine quantitative and qualitative factors relevant to a specific situation. Factors can be assigned different weights according to their relative importance. Factual data or subjective estimates are used to develop factor scores, weighted factor scores, and total location scores so that the best location from among those compared is identified.

Cost Comparisons

This method relies completely on detailed *cost comparisons* of different locations. It completely ignores other non-cost factors and all qualitative factors. As a result, its use is quite limited. It can be used only when all the ignored factors are insignificant, or as a preliminary analysis.

Break-Even Analysis

Break-even analysis can be used to compare the total costs of two or more facilities and identify the location with the least total cost. The annual production volumes must be known. The analysis can also identify the volumes at which other locations become the least-cost locations.

Review of the Operations Situation at ABZ Electronics

"ABZ, Quality With A View!"

THE ABZ OF IT, 1989
Weekly Newsletter

Volume 51, Issue 37
Clarkstown Edition

ABZ'S LOSING MONEY

ABZ Electronics has been losing money for the past three years. ABZ executives attribute this situation to strong competition in the television and videocassette recorder markets. The strong competition comes from foreign firms (Philips and Thompson, for example) that manufacture their products and their American brands such as (Magnavox, Philco, Sylvania, RCA, and GE) in their home countries and in the United States. It comes from foreign firms (Bang und Olufsen, Goldstar, Hitachi, JVC, Matushita, American Kotobuki, NEC, Orion, Sony, and Sanyo, for example) that have plants in the U.S. It comes from foreign firms who export their products to the United States (NAD, Panasonic, Proton, Samsung, Sansui, Tatung, Teknika, Toshiba, and Yamaha, for example). ABZ executives do not want to continue their three-year practice of selling television products below cost just to maintain the current market share.

A decision has been made by ABZ executives to investigate a number of options that would result in increased market share for television and video cassettes. These options would also need to result in lower operations costs and better service.

ABZ executives feel it is time to study the relocation of existing facilities as alternatives to lower labor costs.

ABZ AND BOSE

ABZ and Bose agreed to extend "strategic alliance" for another 5 years announcing the new pact at the Winter Consumer Electronics Show that calls for continued collaboration on new ABZ televisions featuring Bose sound systems. In August of 1986, ABZ introduced 4 digital televisions under the logo, "ABZ Sound by Bose."

PHILIPS AND ABZ TIED

Philips is tied with ABZ for the number 2 spot in U.S. television market share (after Thomson), according to the January 15 *BusinessWeek* profile, which says it has 10% of the world market. The article describes the Dutch company as being on "war footing" in battle with the Japanese and Korean firms for world markets.

ELECTRONIC LEADERS

For the second straight year, ABZ and Tandy were the only two U.S. companies with major consumer electronics interests to be ranked in Electronics News' annual list of top 50 firms. The ranking is based on estimated electronics sales volume for the most recent reported four quarters.

CHECK THOSE SICK LEAVE HOURS

Sick-leave hours taken during the last pay period may not have been correctly recorded on paycheck stubs and accrual reports. Input problems with data for these dates have required that the Human Resources Department resubmit the departmental leave reports to Computer Services for re-keying during the next pay period.

Any employee who used sick leave during this pay period and notices that this is not reflected on the last pay stub should call Maxine or Hilda in the Human Resources Department, Extension 2222. Human Resources apologizes for this inconvenience.

NEW HIRES

Lisa Magana - Trailer Spotter, *Jimmy Gray* - Salvage Attendant, *Jenny Rodriguez* - Audio Pre-Test Operator, *Charles Wright, Jr.* -Plastics Inspector, *Deborah Hall* - Heavy Assembler/Packer, *Michele Heerding* - Latch-Key Supervisor, *Chris Fitch* - Plastics Inspector, *Peter Martinez* - Audio Pre-Test Operator, *Dan Heerding* - Security.

ABZ Electronics
"Quality With A View!"

M E M O R A N D U M

From the Desk of Joe Yehudai
Group Manager, Operations
Consumer Electronics Division

TO: Operations Specialists

A directive from ABZ executives indicates that you should consider all economic, social, environmental, and technical factors in determining where to locate any new manufacturing facility. The executives insist that the major objective of the proposed location analysis is to identify the location that offers the lowest operating cost. Further, the executives remind you that a complete location analysis must integrate the economic or quantitative factors with the qualitative factors. The executives are quick to point out that qualitative factors can be dominant when compared to quantitative ones and that you should consider this in your study of locations. Finally, the executives remind you that location decisions must be sequential--regional, community, and site. Your charge is to develop a combined regional and community analysis.

ABZ Electronics
"Quality With A View!"
M E M O R A N D U M

TO: Joe Yehudai

FROM: Bob Kemper

RE: Location Strategy Guidelines

The ABZ Board of Directors recommend that operations managers adopt the following policy when developing location strategy:
"In deciding whether or not to locate a manufacturing operation, ABZ has a moral obligation to its employees. It also has a moral obligation to the community in which the operation is located. These obligations require that the company:

1.   avoid any relocation if reasonably possible;
2.   take into account the impact of any proposed move on employees and the community;
3.   notify the affected parties as soon as possible if a decision to relocate is made; and
4.   take positive measures to help mitigate the effects of any possible relocation."

Individual Experience 7-1
Determining the Best Location for a New
Assembly Plant and a New Warehouse

ABZ Electronics
"Quality With A View!"

M E M O R A N D U M

From:	Joe Yehudai
To:	Pat Hancock
RE:	Determining the Best Location for a New Assembly Plant and a New Warehouse

ABZ Electronics operates two television assembly plants and three warehouses. Your colleagues have recently completed two location studies. The first study compared several locations for an assembly plant. Two locations were identified as equally desirable. The second study compared several locations for warehouses and identified two equally competitive locations. Your challenge (as noted in the Activities that follow), on the basis of the executive directives above and the following charted information, is to recommend which warehouse and which assembly plant should be built. Your final directive is to minimize the total transportation cost.

Assembly Plant	Monthly Capacity (Units)
Location A (existing)	150,000
Location B (existing)	180,000
Location C (proposed)	200,000
Location D (proposed)	200,000

Warehouse	Monthly Requirements (Units)
Location 1 (existing)	100,000
Location 2 (existing)	120,000
Location 3 (existing)	110,000
Location 4 (proposed)	190,000
Location 5 (proposed)	190,000

Transportation Costs (Per Unit)

Plant	Warehouse				
	Location 1	Location 2	Location 3	Location 4	Location 5
A	1.50	2.00	1.75	2.25	2.00
B	1.75	1.50	2.00	1.50	2.25
C	2.25	1.75	1.00	1.75	2.00
D	2.00	2.25	1.50	1.75	1.75

Here are four activities (see the next three pages) that I want you to complete. I needed this yesterday.

Activity 7-1-1 Use a transportation method such as northwest corner and the stepping stone or any other transportation method to recommend which assembly plant and which warehouse should be built.

Activity 7-1-2 Use the linear programming approach, Simplex, to determine which assembly plant and which warehouse should be built.

Activity 7-1-3 What ethical and cultural factors should be considered in the decision? Explain.

Activity 7-1-4 Upon the completion of activities 1 and 2, what additional factors will need to be incorporated into the final decision-making process? What additional information will be needed?

Group Experience 7-1
Selecting the Best Location for a High-Definition Television Plant

---

ABZ Electronics
"Quality With A View!"

M E M O R A N D U M

From: Joe Yehudai

To: Operations Specialists

RE: HDTV Planning

    ABZ electronics is in the process of developing HDTV (high-definition television). A new production facility may be needed if we are to pursue HDTV. Three states have been identified as potential locations for a new plant. Such a plant would have to be ready in 1993. The states identified as possible sites are Illinois, Indiana, and Missouri.
    Here is what I need by the end of the week.

Activity 7-1-1G Use a factor rating with weighted scores to identify the state that will provide the "best" location. Start your task by preparing a workable relevant location factor list. Your list should include factors for which statistical data are available and/or for which a relative score can be estimated.

Activity 7-1-2G Use group consensus to determine the weights of the factors and their scores. Calculate the total location-weighted score and make a recommendation.

Activity 7-1-3G Note any ethical and cultural factors that should be considered in a final decision.

Activity 7-1-4G Upon the completion of activities 1 and 2, suggest additional factors that should be incorporated into the final decision making process. What additional information needs to be gathered? Explain.

Group Experience 7-2
A New Cabinet Manufacturing Plant in Mexico

ABZ Electronics
"Quality With A View!"

MEMORANDUM

From: Joe Yehudai

To: Operations Specialists

RE: A New Cabinet Manufacturing Plant in Mexico

ABZ electronics is planning the construction of a new cabinet plant in Mexico. The three cities that are finalists in a preliminary analysis are Juarez, Nogales, and Monterrey. Currently, the projected requirement is for 300,000 cabinets per year. The relevant cost data is as follows:

Site	Fixed Cost/Year	Variable Cost/Unit
Juarez	$200,000	$14
Nogales	$300,000	$13
Monterrey	$700,000	$12

Here is what I would like you to determine for my consideration.

Activity 7-2-1G Use a break-even analysis to determine the "best" location for the projected volume. You may use a graph if you prefer.

Activity 7-2-1G (Continued)

Activity 7-2-2G At what projected volumes will the other locations be preferred? Use a break-even analysis.

Activity 7-2-3G What ethical and cultural factors should be considered in the decision? Explain.

Activity 7-2-4G Upon the completion of activities 1 and 2, what additional factors should be incorporated into the final decision-making process? What additional information will be needed? Explain.

CHAPTER 8

Product Strategy Activities

Product strategy is a way of deciding which goods and services an organization will produce and market. Product strategy is a main component of the operations strategy and the link between the operations strategy and the other functional strategies, especially marketing and research and development.

Product, marketing, and research and development strategies fit together to build an effective overall functional strategy. Together, they form the product aspect of the business strategy.

The product strategy and the operations strategy of the business should take into account the strengths and weaknesses of operations, which are primarily internal, as well as those of other functional areas which deal more with external opportunities and threats.

The tendency in the U.S. is to place too much emphasis on marketing and finance. As a result, product strategy is often noncompetitive. In many cases, U.S. companies simply produce the wrong products, that is, products that are at a disadvantage rather than at an advantage in the market place. Moreover, the resources that are allocated to operations are often insufficient to overcome such weaknesses as lack of technology, poorly trained employees, and outmoded equipment.

When many different products must be produced, operations should have enough control of the scheduling process to reduce (not minimize) cost and increase (not maximize) capacity utilization. Obviously, just as customer relations cannot be the only criteria on which to base an effective product strategy, neither can operations criteria be. Still, operations personnel should be among the main players when a decision is made about which products to produce, which products to sell, which products to buy, and which products to resell. They should also be major participants in product design.

Cooperation and coordination between marketing, operations, and research and development from the inception of a new product would be very beneficial to the company. At the very least, it would ensure a smooth transition from research and development to production. Operations people would be able to contribute to the quality of the total product and not just attempt to improve the quality of the components. Even the most sophisticated product can be designed so that it is relatively simple to produce which reduces the number of units that must be scrapped or reworked during production and also reduces the need for highly trained and highly paid employees. The product's price competitiveness or profits would thus be improved.

Another aspect of the contribution that operations can make to product design involves the desirability of standardizing parts and sub-assemblies and therefore reducing cost. It should be noted that one of the main measures of an operations manager's performance is the ability to produce goods at or below the standard cost. Design engineers do not usually have the same kind of incentive for that type of cost savings.

The product strategy is also linked to other components of the operations strategy. Adding or dropping products directly affects capacity needs and could result in capacity expansion or reduction, a decision to add a new product could be determined by the available process or it could create the need for a new process; the company's products could affect plant layout or vise versa. The same relationship exists between the product strategy and the human resources strategy: highly complex products usually require a highly skilled labor force.

Listing and Description of Appropriate OM Tools

A successful product strategy will be aided by the use of the following OM tools: linear programming; break-even analysis; decision trees; payoff tables; and make-or-buy analysis.

Linear Programming

Linear programming attempts to minimize or maximize a mathematical object function subject to a collection of mathematical constraints. The relationships between the variables are expressed in terms of linear equations or inequalities. Linear programming can assist in identifying the optimal solutions to a host of different problems. For example, when resources are limited they could be allocated to the production of an optimal mix of products so that profit is maximized. Each product requires a particular combination of capacity inputs and its sale results in a particular amount of profit. Linear programming could be used graphically or with the aid of a computation method such as Simplex.

Break-Even Analysis

Break-even analysis (a financial statement that enables managers to analyze the relationships among costs, sales volume, and profits) can be used in performing a sensitivity analysis for a new product decision. For example, different estimates for forecasted volumes, optimistic and pessimistic, can be used in the break-even formula. If the proposed product will yield a profit (be above the break-even point) even with the most pessimistic volume estimate, then it should be given serious consideration.

Decision Trees

Decision-tree analysis (graphic aids for making multi-phase decisions) permits a statistical and graphical analysis of a multi-phase situation. The decision is made in an environment of risk. The probabilities of different possible events are known and so are the monetary payoffs that would result from a particular alternative and a particular event. The expected-value concept is used to find the best alternative. An example of a good application of decision-tree analysis would be the decision to use current in-house development personnel or outside consultants for the same purpose in a situation involving possible future in-house production or subcontracting and the sale of a new product.

Payoff Tables

A *payoff table* is a statistical, single-phase decision-making technique. When you are in an environment of risk and want to know the probabilities of different possible events and the monetary payoffs that would result from a particular alternative and particular event, use a payoff table. The expected-value concept helps find the best alternative. Payoff tables can be used when making decisions about adding products based on cost and revenue estimates and possible economic conditions.

Make-or-Buy Analysis

Product strategy decisions can benefit from *make-or-buy analysis* (an analysis that suggests whether a material or part should be made in-house or bought from a supplier). For example, a manufacturing company would like to broaden its product line and its most important criterion is profit. The company can either produce and sell the products itself, or buy the product, put the company label on it, and resell it. Make-or-buy analysis can be used in this type of decision.

Individual Experience 8-1
Making Decisions About New Product Development

ABZ Electronics
"Quality With A View!"

M E M O R A N D U M

From: Joe Yehudai

To: Operations Specialists

RE: Flat-Tension Television Tube

The engineering department is very close to formalizing a new product concept known as a flat-tension television tube. Management must decide on how to capitalize on the new idea. If the idea is sold next year at its preliminary stage, it is estimated that it would sell for the following amounts depending on next year's economic climate:

Economic Conditions	Probability	Proceeds from Sale
Good	.3	$15,000,000
Fair	.6	$10,500,000
Poor	.1	$ 7,500,000

It will cost approximately $6,000,000 and will take approximately three years to complete the new product development. The engineering department estimates that there is only a 40 percent probability that the project will be successful. If the project is unsuccessful, the product development costs will have to be eaten by management--a total loss.

If the project is successful, management will have to decide if ABZ should sell the production and marketing rights to another manufacturer or produce and sell the product itself. If the new product is produced and sold by ABZ, the net present value of the return (cost included) will depend on the market size:

Size of Market	Probability	Returns
Large	.4	$160,000,000
Small	.6	$ 15,000,000

If the production and marketing rights of the developed product are sold, the net present value of the returns (cost included) will depend on the economic climate at the time of the sale:

Economic Conditions	Probability	Returns
Good	.4	$ 90,000,000
Fair	.5	55,000,000
Poor	.1	25,000,000

Now here is what I need to have done before the weekend rolls around! (I have provided space within this memorandum for your analysis.)

Activity 8-1-1 Use a decision tree and recommend a course of action.

Activity 8-1-2 If the probability for a large market is revised to .3, how will it affect your recommendation?

Activity 8-1-3 What ethical and cultural factors should be considered in the decision? Explain.

Activity 8-1-4 Upon the completion of activities 1, 2, and 3, tell me what additional factors should be incorporated into the final decision-making process? What additional information will be needed? Explain.

Group Experience 8-1
Make-or-Buy a 31-inch Color Television Console

ABZ Electronics
"Quality With A View!"

M E M O R A N D U M

From: Joe Yehudai

To: Operations Specialists

RE: 31-inch Color Television Console

    ABZ electronics does not produce or sell a 31-inch color television console. Many of our competitors, such as Hitachi, Magnavox, and Sylvania, do sell such a set. You know that ABZ advertises itself as a full-line television manufacturer. So, we need a 31-inch color television console to complete our full line of color television sets. This will allow us to become more competitive.

    Management does not know whether we should manufacture the set or buy it from another manufacturer and put our name on it.

    The following information was gathered by the planning staff:

Source	Fixed Cost/Year	Variable Cost/Unit
Make	$3,000,000	$1,050
Buy	-----	1,100

The projected volume is 40,000 units per year.

    Now here is what I need to have done before the sun sets tomorrow! (I have provided space within this memorandum for your analysis.)

Activity 8-1-1G What would you recommend as the best course of action?

Activity 8-1-2G What would it take, in terms of projected volume, to get you to change your recommendation?

Activity 8-1-3G In order to compete with Sanyo and Sony, should we sell the console below our costs? Explain.

Activity 8-1-4G Upon the completion of activities 1, 2, and 3, what additional factors do you recommend be incorporated into the final decision-making process? What additional information will be needed? Explain.

Group Experience 8-2
Finding the Optimal Product Mix

ABZ Electronics
"Quality With A View!"

MEMORANDUM

From: Joe Yehudai

To: Operations Specialists

RE: Finding the Optimal Product Mix

In our expanded Clarkstown television assembly plant, we are establishing an assembly line that will be dedicated to our 25-inch (SD2569W) and 27-inch (SD2767H) color television table models. The production process is similar, but the number of labor hours required to assemble and fabricate each set differs.

The 25-inch set takes two hours of assembly and 1.8 hours of fabrication. The 27-inch set requires 2.4 hours of assembly and 1.5 hours of fabrication. This month, we have 8,650 hours of assembly time and 3,460 hours of fabrication time available.

The sale of a 25-inch set is said to yield a profit of $57. The sale of a 27-inch set should yield a profit of $81.

Now here is what I needed from you yesterday! (I have provided space within this memorandum for your analysis.)

Activity 8-2-1G Use linear programming (Simplex or graphic method) to determine the best possible product mix in order to maximize profit.

Activity 8-2-2G Assume that next month's capacity can be increased by 100 percent in the assembly and 50 percent in fabrication. What will be the profit-maximizing mix for that month?

Activity 8-2-3G If our foreign competitors are successful at dumping their 25-inch set for $100 dollars less than our projected price, should we manufacture the set and sell it below our costs to force the competitors to raise their price? Explain. How will our action (selling below cost) force the competition to raise their price? Explain.

P.S. Remember, these sets are necessary if ABZ is to maintain a full line of color television sets.

Activity 8-2-4G Upon the completion of activities 1, 2, and 3, what additional factors should I incorporate into the decision-making process? What additional information will be needed? Explain.

CHAPTER **9**

Process Strategy Activities

Process strategy determines the means and the methods that the organization will use in order to transform resources into goods and services. Materials, labor, information, equipment, and managerial skills are resources that must be transformed. A competitive process strategy will ensure the most efficient and effective use of the organization's resources.

Manufacturing processes may be grouped into three different types. The first type is the *continuous process,* used in producing chemicals, beer, and petroleum products.

The second type is the *repetitive process,* used for producing items in large lots. This mass-production or assembly-line process is used in the auto and appliance industries. The third manufacturing process is used to produce small lots of custom designed products such as furniture and is commonly known as the *job-shop process.* The production of one-of-a-kind items is included in this type of process as is unit production. Space ship and weapons system production are considered job-shop activities.

It is common for an organization to use more than one type of manufacturing process at the same time and in the same facility.

Process strategy is directly linked to product strategy. The decision to select a particular process strategy may be the result of external market opportunities or threats. When this is true, the product takes center stage and the process becomes a function of the product. The corporation decides what it wants to produce then it selects a process strategy to produce it.

When a corporation reacts to an external opportunity, it runs the risk of not having immediate access to the most efficient manufacturing process. To solve such a process and production challenge, the corporation must integrate development and procurement planning into the process strategy.

The formulation of a product strategy may also be based on the manufacturing process capability of an organization. Here, the organization considers it strengths and weaknesses and makes the process and product choice on that basis. A high-skill, labor-intensive product simply cannot be effectively and efficiently produced by a company whose short- and long-range strength is unskilled labor. When the strength of a particular company is the availability of unskilled labor, the process strategy takes center stage and guides the formulation of a product strategy. An organization that knows it strengths and weaknesses and is in touch with the external opportunities and risks will know whether to pursue the "product first/process second" alternative or the "process first/product second" alternative.

The function of process strategy is to determine what equipment will be used, what maintenance will be necessary, and what level of automation will be most effective and efficient. Equipment decisions broadly dictate a plant layout strategy. The type of employees and the level of employee skills needed will also be a rather direct result of the process strategy.

Listing and Description of Appropriate OM Tools

A successful process strategy will be aided by the use of the following OM tools: financial investment evaluation methods; break-even analysis; payoff tables; decision trees; and process planning charts.

Financial Investment Evaluation Methods

The traditional methods of *net present value, payback period, internal rate of return,* and *profitability index* can be used in a variety of process decisions. The most common situations involve a choice between two or more processes and the evaluation of different levels of automation.

Break-Even Analysis

Break-even analysis allows a manager to compare the costs of two or more organizational structures. It can identify the one with the least cost, when annual production volumes are known. It can also identify the annual production volumes that represent points of indifference among the different processes.

Payoff Tables

A *payoff table* provides the manager with single-phase statistical calculations of expected profits or expected costs for each demand level alternative. The probabilities of different possible events in an environment of risk are known and so are the monetary payoffs that result from a particular alternative and a particular event.

Decision Trees

Decision-tree analysis is a statistical and graphical multi-phased decision-making technique used by managers in an environment of risk. The probabilities of different possible events are known and so are the monetary payoffs that result from a particular alternative and a particular event. The expected-value concept is used to find the best alternative. Decision trees are best used where process decisions involve several alternative levels of automation and possible future modifications. The selection of the alternative with the highest expected profit or the lowest expected cost is possible.

Process Planning Charts

Two types of charts are used in process planning. The first type, the *assembly chart*, provides an overall view of the material flow pattern. It also indicates the sequence of operations in the main assembly and sub-assemblies. Process planning charts are based on the information presented in an assembly drawing.

The second type of chart, the *process chart*, provides more detail than the assembly chart. It reduces an operation to steps. Each step is one of five different classes: operation, transport, inspect, delay, and store. A summary of the number of occurrences in each step is provided. The chart could aid in method improvement that is aimed at reducing the number of delay and store elements.

Individual Experience 9-1
Determining the Level of Automation in a HDTV Plant

ABZ Electronics
"Quality With A View!"

M E M O R A N D U M

From: Joe Yehudai

To: Operations Specialists

RE: Determining the Level of Automation in a HDTV
             Plant

    ABZ Electronics is in the process of designing the HDTV
plant to be completed in early 1993. Management must decide on
the level of automation in the assembly operation. Two levels of
automation are considered. These two levels represent a tradeoff
between fixed cost and variable cost.

    For a second-level automated assembly facility, the annual
fixed cost is $5,000,000 and variable assembly cost per unit is $50.

    For a third-level automated assembly facility, the annual
fixed cost is $10,000,000 and variable assembly cost per unit is $40.

    The sales forecast for HDTV is:

Year	Sales Forecast (Units)
1993	700,000
1994	1,800,000
1995	2,600,000
1996	3,200,000
1997	3,500,000
1998	4,300,000
1999	4,700,000

    Here is a list of four activities that I would like you to do
for me as soon as possible.

Activity 9-1-1 Would you recommend a second-level or a third-level automated assembly? Explain.

Activity 9-1-2 If an updated forecast were to show that sales are higher by 30 percent for each year, would you change your recommendation? Explain.

Activity 9-1-3 What ethical and cultural factors should be considered in your decision? Explain.

Activity 9-1-4 Upon the completion of activities 1, 2, and 3, what additional factors should be incorporated into the final decision-making process? What additional information will be needed?

Group Experience 9-1
Attempting to Produce More in America

ABZ Electronics
"Quality With A View!"

MEMORANDUM

From: Joe Yehudai

To: Operations Specialists

RE: Attempting to Produce More in America

All of the ABZ cabinet manufacturing plants are located in Mexico. ABZ's management felt this was necessary if labor costs were to be held to a minimum because cabinet manufacturing is labor intensive.

Now, management has been approached by the union to consider constructing a new cabinet manufacturing plant in the U.S. Management is considering such a plant. If such a plant is to be built, management has decided that it will be an automated plant with an annual volume of 300,000 cabinets. Two different levels of automation will be considered.

Here are some facts for you to consider. First-level automation will cost $3,700,000 and will save $.40 per cabinet in comparison with Mexico. Salvage value will be $370,000. Second-level automation will cost $5,600,000 and will save $.60 per cabinet in comparison with Mexico. Salvage value will be $560,000.

ABZ's tax rate is 45 percent. Depreciation is according to the IRS five-year schedule, and the equipment will have an economic life of six years. A cutoff rate of 15 percent should be used.

Activity 9-1-1G Would you recommend first-level or second-level automation? Explain.

Activity 9-1-2G What is the internal rate of return for each of the two levels of automation? Explain.

Activity 9-1-3G What ethical and cultural factors should be considered in the decision? Explain.

Activity 9-1-4G Upon the completion of activities 1, 2, and 3, what additional factors should be incorporate into the final decision-making process? What additional information will be needed?

Group Experience 9-2
A Robot in the Injection-Molding Operation

ABZ Electronics
"Quality With A View!"

M E M O R A N D U M

From: Joe Yehudai

To: Operations Specialists

RE: Robotics for ABZ?

ABZ's management is considering the introduction of robotics in the injection-molding operation. The union is definitely against the proposal because it will result in the loss of two jobs (one per shift). The project will be approved if the payback period will be six years or less. The total investment is estimated to be $250,000. The annual labor cost replaced by the robot (including benefits and overhead) is $100,000. The robot's annual maintenance cost is approximately $12,000 and the straight-line annual depreciation is $25,000. The robot is 20 percent faster than the workers.

Activity 9-2-1G Should the project be approved? (Use the modified formula in Chase, pp. 61-62.) Explain.

Activity 9-2-2G Can anything be done to save jobs as a result of such automation?

Activity 9-2-3G What ethical and cultural factors should be considered in the decision? Explain.

Activity 9-2-4G Upon the completion of activities 1, 2, and 3, what additional factors should be incorporated into the final decision-making process? What additional information will be needed?

CHAPTER 10

Layout Strategy Activities

Layout strategy is concerned with the location and flow of all organizational resources around, into, and within production and service facilities. A cost-effective and cost-efficient layout strategy is one that minimizes the cost of processing, transporting, and storing materials throughout the production and service cycle.

A layout strategy is very closely linked, directly and indirectly, to the rest of the components of operations strategy--capacity, location, product, process, and human resource. The layout strategy is usually one of the last to be formulated. It must target capacity and process requirements. It must satisfy the organization's product design, quality, and quantity requirements. Finally, it must target facility and location requirements. An effective layout strategy will be compatible with the organization's available quality of work life.

A *layout* is the overall arrangement of equipment, work areas, service areas, and storage areas within a facility that produces goods or provides services. The four basic types of layouts for manufacturing facilities are product, process, fixed position, and group technology.

A product layout is appropriate for organizations that produce and service a limited number of different products. It is not appropriate for an organization that is involved with constant or frequent changes of products. A product layout is most appropriate when production volumes are high, equipment is highly specialized, and the employees' skills are narrow.

A process or a functional layout is appropriate for organizations involved in a large number of different tasks. It best serves an organization whose production volumes are low, equipment is multipurpose, and employees' skills are broad.

The fixed position layout is most appropriate for an organization whose product is stationary while resources flow. A group technology (GT) layout is a cell of a product layout within a larger process layout. It benefits organizations that require both types of layout.

Most manufacturing facilities are a combination of two or more different types of layouts. Various techniques assist in designing an efficient and effective layout that meets the required specifications.

Listing and Description of Appropriate OM Tools

A successful layout strategy will be aided by the use of the following OM tools: process layout analysis, systematic layout planning, assembly-line balancing heuristics, and waiting lines.

Process Layout Analysis Techniques

A design of a *process layout* is primarily aimed at reducing the material handling efforts that are necessary to move materials among departments. Since the number of possible layouts is very large, a satisfactory rather than an optimal layout is the goal of the design.

Block diagram analysis assists in the development of a preliminary layout. The load-distance analysis enables managers to compare two or more layouts in terms of total material flow. This flow takes into consideration the quantities moved and the distances traveled. The comparison between layouts can also be made in terms of cost of material handling. A series of trial and error steps attempt to reduce the total material handling efforts.

Systematic Layout Planning

The *systematic layout planning* technique is also used in the design of process layouts. It is used when the material flow among departments may not be the most important criteria in designing a satisfactory layout. A service operation is a good example where systematic layout planning (SLP) can be used. This technique requires the development of a relationship chart which shows the degree of importance of having each department located adjacent to all other departments.

Once the relationship chart is developed, a diagram is prepared. The diagram consists of an initial departmental layout and reflects the desirable distance between departments that need to be close to each other. The goal of layout planning is to develop a layout that satisfies as much as possible the overall need for proximity among departments.

Assembly Line Balancing Heuristics

A product layout is also known as an *assembly line layout*. The product layout divides work station tasks as equally as possible. If assembly line balancing is done properly, the number of employees needed for a particular level of output is reduced. Due to the complexity of assembly line balancing, it is difficult to arrive at optimal solutions.

Simple-rule heuristic methods are used to arrive at satisfactory solutions. Using more than one heuristic for a particular balancing problem, permits a better and a more efficient solution, one that best uses an employee's time.

Waiting Lines

> *Waiting line models* are best used when designing a layout for a service facility. These models aid in the measurement of service demand and service capacity for an existing facility. Effective waiting line analysis matches service demand and service capacity.

Individual Experience 10-1
Preparing and Improving a Layout for a Sheet Metal Shop

> The Clarkstown plant manager is coordinating a planning effort that will result in a new 20,000 square foot sheet metal shop. The completed shop will produce some sheet metal parts that are required in television set assembly. The shop will consist of eight adjacent departments. Each department will occupy an area measuring 50 feet by 50 feet.
>
> Presently, no designation of particular areas within the building has been made. Further, no decision has been made concerning the overall physical shape of the new building. The production planning department, using projected requirements, determined the number of parts that will travel each month among the eight departments in the shop as shown in the following table. Note that only the upper right part of the table is occupied. If, for example, 10,000 units will travel each month from department five to department six and 15,000 units will travel in the opposite direction, a sum of 25,000 units will appear in a proper upper-right cell.

Dept	Department						
1	2	3	4	5	6	7	8
1	23,000	21,000	2,000	7,000	4,000	2,000	1,000
2			13,000		10,000		
3					21,000		
4					9,000		6,000
5						7,000	
6							23,000
7							
8							

Department Codes:
1=Cleaning 2=Inserting Fasteners 3=Painting
4=Forming 5=Plating 6=Punching
7=Inspection and Packing 8=Shearing

Activity 10-1-1

ABZ Electronics
"Quality With A View!"

M E M O R A N D U M

From the Desk of Joe Yehudai
Group Manager, Operations
Consumer Electronics Division

TO: Pat Hancock

Please develop an initial layout for the new sheet metal shop. Use the attached planning information from the production planning department. Your layout should show the departments as circles. Write the department code inside the department circle. Use lines among the circles to represent the flow of parts from one department to another. The quantities traveling from one department to another should be written above the appropriate flow lines.

Presently, there are no restrictions as to the overall shape of the new shop. You should feel free to arrange the departments in any configuration, e.g., one row of eight departments; two rows of four departments; or any other way.

Hey, be logical with a creative twist! Let me know if I can help you.

Activity 10-1-1 (Continued)

Activity 10-1-2

ABZ Electronics
"Quality With A View!"

M E M O R A N D U M

From the Desk of Joe Yehudai
Group Manager, Operations
Consumer Electronics Division

TO: Pat Hancock

   Your initial layout was satisfactory. Now I want you to make some changes. Please change your layout so that material handling efforts are reduced. This should result in an arrangement where the departments that have the heaviest traffic are adjacent to one another.
   Keep up the good work!

Activity 10-1-3

ABZ Electronics
"Quality With A View!"

M E M O R A N D U M

From the Desk of Joe Yehudai
Group Manager, Operations
Consumer Electronics Division

TO: Pat Hancock

     Your revised shop layout for the sheet metal facility was more than satisfactory. I showed it to several industrial engineers and they like it! There was one question, though, that was raised by one of the engineers. He notes that some of the functions will be performed by union members while others will not. He wanted to know if the layout of the building takes that fact into consideration. What do you think?
     Also, perhaps there are other ethical and cultural factors that should be considered in the layout. Could you briefly list and describe them?

Activity 10-1-4

ABZ Electronics
"Quality With A View!"

M E M O R A N D U M

From the Desk of Joe Yehudai
Group Manager, Operations
Consumer Electronics Division

TO: Pat Hancock

     I am getting ready for a final session with some ABZ executives concerning the new sheet metal shop. Are there any additional factors that I should have them consider when they make a final decision about the construction of the new facility? Are there other factors that I should consider before meeting with them?

Group Experience 10-1
Finalizing the Layout for a Sheet Metal Shop

The Clarkstown plant manager coordinated a planning effort that could have resulted in a new 20,000 square foot sheet metal shop. The completed shop was to produce some sheet metal parts that are required in television set assembly. The shop was to consist of eight adjacent departments. Each department was to occupy an area measuring 50 feet by 50 feet.

The production planning department used some projected requirements to determine the number of parts that would travel each month among the eight departments in the shop as shown in the following table. Note that only the upper right part of the table is occupied. For example, when 10,000 units travel each month from department five to department six and 15,000 units travel in the opposite direction, a sum of 25,000 units appears in a proper upper-right cell.

Dept	Department						
	2	3	4	5	6	7	8
1	23,000	21,000	2,000	7,000	4,000	2,000	1,000
2			13,000		10,000		
3					21,000		
4					9,000		6,000
5						7,000	
6							23,000
7							
8							

Department Codes:
1=Cleaning   2=Inserting Fasteners   3=Painting
4=Forming   5=Plating   6=Punching
7=Inspection and Packing   8=Shearing

After weeks of discussion with his staff concerning the proposed new facility, it was discovered that existing space in the Clarkstown plant could be used for the proposed new sheet metal shop. The discovered area is 200 feet by 100 feet. This indicates that the eight departments will be arranged in two rows, four departments in a row. There are to be no walls between the departments. The plant manager would like a layout plan for the planned area.

Activity 10-1-1G

ABZ Electronics
"Quality With A View!"

M E M O R A N D U M

From the Desk of Joe Yehudai
Group Manager, Operations
Consumer Electronics Division

TO: Operations Specialists

The attached information will bring you up to date on the layout planning that has been achieved over the past few weeks. Please take this information and prepare a final layout for the sheet metal shop area. Note that the travel distance among adjacent departments (center to center, vertically, horizontally, or diagonally) is 50 feet.

Note that there are numerous layout alternatives. Can you tell me how many?

You need to select one that will minimize the material handling among the departments. This could be a very time-consuming task. So, what I am asking you to do is to consider a satisfactory layout.

One of ABZ's engineers has suggested the following arrangement:

----

8   6   2   1

5   3   4   7

Use the load-distance method to calculate the total feet traveled (quantities and distances) each month.

Activity 10-1-1G (Continued)

Activity 10-1-2G

ABZ Electronics
"Quality With A View!"

M E M O R A N D U M

From the Desk of Joe Yehudai
Group Manager, Operations
Consumer Electronics Division

TO: Operations Specialists

       Your initial layout was satisfactory. Now I want you to develop a better layout. I want one that you believe will reduce the flow of materials among departments. You need to state this in terms of total feet traveled each month. This should result in an arrangement where the departments that have the heaviest traffic are adjacent to one another. Please substantiate your claim using the load-distance method.
       Keep up the good work!

Activity 10-1-2G (Continued)

Activity 10-1-3G

ABZ Electronics
"Quality With A View!"

M E M O R A N D U M

From the Desk of Joe Yehudai
Group Manager, Operations
Consumer Electronics Division

TO: Operations Specialists

Your revised sheet metal shop layout was more than satisfactory. I showed it to several industrial engineers and they like it! There was one question, though, that was raised by one of the engineers. He notes that some of the functions will be performed by union members while others will not. He wanted to know if the layout of the area takes that fact into consideration. What do you think?

Also, perhaps there are other ethical and cultural factors that should be considered in the layout. Could you briefly list and describe them?

Activity 10-1-4G

ABZ Electronics
"Quality With A View!"

M E M O R A N D U M

From the Desk of Joe Yehudai
Group Manager, Operations
Consumer Electronics Division

TO: Operations Specialists

I am getting ready for a final session with some ABZ executives concerning the new sheet metal shop. Are there any additional factors that I should have them consider when they make a final decision about the remodeling of the Clarkstown plant? Are there other factors that I should consider before meeting with them to discuss the sheet metal shop?

Group Experience 10-2
Balancing the Television Antenna Assembly Line

ABZ Electronics
"Quality With A View!"

MEMORANDUM

TO: Joe Yehudai

FROM: Chris Smith, Supervisor
Antenna Assembly

RE: Help!

Joe, I am concerned about the antenna assembly line. The flow is not as smooth as it should be. I am sure we are wasting effort and money. The union steward does not seem as concerned as I, but I believe he will endorse any new plan. Pat Hancock observed the line in operation. Here is a table that he constructed:

Task	Task That Immediately Preceded	Time to Perform Task (Minutes)
A. Attach cable 1 to connector 1	-	.20
B. Cut wire	-	.25
C. Form wire	B	.35
D. Attach wire to connector 1	A,C	.40
E. Connect cable 2 to connector 2	-	.50
F. Connect cable 2 to connector 3	E	.50
G. Assemble antenna	F	.65
H. Attach connector 1 to antenna	D,G	.25
I. Fold antenna	H	.40
J. Inspect antenna	I	.45
K. Pack	J	.20

Pat noted that the line must assemble 500 antennas per hour. He also noted that 54 minutes of each hour are productive. Joe, see what your people can do for me!

Activity 10-2-1G

ABZ Electronics
"Quality With A View!"

M E M O R A N D U M

TO: Operations Specialists

FROM: Joe Yehudai

RE: Help for Antenna Assembly

    I received the attached memo from Chris Smith. Please assist Chris by streamlining his operations. Use any line-balancing heuristic method to perform your task. Once you have completed the task, tell me how efficient the line will be.
    Thanks.

Activity 10-2-2G

ABZ Electronics
"Quality With A View!"

M E M O R A N D U M

TO: Operations Specialists

FROM: Joe Yehudai

RE: Antenna Assembly

    Chris Smith reports that he has discussed your antenna assembly layout with his union steward. The steward apparently objected to the number of tasks per work station. He believes the number of tasks per work station should be only two.

    Please revise your proposal accordingly. Once you have accomplished this, tell me how the union request has affected efficiency. Then I have two more assignments.

Activity 10-2-3G Tell me what ethical and cultural factors are in play when we design a layout for an assembly line.

Activity 10-2-4G Tell me what additional factors should be considered in assembly line layout planning. Tell me what additional information is needed for effective assembly line layout planning.

CHAPTER 11

Human Resource Strategy Activities

Human resources are individuals engaged in any of the organization's activities. There are two human resource imperatives: (1) the need to optimize individual, group, and organizational effectiveness; and (2) the need to enhance the quality of organizational life. A *human resource strategy* is a plan to use the organization's human resources effectively and efficiently while maintaining or improving the quality of work life.

The human resource management function is about employees. Employees are the means of enhancing organizational effectiveness. Financial management attempts to increase organizational effectiveness through the allocation and conservation of financial resources. Human resource management (personnel management) attempts to increase organizational effectiveness through the establishment of personnel policies, procedures, and management methods.

Operations management attempts to increase organizational effectiveness by the methods used in the manufacturing and service processes. The skill level of the operations employees must be compatible with operations tasks. Tasks are defined in terms of products produced (Chapter 8) and processes used (Chapter 9). Working conditions are affected by location (Chapter 7), layout (Chapter 10), and work schedule (Chapter 11).

Manpower planning is the primary focus of the operations human resource strategy. Hiring the right employees for a job and training them to be productive is a lengthy and costly process. Fair treatment and trust are the basis of a human resource strategy. The employee, not operations, takes center stage.

Job design is concerned with who will do a specific job and with how and where the job will be done. The goal of job design is to facilitate productivity. Job design must take into account efficiency and behavior if it is to succeed. Job design must also guarantee that working conditions are safe and that the health of the employees will not be jeopardized in the short or long run.

Work methods analysis is used to improve productivity and can be performed for new or existing jobs. *Motion study techniques* are also used to improve productivity.

Work measurement methods are used to establish labor standards. These standards can be used for planning, control, productivity improvements, costing and pricing, bidding, compensation, motivation, and financial incentives.

The design of adequate compensation systems is also an important part of the human resource strategy. Compensation can be time-based or output-based. Output-based systems can provide an incentive to improve productivity. Incentive plans may be based on measured standards and may cover groups or individuals. A popular incentive plan that is not based on measured standards is known as profit sharing.

Where employees are represented by a union, the relationship between the union and management are of strategic importance. The relationship is one of conflict--sometimes hostile, sometimes friendly. Do not underestimate the importance of the collective bargaining unit in conflict situations.

Ethical and Cultural Considerations

The question of ethics in business conduct has become one of the most challenging issues confronting the corporate community in this era. Major corporations throughout the United States are vigorously addressing the challenge.

One manifestation of this concern for ethics has been the widespread development of codes of ethics (or conduct) and statements of values in business organizations. More recently, there has been open discussion among corporate executives about ethical issues and how to deal with them and creative efforts by business executives to implement and institutionalize support for ethics policy to ensure ethical action.

The increasing discussion and the growing number of programs to make corporate ethics work, resulted in 1988 report by The Business Roundtable. Since its founding in 1972, The Business Roundtable has included corporate responsibility and ethics among its concerns. A report on business conduct guidelines among member companies was published in 1975. A statement on corporate responsibility was issued in 1981. *Corporate Ethics: A Prime Business Asset*, the 1988 Roundtable report, was based on information compiled from member companies.

It was the hope and intention of The Business Roundtable that the information in the 1988 report would be helpful to all corporations seeking to develop, improve, refine, and renew their efforts toward more ethical policies and conduct throughout their organizations. The remainder of this section discusses the findings of the report (Keough).

The Role of Top Management

To achieve results, the chief executive officer and those around the CEO must be openly and strongly committed to ethical conduct. They must give constant leadership in tending and renewing the values of the organization. Companies find it necessary to communicate that commitment in a wide variety of ways--directives, policy statements, speeches, company publications, and especially actions.

One of the myths about business is that there is a contradiction between ethics and profits. That myth was thoroughly debunked by the attitudes and actions of top managers in the companies that contributed to *Corporate Ethics: A Prime Business Asset.*

The researchers found that a good reputation for fair and honest business is a prime corporate asset that all employees should nurture with the greatest care.

Among managers, there is a widespread recognition that corporate obligations extend to a variety of constituencies or stakeholders and that these responsibilities are central to the ethics of a corporation. Customers, shareholders, employees, suppliers, local communities, and the larger society are basic constituencies that are considered in planning and evaluating corporate policy and action.

Carrying out all corporate obligations requires a comprehensive ethical perspective. This perspective must be understood and acted on in every sector and at all levels of the company (Keough, pp. 4-5).

Importance of a "Code"

Companies take different approaches to establishing sound principles upon which to base their corporate conduct. Some, with long and largely unwritten traditions of integrity, rely on a relatively informal approach. Others have codes that spell out requirements in great detail. The general and growing approach is to set forth principles of conduct for the whole organization in some written form.

Whatever they are called, these documents exemplify the root meaning of ethics--good customs and character. The importance of a "code" is twofold: first, it clarifies company expectations of employee conduct in various situations. Second, it makes clear that the company intends and expects its personnel to recognize the ethical dimensions of corporate policies and actions. When people are affected, when interests collide and choices must be made between values, ethical considerations are at stake. For people in business, that means nearly all the time.

While the areas covered in codes and standards vary from one industry to another, a general list of topics covered includes (Keough, p. 5): fundamental honesty and adherence to the law; product safety and quality; health and safety in the workplace; conflicts of interest; employment practices; fairness in selling/marketing practices; financial reporting; supplier relationships; pricing, billing, and contracting; trading in securities/using inside information; payments to obtain business/Foreign Corrupt Practices Act; acquiring and using information about others; security; political activities; protection of the environment; and intellectual property/proprietary information.

Some companies have had codes for decades. A prime example is the widely noted *Credo of Johnson & Johnson,* reproduced in full in Section VIII of the report.

While no code can cover all situations, explicit standards can be helpful and guide the judgments and consciences of people as they make specific decisions. Codes must be "living documents." They must be reviewed periodically to meet new circumstances and renewed with personnel to assure understanding and "ownership" of the company's values.

Codes are important for communicating clear expectations. Companies have found that more is needed. To develop and improve an ethical climate, a vigorous and continuously renewed process of implementation is essential.

Making Ethics Work

In the growing movement among major U.S. corporations to develop and refine mechanisms to make their ethics effective, there are two interrelated purposes: First, there is the aim to ensure compliance with company standards of conduct. At work is the realization that human consciences are fragile and need the support of institutions. Second, there is the growing conviction that strong corporate culture and ethics are a vital strategic key to survival and profitability in a highly competitive era (Keough, p. 6).

Some of the varied approaches that illustrate the first purpose include mechanisms designed to provide: management involvement and oversight down the line; attention to values and ethics in recruiting and hiring; emphasis on corporate ethics in education and training; communications programs to inform and motivate employees; recognition and reward for exemplary performance, including pay and promotion; ombudsmen and hotlines for employee comment and complaint; special focus on vulnerable sectors and jobs; periodic certification of adherence to standards; auditing to ensure compliance; and enforcement procedures, including discipline and dismissal (Keough, pp. 6-7).

The second purpose is clearly apparent in the corporate ethics programs at Champion International. *The Champion Way*, a statement of corporate values, has been implemented through *The Champion Way In Action* with the specific aim of strengthening the ability of the company to survive and to enhance profitability.

Within the spectrum of programs to manage corporate ethics, a well-developed structure can include an oversight committee of the board of directors. This is usually made up of outside directors, a committee of top managers, an ethics program staff, and one or more ombudsmen.

The work of the program permeates all sectors of the company and flows down through all organizational levels. The process starts with weighing the attitudes and history of prospective employees. The process involves all training programs and the serious and continuous attention of line managers at all levels and employees in every division. Wide-ranging activities and methods are used, focusing on the values of the company and their applicability in specific locations. The strong endorsement of the program by the CEO is conveyed either in person or through well-done videos.

"Openness" in communication is fundamental. No less important is the building of an atmosphere of trust. Employees should report violations and feel it their duty to do so. Channels of communication should be provided for making such reporting possible. These open channels of communication will encourage free communication about employee concerns to various levels of management.

Many companies give special attention to areas of particular vulnerability--purchasing, for example--to diminish temptation and to improve detection of violations. Companies generally require personnel to sign documents periodically certifying compliance with company standards.

While there are provisions for disciplining those who are found in violation, the point is made that the purpose of enforcement is to encourage compliance with standards rather than to administer punishment. A general principle is to "punish in private" unless prosecution is necessary. On the other side of the coin, praise is designed to be public. Some programs include honors for employees with exemplary performance.

In total, the efforts to implement and institutionalize corporate ethics are widespread and impressive. Companies have programs designed to create an environment of values and to make ethical awareness and conduct a way of life. The drive toward effective implementation is fueled both by the recognition that corporate culture can be nurtured and by the conviction that corporate ethics can add a competitive edge to company performance (Keough, pp. 6-7).

Involvement and Commitment of Personnel at All Levels

In addition to leadership by top executives, an effective program of corporate ethics requires the involvement and commitment of personnel at all levels. This participation can be achieved only by programs that work through the various levels of management and involve all work groups.

Participation and decentralized involvement are not intended to imply that a company will or can be run as a democracy. Participative involvement does mean that each level of the business and every work group accepts appropriate responsibilities that cannot be taken on by those above or below. No ethics program can be successful without the strong leadership of the CEO, and no CEO can ensure high standards of conduct in the organization without the strong personal contribution of each manager.

As a central component of an effective corporate ethics program, participation produces several important effects. These results add up to a stronger organization and improved performance.

First, as employees join in discussions of corporate values and goals, they come to understand what the company stands for and how they are important parts of this business community. Through participative sessions, ethics ceases to be a set of abstract concepts and instead emerges as the way to develop better working relationships and deal with various constituencies on a day-to-day basis.

Second, as employees interact with one another about what is valuable for them and the company, they develop higher levels of trust and take more pride in the business that they are a part of. A program of corporate ethics can, through participative methods, strengthen the culture and values of the company.

Third, as the level of trust in the work groups increases and employees feel more involved in the company, their experiences and skills can be focused on job-related improvements in product and quality. Ways to do their jobs better are more likely to occur to them and they are far more likely to share those ideas with their supervisors and colleagues. The outcome can be more efficient ways of operating, improved quality and productivity, and better performance overall.

In those and other ways, decentralized involvement leads toward better adherence to standards of conduct. Beyond that, there is an increased commitment and a release of imagination and energy. Involvement of personnel, therefore, can become a crucial part of a program of corporate ethics that makes a key contribution to corporate success (Keough, pp. 8-9).

Measuring Results

There are no precise ways to measure the end results of the widespread and intensive efforts to develop effective corporate ethics programs. Companies use various methods, such as surveys and auditing procedures, to monitor compliance with standards of conduct. A sense about the extent that a company's culture has been strengthened can also be achieved. Additionally, there are evidences of performance that can be measured to a certain degree, though the relation of improvements to a corporate ethics program may be difficult to trace.

Company executives will make judgments about the effectiveness of their corporate ethics programs based on their own observations of the climate within the corporation, their appraisal of the company's reputation in the communities where it operates, and performance in the marketplace. In addition, corporate leaders can be confident that the probability of problems is greatly reduced and company performance enhanced because of the efforts they have made. The ultimate measurements will emerge only over a longer period of time (Keough, p. 9).

Self-Interest, Survival, and Achievement

The impressive efforts of a broad cross-section of companies, illustrated in detail in *Corporate Ethics: A Prime Business Asset*, show that major U.S. corporations have stressed ethical behavior for a long time and are addressing the recent challenges with vigor, skill, and determination.

The corporate community should continue to refine and renew efforts to improve performance and manage change effectively through programs in corporate ethics. In one sense, the ultimate reward will be that the public has greater confidence in business.

In the view of the top executives represented in The Business Roundtable study, there is no conflict between ethical practices and acceptable profits. Ethical practices are a necessary precondition for acceptable profits. Sound values, purposes, and practices are the basis for long-range achievement.

In striving for improved ethics in corporate action, perfection should not be expected. Human endeavors, those in which corporations are involved, will not be perfect. This should not be reason for despair or cynicism. Companies that have suffered serious breaches of ethics and legality have found it possible to develop strong programs of corporate ethics and thus to embark on a path of renewal and improvement.

Effective leadership by the management of corporations is the best way to support and advance the cause of private enterprise. Basic to such leadership is the insight that corporate ethics is a strategic key to survival and profitability in this era of fierce competitiveness in a global economy (Keough, p. 10).

Listing and Description of Appropriate OM Tools

There are a number of quantitative operations tools available to the operations manager. Among the ones to be discussed in this chapter are work methods analysis; work measurement methods; behavioral job design methods; compensation methods, learning curves analysis, and linear programming.

Work Methods Analysis

The principal approach to the study of work methods is the construction of charts. The choice of which charting method to use depends on the activity level of the task and whether the focus is on (1) the overall productive system, (2) the stationary worker at a fixed work place, (3) a worker interacting with equipment, or (4) a worker interacting with other workers.

Charting may be used for new or existing jobs. The need for work methods analysis is often the result of changes in tools, materials, product design, or government regulations. The use of several different charts facilitates the performance of the analysis.

The *process chart* breaks down an operation into steps. Each step is one of five different classes: operation, transport, inspect, delay, store. A summary of the number of occurrences in each class is provided. The process chart can assist in method improvement that aims for the elimination of unnecessary steps.

A *worker-machine chart* is helpful for visualizing the parts of a work cycle during which a machine and an operator are busy or idle. It may assist in making changes that will improve productivity. It may help to determine the number of machines that an operator can manage effectively and efficiently.

A third chart, the *multi-activity chart*, can assist in analyzing and coordinating team work. Motion studies are aimed at eliminating unnecessary human motions. Motion studies may identify the sequence of motions that will improve productivity.

Work Measurement Methods

Work measurement (the process of estimating the amount of worker time required to generate one unit of output) focuses on the length of time that it takes to complete a job. Standard job times can be used for planning, control, budgeting, scheduling, and compensation systems. Standards can be established for existing or proposed jobs.

There are four common methods of work measurement: *time study* (the method of establishing time standards by using stopwatches to time operations being performed by workers), *historical data, predetermined time standards,* and *work sampling* (a work measurement technique that randomly samples the work of one or more persons at periodic intervals to determine the proportion of the total operation that is accounted for by one particular activity).

Behavioral Job Design Methods

The behavioral approaches to job design include: *job enlargement* (the combining of various operations at a similar level into one job to provide more variety for workers and thus increase motivation and satisfaction), *job rotation* (a method of increasing employees' job satisfaction by regular and recurring rotation of duties), and *job enrichment* (the vertical combination of tasks that increases one's duties and responsibilities; job depth is enhanced to improve job satisfaction). These approaches assist in reducing boredom. They may also be used when the focus is on making jobs more interesting, meaningful, and stimulating. As a result of a successful implementation of these job design methods, a quality work life is possible for each employee.

Compensation Methods

The most common compensation method is *time-based*. While time-based compensation is simple and easy to implement, it provides very little incentive for improved performance. Both salaried and hourly employees can be compensated via the time-based method.

A second method of compensation is *output-based compensation*. An increase in output results in an increase in earnings. This method can be applied to individuals or to groups. If properly applied, output compensation can provide a strong incentive for productivity improvement. Output compensation should be labor-standard oriented.

A common incentive system that is not based on any labor standard is called *profit sharing*. It is applied to all the employees as a group. While easy to implement, it does not provide a strong incentive to improve performance. The challenge is to identify the large number of variables that affect profit. Many incentive plans may be considered when cost reduction is a high priority.

Learning Curves

Learning curve (a curve illustrating the relationship between the number of units produced and the amount of labor required per unit) analysis is suitable when a repetitive task is cited for improvement. The time it takes to perform a task is reduced as the task is performed over and over again.

Improvements in the performance of complex and long tasks may be significant. Generally, the larger the number of repetitions, the more significant the learning. Improvements in simple and short tasks are less significant and occur during the first repetitions. Managers who are familiar with the learning curve analysis find the results useful in preparing cost estimates for new products, in preparing bids, and in establishing labor standards and compensation systems.

Linear Programming

Linear programming is a mathematical technique for applying scarce resources optimally to competing demands. It can assist in identifying the optimal solution to a host of different problems. For example, linear programming can help assign workers to jobs according to performance and time required to complete the job. An optimal assignment minimizes total time or total cost and maximizes efficiency.

Linear programming could be used with the aid of a computation method such as Simplex. The graphical method is not appropriate because it is limited to two-variable situations. There is also a modified method for the assignment problem described in this chapter. This method is known as the assignment method of linear programming.

Individual Experience 11-1
Manpower Planning in the HDTV Plant

Earlier this year, you provided ABZ's management with a recommendation concerning the appropriate level of automation for the planned HDTV assembly plant (See File 10-1-1). Yesterday, Jack Dustman, Director of Human Resources, determined that it was time to do manpower planning for the new HDTV assembly operation. He sought permission to directly contact various operations specialists to determine the amount of direct labor that will be needed to assemble a typical HDTV set. He will expect the operations specialists to use any original forecast material (File 10-1) and accompanying recommendations as input for the manpower planning study. ABZ production records indicate that ABZ workers generally experience an 85 percent learning curve for similar production activities. The industrial engineering department estimates that the assembly of the first HDTV set will require approximately three man hours. Assembly employees are expected to contribute 1,900 hours per year.

Activity 11-1-1 Jack: Pat. I believe Joe told you that I would be contacting you concerning manpower planning for the new HDTV assembly operation. What I need is a forecast of the number of assembly line employees needed for each year from 1993 to 1999. Please review the original forecast (File 10-1) and other pertinent data.

Activity 11-1-2 Jack: Pat. I received your data on the number of direct labor employees that will be needed to assemble HDTV sets in 1993-1999. I sent it, some additional manufacturing cost information, and your recommendation to the marketing people. Today, the marketing people told me that labor costs must be reduced if ABZ is to stay competitive. In fact, they told me that our top brass told the union representatives that the future of the company hinges substantially on HDTV and lower labor costs. Please revise your manpower forecast to reflect an 80 percent learning curve.

The union representatives are fully aware of the competitive situation and we may be able to get them to commit to an 80 percent learning curve. Could you get me this data in a hurry? Let's not allow the union to change their mind.

Activity 11-1-3 Todd Madrid (ICEU): Hey Pat. I got a bone to pick with you. Jack Dustman let me see some forecasts that you prepared for the manpower planning document regarding the new HDTV plant. I really object to you using an 80 percent learning curve to establish labor standards. This isn't Japan. You can't just come in here and inflict the Japanese culture on our workers. Come on. Explain yourself!

Activity 11-1-4 Todd Madrid: Give me a break, Pat. Name and describe three or four other methods that could be used to establish labor standards. Let me be the judge as to which one you should use to establish labor standards. What do I need to read to understand your point of view regarding labor standards?

Group Experience 11-1
Choosing a Compensation Method

ABZ Electronics
"Quality With A View!"

M E M O R A N D U M

From: Bob Kemper

To: Jack Dustman

RE: Employee Motivation

We cut costs. We controlled rejects. We explored different production methods to cut costs. We tried to sue Japanese firms who dumped television sets on the market below costs. However, we still are having difficulty maintaining our market share.

Do we need a motivational tool such as a profit sharing program or an incentive system based on (labor) standards to motivate our people? Have any ideas? Let me hear from you! P.S. Whatever you recommend, make sure all our employees are covered by your plan.

Activity 11-1-1G Jack Dustman: You all have a copy of the memo Bob Kemper sent to me. I have selected you people to be a profit sharing/incentive system ad hoc committee. First, I want you to assist me by preparing a detailed position paper on the pros and cons of profit sharing.

Activity 11-1-2G Jack Dustman: Next, I want you to prepare a similar analysis for an incentive system.

Activity 11-1-3G Jack Dustman: If we limit profit sharing to salaried personnel, are we being fair to operations personnel? Tell me what you think.

Activity 11-1-4G Jack Dustman: Finally, tell me if you think we should consider using profit sharing for some employees and incentive standards for the others. What additional factors should we consider? Is there any additional information we will need?

Group Experience 11-2
Job Design

ABZ Electronics
"Quality With A View!"

M E M O R A N D U M

From: Joe Yehudai

To: Operations Specialists

RE: Productivity, Quality, Turnover, Tardiness, and Absenteeism

     The control system in ABZ's assembly plant has identified some troubling facts. Productivity and quality are down. Employee turnover, tardiness, and absenteeism are up. The plant manager would like to use job design techniques to combat the problems. He chose to start with the final assembly. The tasks in this department are very simple, involving manual operations, the use of power, no power hand tools, and simple support machinery.

Activity 11-2-1G What steps should be taken in order to identify the problems behind the troubling symptoms.

Activity 11-2-2G How may job enlargement and/or job enrichment concepts be used?

Activity 11-2-3G What ethical and cultural factors should be considered when dealing with such problems? Explain.

Activity 11-2-4G Could other approaches be used? What additional information will be needed? Explain.

EXHIBIT IV.1 Operations Management System

TACTICAL SUPPORT ACTIVITIES

Once a decision is made to design, change, or review an operational plan of action (Chapter 5), resource allocations are considered (Chapters 6 through 11). This activity is followed by an attempt to design, change, or review specific tasks--tactical programming. Tactical programming (Chapters 12 through 21) specifies the activities to be carried out.

We have divided the tactical programming activities into two groups. The first group, Chapters 12 through 17, is covered in this section. The second group is covered in Section V.

Chapter 12 focuses on quality assurance activities. *Quality assurance* involves a broad group of activities aimed at achieving the organization's quality objectives. If you concentrate on this chapter, you should be able to apply acceptance sampling and process control techniques to operations management challenges.

Chapter 13 considers maintenance strategy. *Maintenance strategies* are what keep an organization's facility and equipment at predetermined work levels. Once you have participated in the activities of this chapter, you should be able solve maintenance operations challenges by applying such tools as simulation, waiting lines, financial investment evaluation, preventive maintenance, and payoff tables.

Chapter 14 introduces you to operations cost control. Cost control is an important responsibility of every manager. You will be introduced to such operations tools as cost standards, cost-variance analysis, value analysis, standardization, and learning curves. If you concentrate on this chapter, you should be able to establish standard costs, measure actual costs, compare actual costs to standard costs, and implement needed cost changes.

Material management is the subject of Chapter 15. Material management activities support the flow of materials from vendors through an operations system to customers. If you complete the exercises in this chapter and integrate the recommended tools into your decision-making thought process, you should be able to effectively participate in such operations activities as purchasing, receiving, inventory control, shop floor control, traffic, shipping, and distribution.

Chapter 16 covers advanced manufacturing support activities. If you concentrate on this chapter, you should be able to understand how operations managers select a right computer-integrated manufacturing system for the right company at the right time.

Chapter 17 addresses project planning and control systems. If you give this chapter a chance, you will become a stronger, more effective operations planner. You will be able to apply network based planning and control techniques to large and complex operations projects using PERT and CPM.

As an ABZ operations specialist, you should have noted as early as Chapter 11 a change in the degree to which you became personally involved in operations decisions. In earlier chapters (Chapters 2,3, and 4), operations specialists were observers of the external environment and ABZ's strategic activities. Your participation in functional operations activities (Chapters 6-11) was highly impersonal. Instructions were contained in or prompted by memorandums from above. You responded to requests such as, "Use a time series to determine . . ."

Then, in Chapter 11, a director of human resources came to the shop or service floor. He literally grabbed you by the arm saying, "I want you to assist me by preparing a detailed . . ." In Chapters 12 through 17, the activity focuses on face-to-face negotiations, "Tell me what you think . . .," "Tell me if you think we should . . .," "Pat this is Joe. Say, I want you to meet with . . ."

CHAPTER 12

Quality Assurance Activities

Quality assurance involves a broad group of activities that are aimed at achieving the organization's quality objectives. An organization's interpretation of quality is expressed in its strategies--grand, corporate, business, operations, and marketing. Quality, cost, availability, flexibility, and dependability are competitive weapons.

Quality assurance is a much broader concept than quality control. Quality is a characteristic that makes something what it is. Product quality determines an organization's reputation. It is the customer who determines what quality is. Customers define quality in terms of appearance, performance, availability, flexibility, and reliability.

Quality assurance is a continuum of activities that start when quality standards are set and finish when quality goods and services are delivered to the customers. An effective quality assurance strategy reduces the need for quality control and subsequent corrective actions.

Quality assurance is best when a "no rejects" philosophy is adopted by management. Unfortunately, for most mass-produced products this is not economically feasible. Employees should approach production with a "do not make the same mistake once" mind-set. Mistakes are costly. Detecting defective products in the final quality control inspection might be too late and too costly. Emphasizing quality in the early stages--product and process design--will reduce rejects.

A successful quality assurance program must rely on a total organizational commitment. Commitment to quality begins at the top. First, there is the aim to ensure compliance with company quality standards. At work is the realization that human consciences are fragile and need the support of the organization. Second, there is the growing conviction that quality is a vital strategic key to survival and profitability in a highly competitive era.

In addition to leadership by top executives, an effective program of quality assurance requires the involvement and commitment of personnel at all levels. This participative element can be achieved only by programs that work through the various levels of management and involve all work groups. The commitment to quality by skilled and motivated employees is as important as sophisticated equipment and quality materials.

Quality circles are proven vehicles for promoting organizational commitment to quality. A quality circle is a small group of volunteer employees from all organizational levels who meet regularly to discuss a particular production project in terms of quality assurance.

Quality is a main component of the just-in-time (JIT) concept and is the main criterion in establishing a vendor as a JIT vendor. A JIT vendor is expected to deliver an order of parts on time in the quantity and of the quality promised. The customer trusts the vendor to deliver quality products that do not need inspection, and so the customer does not carry an inventory of additional parts to be used when defective components are delivered. Targeted delivery dates by JIT vendors are matched with a customer's production schedule and very little time is allowed for replacement orders. This commitment to quality on the part of the vendor improves the customer's competitive position because the dollars the customer saves through inventory reduction can be directed toward improved product quality, reduced prices, and increased profits.

Quality has not been a strong suit of U.S. manufacturers in recent years which has contributed to the inability of U.S. manufacturers to compete in the international market. Restoring a competitive edge for U.S. manufacturers will require a major strategic restructuring of the quality assurance process.

Listing and Description of Appropriate OM Tools

There are a number of quantitative operations tools available to the operations manager. Among the ones to be discussed in this chapter are acceptance sampling and process control.

Acceptance Sampling

Acceptance sampling is a statistical quality-control procedure that is used to determine whether a group of items should be accepted or rejected. The procedure can be applied to incoming purchased raw materials and parts, to parts and sub-assemblies produced internally; and to outgoing finished goods.

Since a 100 percent inspection of a large lot of is too costly, sampling is used to determine the quality of the lot. A lot is accepted if it meets predetermined quality standards and it is rejected if the standards are not met. The disposition of rejected lots is predetermined. Rejected lots of purchased parts, for example, could be subjected to 100 percent inspection by the customer at the vendor's cost. The other alternative is to return the rejected lots to the vendor for credit.

Sampling by attributes is accomplished when an item, or one or more of its characteristics, can be observed as good or bad. Sampling by variables is a procedure used to measure the characteristics of items against predetermined standards.

Process Control

Statistical process control, known as process control, is a technique that assists in monitoring production processes. Production processes must be monitored continuously in order to assure that the quality of their output will be acceptable. An early detection of a faulty production process is preferred. It is less costly than the detection of parts that do not meet quality standards and must be scrapped or reworked. If a production process is out of control or shows unstable performance, corrective action must be taken. Process control can be implemented with the aid of graphical charts known as control charts.

Individual Experience 12-1
Acceptance Plan (by Attributes) for a Switching Diode

ABZ Electronics purchases a mass-produced switching diode that is assembled into a tuner control sub-assembly used in ABZ color television sets. Since the diode must be inserted into the tuner control sub-assembly prior to attaching the sub-assembly to the chassis of the television set, it is important that diode rejects are found prior to assembly. If by chance a defective diode is inserted in the tuner control, the television set would need to be dismantled which would be a costly operation.

The vendor that supplies the switching diode is a JIT vendor. ABZ and the vendor have agreed that lots (one lot equals 1,000 components) containing 3 percent of defective diodes will be considered normal. Lots containing more than 3 percent of rejects should never be shipped by the vendor to ABZ. The probability of rejecting a good lot is set at .10 and the sample size for inspection is set at 200 as part of the purchase agreement. The inspection is performed by the vendor. ABZ uses vendor shipments in its assembly without additional inspection.

Activity 12-1-1   Pat, this is Joe. Say, I want you to meet with Kelly Chambers and Leslie Malloy tomorrow morning as part of an ad hoc group assigned to help our switching diode vendor establish a new quality acceptance plan. See if you people can help him establish a new plan. Go to the meeting with at least one major question that you think the group should consider. (Question)

Activity 12-1-2 Leslie Malloy: Kelly and Pat, it seems to me that ABZ has the switching diode vendor by the tail. He knows that we could dump his company for a new vendor if they do not cooperate on the acceptance plan issue. So let's develop an acceptance plan that allows for no rejects.

Kelly Chambers: No rejects? Given the technology, I can't see how we can require no rejects!

Pat Hancock: Leslie, Kelly is right. We are not going to be able to devise an acceptance plan the will reduce the probability of finding defective switching diodes to zero. The vendor is aware that he could lose his contract with us. I say we cooperate with him on this.

Leslie Malloy: You're right, Kelly and Pat. Good vendors are hard to come by. In order to accomplish our goal, a new acceptance plan should be established utilizing a different alpha. The vendor doesn't know whether a .05 or a .25 alpha should be used. Let's select the proper alpha and establish the new acceptance plan.

Activity 12-1-3 Kelly Chambers: Leslie and Pat, what ethical and cultural factors should be considered if quality assurance needs are to be satisfied?

Activity 12-1-4 Leslie Malloy: Pat, what are the factors we should incorporate into the quality assurance plan if we implement the new acceptance plan?

Group Experience 12-1
Acceptance Plan (by Variables) for a Capacitor

ABZ is purchasing a 4pF capacitor for its tuner control sub-assembly. The vendor presently does not employ a just-in-time production system. This forces the vendor to jointly inspect with ABZ all production shipments. Past records indicate that the standard deviation of the production population is .25pF and that the mean is 4pF. The sample size for the tuner capacitor has been 150.

Activity 12-1-1G Leslie, Pat, Sandy, I'm glad I found you all together because I could use some quick help regarding the acceptance plan for the 4pF capacitor. You know that we use an alpha of .10 to set our acceptance plan for lots that are received from the vendor. A sample from one of the most recent lots that we received was tested and the mean was found to be 4.05pF. Should we accept or reject the entire lot? Why?

Activity 12-1-2G What if we change the alpha? Will this change whether or not we accept the lot? Why or why not?

Activity 12-1-3G Kelly Chambers: Wait a minute Joe, Leslie, and Pat. Aren't there some ethical factors that we should be considering before we implement this action? Before we satisfy ABZ's quality assurance needs, don't we need to consider some ethical and cultural factors? Aren't we placing our vendor in a vulnerable position? How are we going to explain our actions to the vendor?

Activity 12-1-4G Leslie Malloy: Should we be concerned about what the vendor does with a lot that he rejected prior to shipping it to us? What should we do with a lot that we reject after it has been shipped to us? What factors should be incorporated in such decisions? Do we need additional information?

Group Experience 12-2
Control Chart for Plastic Knobs

ABZ is producing the plastic knobs it uses for all of its television sets. ABZ uses the injection-molding technique. The knobs have a cavity that is designed to fit over the metal shaft of the television control apparatus. The inside diameter of the cavity must be within a specified range to allow for proper assembly. Diameters are checked with a go-no-go gauge. Rejected knobs are scrapped. Five percent defects per sample is considered normal.

Activity 12-2-1G Leslie, Kelly, and Pat, do I have a job for you! I need you to construct a three-sigma control chart for the plastic knobs that we produce for our television sets. Use a sample size of fifty. Justify our claim that seven defects per fifty knobs is an indication that our production process and production department are in control.

Activity 12-2-2G Leslie, Kelly, and Pat, do you remember that project you worked on concerning a three-sigma control chart? I would like you to review the action you took at the time. Once you finish your review, I would like you to consider quality control for a larger sample. Please construct a new three-sigma control chart for sample size 100. Justify our claim that fourteen rejects per 100 knobs is an indication that our production process and production department are out of control and are inefficient.

Activity 12-2-3G What do you folks believe are the factors that should be incorporated into a decision about the sample size?

CHAPTER 13

Maintenance Activities

The goal of maintenance activities is to keep the organization's facility and equipment at predetermined work levels. Maintenance activities include planning, implementing, and control. In the planning stage, managers must select a strategy that will direct personnel to fix equipment before it malfunctions or after it malfunctions. Fixing equipment before it malfunctions is referred to as a pure-preventive maintenance policy. At the other end of the maintenance continuum is the a pure-breakdown (repair) policy--fix equipment after it malfunctions.

Most organizations implement a maintenance strategy somewhere in the middle of the maintenance continuum. Management faces a trade-off situation. An attempt is made to select a level and a frequency of maintenance that minimizes the cost of preventive maintenance and of breakdowns (repair). Since no level of preventive maintenance can eliminate breakdowns completely, repair is always an important activity.

The maintenance control process finds management deciding whether to repair or replace a piece of equipment. A replacement is considered a new investment. New equipment investments must be made on the basis of preventive maintenance and anticipated breakdown costs.

Whether management decides on a pure-preventive or pure-breakdown policy, the prerequisite for a successful maintenance program is the availability of maintenance parts and supplies or replacement (standby) equipment. The maintenance department is a major participant in this aspect of maintenance policy decision making. The maintenance manager must control inventory (parts, supplies, replacement machines) activities. Some organizations choose to keep standby machines to protect themselves against the consequences of breakdowns. Plants that use special-purpose equipment are more likely to invest in standby equipment than plants that have general-purpose equipment.

Maintenance activities directly affect the organization's ability to compete. Poor maintenance results in excessive numbers of breakdowns. A breakdown idles machines and employees and reduces the total output capacity of the organization. During the breakdown, labor and overhead costs per unit increase and profits decrease. Additionally, goods cannot be shipped on schedule. The direct result of continual breakdowns is a not-on-time delivery reputation.

Poorly maintained machines increase the amount of scrap and rework efforts. Increased levels of scrap and rework projects increase unit material and labor costs. Equipment that is not performing at peak levels affects product quality. Additionally, equipment that is not performing at peak levels affects the people operating the equipment because it places these employees at risk. Injuries are often the result of management's failure to replace or adequately maintain equipment.

The final challenge to managers of maintenance activities involves maintenance personnel. Skilled maintenance personnel have always been in short supply, which has caused wages to be high. In a high-wage situation, management must make sure that maintenance personnel are used effectively and efficiently. Tracking maintenance personnel is a major concern because they are generally isolated from other employees and work with little supervision.

Employee turnover must be held to a minimum. Losing a well trained maintenance employee to a competitor or to another organization is costly.

Listing and Description of Appropriate OM Tools

There are a number of quantitative operations tools available to the operations manager. Among the ones to be discussed in this chapter are simulation, waiting lines, financial investment evaluation methods, preventive maintenance versus breakdown policy, and payoff tables.

Simulation

A *simulation* is a process of experimentation using a model of a real system or an activity. As a result of the experimentation, an understanding of the system's behavior under different conditions is gained. Simulation is used as a problem-solving tool in many different situations. In maintenance studies, simulation can assist in determining optimal crew size, spare-parts inventory levels, and maintenance policy. Monte Carlo is a simple and easy-to-use probabilistic simulation technique.

Waiting Lines

Waiting line models can be used to solve a variety of maintenance challenges. The same type of challenges that were listed for the simulation process can be solved with the aid of waiting line models. To be effective, a queuing model that represents the study situation at a reasonable level of accuracy must be available. The use of waiting line models is therefore much more limited than that of simulation.

Financial Investment Evaluation Methods

The traditional methods of net present value, payback period, internal rate of return, and profitability index can be used in a variety of maintenance challenges. The most typical challenge involves a decision to replace an old machine with a new machine rather than continue with frequent preventive maintenance and repairs.

Preventive Maintenance Versus Breakdown Policy

Preventive maintenance (activities such as machine adjustments, lubrication, cleaning, parts replacement, painting, and needed repairs and overhauls, that are performed before malfunction of facilities or machines occurs) versus *breakdown policy* (an anti-preventive maintenance policy that requires the servicing of facilities and machines only when there is a breakdown) is a typical choice faced by maintenance managers. If the frequency of preventive maintenance is increased, the number of breakdowns is decreased. Each frequency level is associated with different preventive maintenance and breakdown costs. An optimal preventive maintenance policy minimizes the sum of these two costs. A trial-and-error cost comparison is most commonly used to aid in making maintenance decisions.

Payoff Tables

A *payoff table* is a statistical, single-phased decision-making technique. A decision is made in an environment of risk. The probabilities of different possible events are known and so are the monetary payoffs that result from a particular alternative and a particular event. The expected-value concept is used to find the best alternative. Payoff tables can be used to determine the optimal number of standby machines. They can also be used to determine the optimal level of spare-parts inventory. The use of payoff tables is also appropriate for other challenges that require the selection of the alternative with the highest expected profit or the lowest expected cost.

Individual Experience 13-1
Determining Maintenance Crew Size

ABZ operates thirty-five injection-molding machines seven days per week, three shifts per day. Each shift is assigned one Repairman IV (top grade, top pay level) to provide on-site maintenance of equipment. A Repairman IV costs the company $45 per hour.

When one injection-molding machine is taken off line for repairs for one hour, the cost to ABZ is $200. This cost is sufficient enough to cause ABZ's maintenance management to view equipment breakdowns as a sign of trouble. It is a sign of serious trouble when a second or third injection-molding machine is taken off line to sit idle while a Repairman IV works at bringing a first offline molding machine to on-line status. To keep tabs on maintenance costs, maintenance management initiated a random statistical sampling program to monitor the time between machine breakdowns, the number of breakdowns, and the repair time required.

EXHIBIT 13.1
Repair and Breakdown File

Time Between Machine Breakdowns (Hrs)	No. of Times Observed
1.0	13
1.5	15
2.0	30
2.5	22
3.0	20

Repair Time Required (Hours)	No. of Times Observed
1	20
2	25
3	45
4	10

Activity 13-1-1 Joe: Pat, I need some maintenance information in a hurry. Please go to the repair and breakdown file. Retrieve what information we have concerning time between machine breakdowns and repair time required. Then, calculate for me the repair labor costs, the machine breakdown costs, and a combination of the two costs.

Pat: How do you want me to calculate these costs.

Joe: What do you recommend?

Pat: I would prefer a twenty-breakdown* Monte Carlo simulation. I will use a two-digit random numbers calculation. This will improve accuracy.

Joe: Great!
*(If you have a computer program for this simulation, simulate 100 breakdowns rather than twenty.)

Activity 13-1-2 Joe: Pat, while you are doing your calculation, you may as well perform a twenty-breakdown Monte simulation using a two-Repairman IV crew per shift (To improve accuracy, if you have a computer program for this simulation, simulate 100 breakdowns rather than twenty).

Pat: How should I figure the repair time?

Joe: Figure that the time to repair a breakdown with a crew of two will be 75 percent of the time that it takes one repairman to repair a comparable breakdown (.75, 1.5, 2.25, and 3 hours).

Pat: Anything else?

Joe: Sure! Why don't you use the same probability distribution as before for repair time required. Calculate the same costs as in the first simulation. Which crew size is less costly?

Activity 13-1-3 Joe: Leslie, Pat, and Kelly, what ethical and cultural factors should be considered if new maintenance standards are to be satisfied?

Activity 13-1-4 Joe: What additional factors should we consider when we determine the crew sizes? What additional information will we need? Explain.

Group Experience 13-1
Determining the Number of Standby Machines

The maintenance manager is considering having standby wire-connecting machines to combat the negative effects of machine breakdowns and malfunctions. When a breakdown or malfunction occurs and a standby machine is not available, the cost incurred by the company is $120 per hour. When a standby machine sits idle the cost is $60 per hour. A statistical data file is available.

EXHIBIT 13.2
Machine Breakdowns and Malfunctions
Statistical File

Number of Machines Broken Down or Malfunctioning per Hour	Number of Times Observed
5	60
4	90
3	120
2	30

Activity 13-1-1G Joe: Pat? Hey, this is Joe. I need a payoff table to determine the number of standby machines it will take to minimize the cost of machine breakdown and malfunctions. I think there is some statistical data in the file that you can use. Thanks.

Activity 13-1-1G (Continued)

Activity 13-1-2G Joe: Pat, I read your report that included a payoff table concerning the number of standby machines it will take to minimize the cost of machine breakdown and malfunctions. What I want to know is, if a more effective rescheduling of operations could result in the reduction of breakdown and malfunctioning cost to $100 per occurrence, would you change your recommendation? If so or if not, please explain.

Activity 13-1-3G Joe: Leslie, Pat, and Kelly, what ethical and cultural factors should be considered if we are to implement a new maintenance strategy that calls for the use of standby machines? Explain.

Activity 13-1-4G Joe: Leslie, Pat, and Kelly, what additional factors should be incorporated into a new maintenance strategy? What additional information will be needed? Explain.

Group Experience 13-2
Preventive Maintenance vs. Breakdown Policy

ABZ operates twenty wire-cutting machines. The machines are serviced on a preventive maintenance schedule at a cost of $100 each. When a machine breakdown occurs, it costs $300 to get the machine back into service. The probability of machine failure after maintenance is shown in the following maintenance file.

EXHIBIT 13-3
Machine Maintenance File

Number of Months Since Maintenance	Number of Machine Failures
4	80
3	60
2	40
1	20

Activity 13-2-1G Joe: Pat, could you or one of your group members pull the machine maintenance file and tell me how often the machine should be serviced? Don't just tell me, show and explain your calculations. Thanks.

Activity 13-2-2G Joe: Pat. Hey, I found your machine maintenance calculations and explanation helpful. Now I want to know what the cost of a breakdown policy is. I want to know if it is less costly than a preventive maintenance schedule. Please calculate and explain the costs.

Activity 13-2-3G Joe: Pat, now that you have calculated and explained the preventive maintenance and breakdown policies, do you see any possible ethical and cultural conflicts in using any one of them? Could you explain your position?

Activity 13-2-4G Joe: Pat, are there any additional factors that we should be incorporating into our final maintenance policy decision-making process? Is there any additional information we will need? Please explain.

CHAPTER 14

Cost Control Activities

Cost control is an important responsibility of every manager. Operations functions are cost intensive--the most cost intensive of all management functions. When cost savings are realized, they are realized at the operations level. The importance of cost control cannot be overstated.

Operations managers, in general, are responsible for the cost of goods sold. Producing goods and services at or below standard costs is the prime objective of operations managers. An operations manager is evaluated on the basis of cost. When costs are above expectations and standards, a change in leadership may be necessary.

Cost control is a major component of an organization's business strategy. This emphasis on cost must filter into each functional activity of an organization--research and development, operations, marketing, finance. Managers in each functional area must focus on cost control.

Any control process involves four stages: establishing standard values, measuring actual values, comparing actual values to standard values, and implementing needed changes. Either the standard or the performance must change.

To control the cost of goods sold, cost standards must be established for labor, material, and overhead. The collection and allocation of costs into different accounts are part of the measurement process. There are two basic methods--job costing and continuous processing--of compiling costs. Each depends on the type of production process being used. Job costing requires data appropriate to a specific job or specific customer. Continuous processing costs are compiled for a specific operations activity or a specific department.

Labor and material costs are direct costs and they are product specific. Direct costs vary with the volume of production and may be classified as variable costs. Overhead costs are not product specific. They are classified as indirect costs and also as fixed costs since they do not vary with the volume of production.

Operations managers use an *operations budget* to plan and control costs. This budget shows fixed, semi-variable, and variable costs for a specific period. The budget item costs are the result of cost standards and projected production volumes. An operations budget reflects organizational goals and guides the organization toward its goals. The budget also provides valuable information for other functional areas-- marketing, finance, and research and development.

Budgets can also be classified as fixed or variable. Fixed budgets are prepared for a particular projected level of activity (volume). Variable or flexible budgets project costs for various levels of activity.

Listing and Description of Appropriate OM Tools

There are a number of quantitative operations tools available to the operations manager. Among the ones to be discussed in this chapter are cost standards, cost-variance analysis, value analysis, standardization, and learning curves.

Cost Standards

An effective operations budget must be based on *cost standards* (an established set of cost decisions used by managers to deal with recurring labor, material, and overhead expenses). The three types of cost for which standards are established are labor, material, and overhead. Labor costs are based on wages and labor standards. Labor standards are based on estimates or work measurements. Methods of work measurement are discussed in Chapter 11.

Material cost standards are based on engineering drawings, engineering specifications, and bills of materials.

Overhead cost elements can be classified as fixed or semi-variable. Variable or flexible budgets treat semi-variable components of the overhead as variable costs. Fixed budgets present the semi-variable component as one level and attach it to the fixed projected level of activity.

Cost-Variance Analysis

When actual costs are compared to budgeted or standard costs, deviations are usually detected. Analysis of cost variance is performed in order to identify the cause of the deviation. *Cost-variance analysis* is necessary whether the deviation is desirable or undesirable. An undesirable deviation occurs when actual costs exceed budget costs. In this case, the analysis helps to determine the proper corrective action that must be taken.

A desirable deviation occurs when actual cost is lower than the budgeted cost. In this case, the analysis helps to determine if the deviation is a result of inaccurate standards or successful operations. If the deviation is a result of successful operations, then an effort to replicate the operations process is in order.

Value Analysis

Value analysis is a cost control and cost reduction technique that focuses primarily on material costs. The analysis is performed by examining all the parts and materials, and their functions. The analysis is aimed at reducing costs through cheaper components and materials in a way that will not affect product quality or appeal. Simplification of parts is also included in these efforts. Value analysis can result not only in cost savings, but sometimes in an improved product at the same time. Value analysis requires a team (companywide) effort. At the least, the team should include personnel from operations, purchasing, engineering, and marketing.

Standardization

Standardization, the use of the same parts and sub-assemblies, is a cost control and cost reduction technique. Standardization can be implemented via value analysis or as an independent project. The standardization of parts enables an organization to purchase fewer different parts and those parts that are ordered will be ordered in larger quantities. This will allow a company to receive quantity discounts. If fewer different parts are purchased, administrative efforts and inventory levels are reduced. Collectively, these changes result in lower product costs.

The standardization of sub-assemblies that are produced internally will have similar positive effects. An accompanying reduced labor cost should result from less frequent but larger production runs.

Learning Curves

The learning-curve concept deals with repetitive tasks. Learning-curve logic recognizes the principle that states, "a repetitive task improves the more the task is repeated." That is, the time it takes to perform any task is reduced as the task is performed again.

Implementation of the leaning-curve concept allows an operations manager to prepare cost estimates for new products and to establish labor standards and compensation alternatives. A learning curve can also be used to control costs. The learning-curve concept can be applied throughout an organization. It can be used to improve an organization's competitive position by focusing on ways to increase performance and decrease costs.

Individual Experience 14-1
Establishing Standard Material Cost for Purchased Parts

ABZ Electronics is in the process of reviewing its manufacturing cost control system as part of its efforts to improve its global competitiveness. ABZ executives have determined that the existing cost control system must be reviewed. If the cost control system proves to be ineffective, the executives will require that changes be made.

Activity 14-1-1 Mac Bosse: Pat, the big cheeses want the operations managers to review the existing cost control system. You're the expert on the subject so I would appreciate your conducting this review for me. Here is what I need to get us started.

First, I need you to prepare a new detailed cost control procedure that clearly describes how to establish, maintain, and update standard material costs. You will need to consider standard material costs for parts we have already purchased and new parts to be purchased.

Activity 14-1-2 Mac Bosse: Pat? Are you still with me? Okay. The second need I have is for you to tell me how the cost control procedure is related to the concept of quality. Specifically, tell me what I should include in the cost control system that will ensure that quality is not compromised.

Activity 14-1-3 Mac Bosse: Pat, once you have described the new cost control system and told me how the cost control procedure is related to the concept of quality, I want you to review your work and tell me what ethical and cultural factors have and have not been considered in your cost control strategy.

Activity 14-1-4 Pat Hancock: Anything else?

Mac Bosse: Yes. You could tell me what additional factors I should incorporate into the final cost control document that I need to submit to my supervisor. Also, note any additional information that you think I will need.

Group Experience 14-1
A Fixed or Flexible Manufacturing Budget?

ABZ Electronics is in the process of reviewing its manufacturing cost control system as part of its efforts to improve its global competitiveness. ABZ executives have determined that the existing cost control system needs to be reviewed. If the cost control system proves to be ineffective, the executives will require changes.

An ad hoc committee of operations specialists will be asked to contribute to the review of the cost control system. The committee will be asked to review fixed and flexible (variable) manufacturing budgets. Some operations managers in the manufacturing group feel that the simultaneous use of fixed and flexible budgets are unnecessary and is wasteful. They recommend that one of the budget systems be dropped.

Activity 14-1-1G Larry Gardner (Budget Director): As you know, top management has asked the operations managers to review the existing cost control system. I'm asking this group of operations specialists to prepare a comparison between fixed and flexible manufacturing budgets. I want you to make a recommendation as to whether we should (1) stay with the existing dual system, (2) change to a fixed budget system, or (3) change to a flexible budget system. Personally, I believe that if something isn't broken you don't fix it. However, top management isn't interested in my opinion. They want a systematic review and an accompanying functional recommendation.

So, get to it. Make us look good.

Activity 14-1-2G Joe: Hold it! Hold it! Before you get away from me I have one other challenge for you. As you know the manufacturing budgeting process involves the establishment of cost standards. So that top management understands our position on the subject, discuss among yourselves the consequences of setting the cost standards too high or too low. When I say cost standards, I mean material, labor, and overhead costs. Give me a laundry list of different cost standards and a brief pro-and-con discussion on each.

Additionally, give me a consensus opinion as to what you think can be done to improve the accuracy of the standards.

Activity 14-1-3G Pat: Whoa Larry! It sounds as if you are going to drag us into that union-versus-management squabble where nobody is the winner. We're wrong according to the union if the units per hour labor standards are too high. We're wrong according to top management if the units per hour labor standards are too low.

Larry Gardner: Good point, Pat. Why don't you people discuss cost standards in terms of budgets, ethics, and values. Give me a page of your thoughts on the subject.

Activity 14-1-4G Larry Gardner: Pat, regarding the assignments I made this morning concerning cost control and budgeting, act as the devil's advocate and tell me if there are additional factors that I should have incorporated into the process of establishing and reviewing manufacturing budgets. Is there some additional information I should have asked for? Please explain.

Group Experience 14-2
Value Analysis: A Cost Control Tool

ABZ Electronics is in the process of reviewing its manufacturing cost control system as part of its efforts to improve its global competitiveness. ABZ executives have determined that the existing cost control system must be reviewed. If the cost control system proves to be ineffective, the executives will require changes.

During the executive discussions on materials cost control and materials cost reduction, the concept "value analysis" was introduced. Most executives and functional managers were not familiar with the concept. Some had read an article about it in *Fortune* or had heard the concept discussed in meetings with outside executives, but none had a hands-on experience with it.

Activity 14-2-1G Larry Gardner (Budget Director): As you know, top management has asked the operations managers to review the existing cost control system. I'm asking this group of operations specialists to prepare a document aimed at familiarizing management with the concept of "value analysis." The purpose of this exercise is to prepare a "value analysis primer" for ABZ's executives and functional managers. Your document will be used to launch an executive and management discussion that may lead to the use of value analysis as an ABZ management tool.

Please include in your brief position paper an actual value analysis. To achieve this, perhaps you could locate a retail store that carries ABZ color television sets and Sony television sets. If the retail store does not have an ABZ set, compare the Sony with a Zenith. Using a small number of simple external television components on the two television sets, demonstrate a simple value analysis.

Activity 14-2-2G Pat: Larry, while it is very beneficial to use value analysis during product design, in many instances it is not possible.

Larry Gardner: True, so the next best thing to do is to employ value analysis for products that are already on the market. Perhaps your group could give me a list of the risks that could result from using value analysis for products on the market. In addition, perhaps you could note what could be done to reduce those risks?

Activity 14-2-3G Pat: Larry, are you interested in our opinion as to the ethical and cultural impact that value analysis could have on ABZ's corporate culture?

Larry: Yes, I am. Let me have a page, via group consensus, concerning ethics and values.

Activity 14-2-4G Larry: Additionally, when you finish your work on value analysis, give me a page that discusses additional factors that I should incorporate into a value analysis strategy. Please note what additional information I will need.

CHAPTER **15**

Materials Management Activities

Materials management activities support the flow of materials from vendors through an operations system to customers. The ability to achieve the desired level of product cost, quality, availability, dependability, and flexibility depends heavily on the effective and efficient flow of materials. In its broadest form, materials management activities can be organized into six groups or functions: purchasing, receiving, inventory control, shop floor control, traffic, and shipping and distribution. This structure is a result of a long process of organizational evolution. Not all organizations are at this stage of development. Separate chapters in this book are dedicated to inventory (Chapter 19 and part of Chapter 20) and shop floor control activities (Chapter 21).

Over 50 percent of the expenditures of a typical manufacturing company are spent on procurement of materials, including raw materials, parts, sub-assemblies, and supplies, and the purchasing department is engaged in several activities.

Selection of vendors and evaluation of their performance is done on a continuous basis. Purchasing of production materials is largely automated and linked to a materials requirement planning system. Purchasing of all other materials is based on a requisition from the user. Purchasing does not end with the placement of an order; order follow-up is equally crucial.

Receiving activities may include unloading, identifying, inspecting, reporting, and storing inbound shipments. Shipping and distribution activities are similar to receiving. They may include preparing documents, packaging, labeling, loading, and directing outbound shipments to customers and to distribution centers.

Shipping and receiving activities are sometimes organized as one unit. A traffic manager's main activities include selection of the transportation mode, coordination of arrival and departure of shipments, and audit of freight bills.

Inventory control activities ensure the continuous availability of purchased materials. Work in process and finished goods inventory are inventory control subsystems. Inventory control specifies what, when, and how much to buy. Held inventories buffer a variety of uncertainties that can disrupt supply. Since holding inventory is costly, an optimal inventory control policy must provide a predetermined level of certainty of supply at the lowest possible cost.

Shop floor control activities include input/output control, scheduling, sequencing, routing, dispatching, and expediting.

While many materials management activities can be programmed, it is the human factor that is the key to a competitive performance. Skilled and motivated employees are crucial.

Listing and Description of Appropriate OM Tools

There are a number of quantitative operations tools available to the operations manager. Among the ones to be discussed in this chapter are vendor selection systems, marginal analysis (single-period inventory), distribution requirements planning, payoff tables, make-or-buy analysis, and linear programming.

Vendor Selection Systems

Vendor selection systems assist in the selection and continuous evaluation of vendor performance. A master list of vendor evaluation criteria or factors is reduced to a list of item-relevant criteria or factors. The resulting list of factors is then arranged according to importance. The factors are then assigned weights. Each vendor is given a factor score according to performance. Vendors are ultimately ranked according to the total weighted score.

Marginal Analysis (Single-Period Inventory)

Marginal analysis is a technique that can be used to determine the stock level of a single- period inventory item. This includes items that have a short shelf life, are seasonal, or are special-promotion oriented. Such items are not carried in inventory from one period to another. They must be discarded or sold at a loss at the end of the period.

Distribution Requirements Planning (DRP)

Distribution requirements planning applies MRP (material requirements planning) logic (see Chapter 20) to distribution challenges. It assists in translating regional warehouse requirements to central distribution requirements to orders that are released to the plant.

Payoff Tables

A *payoff table* is a statistical table used in decision making to show the expected profits or expected costs for each alternative level of demand. Payoff tables are used for decisions subject to risk. The probabilities of different events are known, as are the monetary payoffs that result from a particular alternative and a particular event. The expected-value concept finds the best alternative. Payoff tables can be used to determine how many units of a single-period inventory item should be stocked.

Make-or-Buy Analysis

Make-or-buy analysis is used in materials management to evaluate the economic consequences of switching from a make-it-yourself strategy to a buy-it-from-someone-else strategy (or vice versa). The make-or-buy analysis technique is particularly useful in situations where suppliers are not reliable.

Linear Programming

Linear programming can assist in finding an optimal shipping schedule. This schedule will specify what quantities will be shipped from certain plants to certain warehouses at minimum transportation costs.

Linear programming may be used graphically or with the aid of a computation method such as Simplex. There is also a modified method, applicable to certain transportation challenges, that is known as the transportation method of linear programming.

Individual Experience 15-1
Improving a Vendor Selection System

ABZ's management has determined that the purchasing department will be able to improve its performance if the vendor selection system were more accurate and efficient. Materials Manager, Joyce Poe, is to assign one of his senior assistants to spend time on this project. ABZ's management views material cost reduction as an important measure of organizational success. In addition, they believe that improved vendor selection would provide other benefits as well.

Activity 15-1-1 Joyce Poe (Materials Manager, Clarkstown Plant): Pat, I'm sure you know that I selected you to help me study the vendor selection system here at Clarkstown. There are a number of activities that will involve you. The first task in the project is the development of general performance criteria for domestic and international vendors. When I say criteria I mean such items as timeliness, quality, price, and so forth. The performance criteria you select will serve as a master-vendor, evaluation checklist. A materials manager could use your checklist to determine how good a particular vendor is.

At this stage of the project you are concerned with vendors in general. Later, I will ask you to make your vendor checklist product-specific.

Activity 15-1-2 Joyce Poe: Pat, you did a great job when you developed the general performance criteria for domestic and international vendors. Now we are ready to embark on a second task--product-specific vendor checklists. These product-specific vendor lists will be used to train our purchasing agents so that they may be more effective and more efficient in product specific vendor selection.

To do what I need done, you first must prepare two product-specific vendor checklists. The first checklist will include vendor criteria for the lumber used in television console cabinets.

The second checklist will include vendor criteria for large color television picture tubes. These tubes will be larger than thirty inches because ABZ currently does not manufacture a thirty-inch or larger color television tube although we do sell color television sets that have picture tubes larger than thirty inches.

My expectation is that each of the two checklists will be shorter than the general checklist you previously developed. These new checklists will include only the factors that are the most relevant to the particular product.

Your checklist should be arranged according to importance with the most important criterion first and the others listed in descending order. A relative weight of importance should be assigned to each criterion. The sum of the weights in each list should equal the value one.

Activity 15-1-3 Pat: It sounds to me as if you are asking me to develop a checklist based on rational criteria. I suspect, however, that vendor selection is often made on the basis of whom a purchasing agent knows and how the purchasing agent gets along with a particular representative of the vendor. I expect that my checklist will become a matter of controversy among our purchasing personnel.

Joyce: I see what you mean. You're worried about ethical and value considerations!

Pat: Yes, I am.

Joyce: Okay. So include in your recommendation a list of ethical do and do nots. Maybe you should have a separate list for domestic vendors and for offshore vendors. What do you think?

Activity 15-1-4 Joyce: Prepare a statement that I can distribute to our purchasing agents concerning the new vendor selection system. I plan to distribute it once the new system is implemented. Be sure you note what some of the special problems are going to be when a purchasing agent deals with new vendors. In addition, would you please tell purchasing agents what we expect in terms of selecting potential vendors who have been in business only a short period of time?

Group Experience 15-1
Single-Period Inventory

ABZ's marketing executives believe that ABZ can penetrate the color television market in the Sacramento area. Foreign competitors captured a majority of the Sacramento market in the early 1980s, mostly because of price and availability. ABZ had no distribution in the area.

The marketing manager assigned to the Sacramento area is considering a three-week Christmas promotion in several shopping malls in Sacramento. The purpose of the promotion is to make ABZ an active competitor in the local market. ABZ's marketing research group provided forecasts for several television models.

The Christmas promotion will target ABZ's 13-inch color portable model D1382W. A marketing group forecast for the model D1382W is:

Probability of Demand for Model D1382W
Christmas Promotion—Sacramento, CA

Demand (sets)	Probability of Demand
500 or less	0.00
600	0.05
700	0.10
800	0.15
900	0.25
1,000	0.20
1,100	0.15
1,200	0.10
1,300 or more	0.00

The expected profit from the sale of one set is $30. Television sets not sold by the end of the promotion period will have to be shipped back to the factory. This will result in an additional cost (loss) of $12 per set. The $12 includes shipping, administrative, and other costs.

Activity 15-1-1G Daniele Kemper (Distribution Specialist): Group, you have received information about a color television promotion for the Sacramento area. You have a copy of a marketing forecast for the Model D1382W set. What I need from you is a recommendation as to how many sets of the D1382W should be shipped to Sacramento.

Activity 15-1-2G Pat: What our group needs to know is what will happen to the unsold sets if the marketing promotion fails. Shouldn't we be looking at a way to reduce the loss?

Daniele Kemper: The unsold sets could be shipped to the Los Angeles warehouse if space is available there. In that case the additional cost (loss) that will be incurred by ABZ will be reduced from $12 to $9 per set. Does this change your recommendation as to how many sets of D1382W should be shipped to Sacramento? Explain.

Activity 15-1-3G Pat: Daniele, now that we have made a recommendation concerning the Sacramento promotion, do you want to hear what our group believes are additional factors you should incorporate into the final decision-making process?

Daniele Kemper: Yes, and also make a statement about what additional information will be needed.

Group Experience 15-2
Distribution Requirements Planning (DRP)

ABZ is shipping its projection television sets (PV4049H, PV4051H, PV4055Y, PV4553P, PV4557P, PV820X, and PV855P) from the central distribution warehouse in its Clarkstown factory to its warehouses in Los Angeles and New York City. Los Angeles and New Your City warehouses are the only warehouses that receive these sets from Clarkstown. The DRP data base for projection television model PV4049H is shown in the following three charts.

New York City Warehouse

	Week -1	1	2	3	4	5
Forecast Demand		2,800	3,000	1,800	2,600	3,200
Scheduled Receipts		3,000				
Projected Ending Inventory	3,200					
Planned Receipt of Shipments* Planned Order Releases*						

Safety stock is 1,000 sets, shipments are made in lots of 3,000.
Lead time* is one week.

Los Angeles Warehouse

	Week -1	1	2	3	4	5
Forecast Demand		1,500	2,000	2,800	3,500	3,000
Scheduled Receipts		4,000				
Projected Ending Inventory	2,500					
Planned Receipt of Shipments* Planned Order Releases*						

Safety stock is 1,500 sets, shipments are made in lots of 4,000.
Lead time* is two weeks.

Central Distribution Warehouse

	Week -1	1	2	3	4	5
Gross Requirements						
Scheduled Receipts		5,000				
Projected Ending Inventory	10,000					
Planned Receipts of Orders** Planned Order Releases**						

Safety stock is 2,000 sets. The production lot size is 5,000.
Lead time** is one week.
* Related to the central distribution warehouse
** Related to the factory

Activity 15-2-1G Joe: Group, I need you to complete the DRP data base information regarding the New York City, Los Angeles, and Clarkstown warehouses. I needed this information yesterday.

Activity 15-2-2G Joe: Now that I have your completed DRP data base information, I need to know what type of changes in the system would result in reduced distribution costs.

Activity 15-2-3G Pat: Joe, what is it about ABZ's value system that necessitates the location of projection television warehouses only in New York City and Los Angeles?

Joe: You tell me!

Activity 15-2-4G Joe: Now that this group has raised the question of location of PV warehouses, please tell me what additional factors I should incorporate into the DRP decision making. What additional information do I need?

CHAPTER **16**

Advanced Manufacturing Support Activities

Over the past twenty years a host of advanced manufacturing systems have been developed and implemented to support operations. Most of these advanced systems are automated systems that combine hardware-industrial robots and computers--and software.

Automation means that electro-mechanical devices replace human effort (see Chapter 1). Human effort in operations includes welding, materials handling, design, drafting, and decision making. *Computer-integrated manufacturing (CIM) systems* integrate product and process design (automation) activities, planning and control (manufacturing) activities, and manufacturing activities. CIM systems are used to improve the manufacturing process by improving work flow and productivity. Consistent levels of quality may thus be achieved and maintained, resulting in reduced costs.

CIM systems often have to be customized to fit a particular manufacturing process and facility. Customizing increases implementation costs, but the costs are often justified by increased demand for the product. You should keep in mind, however, that CIM systems are not known for their flexibility, and modifying a particular CIM system to accommodate different products can be very expensive and time-consuming.

There is an appropriate CIM system for the right company at the right time. Ethical, cultural, and skill considerations may preclude a company from implementing a CIM system, or a company may not be ready to replace employees with robots or computers. In the long run, the use of CIM systems may be the only way that U.S. companies can regain global leadership, but for any given company, the circumstances and the timing are crucial considerations in the decision-making process.

Listing and Description of CIM Systems and OM Tools

There are a number of CIM systems available to the operations manager. Among the systems to be discussed in this chapter are computer-aided design (CAD), computer-aided manufacturing (CAM), and flexible manufacturing systems. Some of the OM tools are manufacturing resource planning (MRPII), just-in-time system, financial investment evaluation, and cost-benefit analysis.

Computer-Aided Design (CAD) and Computer-Aided Manufacturing (CAM)

Computer-aided design (CAD) systems include several automated design technologies. *Computer graphics* is used to design geometric specifications for parts. *Computer-aided engineering (CAE)* is used to evaluate and perform engineering analyses on a part. CAD also includes technologies that are used in process design. The design of parts for computer-controlled machine tools is an appropriate CAD function.

Computer-controlled machine tools and computer-aided inspection are examples of *computer-aided manufacturing (CAM) systems*. CAD and CAM processes can be linked through a computer, which can be very beneficial when production processes must be altered. The linkage enables design changes to be implemented in a very short period of time because CAD and CAM systems have the ability to share information easily.

Flexible Manufacturing Systems

A *flexible manufacturing system* uses a computer to control linked machines. For example, Robot 1 welds two parts together. The computer then tells Robot 1 to pass the welded part to Robot 2. Robot 2 takes the part from Robot 1 and then drills three holes into the welded part. The computer controls the transfer of parts from one machine to another.

Flexible manufacturing systems can be used efficiently in a group-technology environment where machines are arranged in small cells within a larger system. For example, five robots may be linked together to manufacture and assemble a tuning apparatus for a television set. The materials are passed from one machine to another until the system is built and assembled. Then, the last robot places the tuning system on an assembly-line belt that transfers it to the next stage of manufacturing.

Manufacturing Resource Planning (MRPII)

MRPII or *manufacturing resource planning,* is an effective method of planning involving all the resources of a manufacturing company. Prior to the development of MRPII, the focus of planning was on materials requirements (MRP) and capacity requirements (CRP) (see Chapter 20). The current state of the art, MRPII, integrates such functions such as marketing and finance into the planning process.

Just-in-Time (JIT) Production System

A *just-in-time (JIT) production system* is a Japanese innovation that is now being gradually adopted by U.S. companies. Also called zero inventories, it is perceived as a purchasing system although it does have its own production planning and control technique, known as the kanban. What is even more important, perhaps, is that the JIT approach requires a high degree of reliability on the part of suppliers and sophisticated planning at the manufacturing end. Such an approach can be applied to problem solving in general.

In the U.S., inventory is held as a buffer against uncertainties. For example, raw materials or purchased parts are kept in stock to offset the risk of receiving defective parts or insufficient numbers of parts from vendors. A company using the JIT approach seeks to eliminate excess inventory by removing uncertainty, that is, by requiring the vendor to improve his performance in regard to quality and on-time delivery of the right quantities. A JIT approach is an attitude that supports the continuous improvement of the entire manufacturing process.

Financial Investment Evaluation Methods

The traditional methods of net present value, payback period, internal rate of return, and profitability index can be used to evaluate a variety of manufacturing investment projects, such as choosing between two or more advanced manufacturing support systems or determining the financial advantages of a single purchase of automated equipment.

Cost-Benefit Analysis

Cost-benefit analysis is used when the total effect of each alternative on costs or profits is not completely clear. Choosing among several possible advanced manufacturing support systems is a situation in which cost-benefit analysis can be applied.

Individual Experience 16-1
Just-In-Time: Reducing Setup Times

ABZ's management requires supervisors to continually study operations for potential cost savings. The desire to use new technology often prompts in-house operations analyses. Presently, ABZ management is trying to assess the potential benefits of the JIT concept.

As a result of management's desire to employ the most advanced and efficient technologies and processes, operations specialist Pat Hancock was asked to study operations in one of ABZ's Mexico plants to investigate potential savings from a reduction of inventory levels.

The Mexico plant manufactures chassis parts and assembles these parts into finished television chassis which are then shipped to the Clarkstown plant where the complete color television set is assembled.

Management believes that reducing setup times for part manufacturing would also reduce setup costs. Reduced setup times and costs would allow for smaller production runs (lots) which would reduce inventory levels.

Pat focused his attention on a metal bracket used in the chassis assembly. The annual demand for the bracket is 100,000 units, 400 brackets are used daily.

The bracket is stamped on a punch press using a die at the rate of 800 units daily (excluding setup time). Setup time is 90 minutes; a setup man costs ABZ $30 an hour. The annual carrying cost of one bracket is $.50.

Activity 16-1-1 Pat: Jim (Tool and Die Supervisor, Clarkstown Plant), have you thought about my idea to modify the die that is used to produce brackets at the Mexico plant? You know I believe that such a change will result in a considerable reduction in setup time.

Jim: I have thought about it and I have an estimate that the new setup time will be one hour. I also estimate that the cost of modifying the new die will be $400.

Pat: Great. I'll determine what the first-year net savings will be if the new die is used. I'll also determine the payback period.

Activity 16-1-1 (Continued)

Activity 16-1-2 Pat: Hello, Mr. Yap? This is Pat Hancock of ABZ. I'm calling to find out if you have the estimates that I asked for. I had requested that you give me one more cost estimate on modifying the die and an estimate on the new setup time that will be realized from the use the modified die.

Mr. Yap (Representative of World-Wide Machine Tools PTE LTD, 178 Gul Circle, Jurong Town, Singapore 2262): Yes, I have the information. We can modify the die for $800. If you use this modified die, it will reduce your setup time to 30 minutes.

Pat: Great, I'll do some figuring and get back to you. Thank you.

Activity 16-1-3 Pat: Joe, you have my calculation of the cost saving we would realize by using a die modified by an outside firm. You also have my calculations based on modifying the die in-house in our tool and die shop. What's next?

Joe: Okay, now that you have two sets of costs, I want you to recommend the alternative you believe we should select.

Activity 16-1-4 Joe: Pat, before you go there is one other consideration you had better address. You need to discuss the impact of a decision to select an outside vendor on the in-house die shop, the union, and the community.

Activity 16-1-5 Joe: Additionally, why don't you tell me what additional factors I should incorporate into the final decision-making process? Tell me what additional information I will need so that I can make the best decision.

Group Experience 16-1
Just-In-Time Prerequisites

Some ABZ executives are not certain that JIT is really the solution for all of its operations challenges. They are aware of the great success the Japanese have had with JIT, but they are of the opinion that while JIT might be suited for some operations, it would not be suited for others. Any decision to implement JIT will occur only after management has reviewed additional information.

Activity 16-1-1G Joe: Group, here is what I needed yesterday. I want you to prepare a comparative study of the conditions relevant to JIT implementation in the U.S. and Japan. Once you have done this, I want you to reach some conclusions. Make recommendations on possible actions for the U.S. in general and the electronics industry and ABZ in particular. Tell me just what actions are necessary to improve our chances of successfully using JIT.

Activity 16-1-2G Joe: I have a challenge that requires your best thinking. Here is the situation: The ABZ assembly plant in Missouri has serious production challenges as a result of operational practices at several of ABZ's Mexico plants. As vendors, the Mexico plants are inefficient.

Frequently, parts are not shipped on time and the quantities shipped are not always correct. Moreover, lots are sometimes rejected for poor quality. All of these factors disrupt production at the Missouri plant and unnecessary costs are incurred.

Here is what I would like you to do for me. Tell me whether JIT is the answer to our problems. If you say yes, briefly discuss a strategy for implementation.

Activity 16-1-3G Pat: Joe, JIT is most effective when suppliers are located near the manufacturing plant. Do you think we should think about the impact a JIT system would have on the ABZ culture?

Joe: That's a good point. Give me a paragraph or two on the topic.

Activity 16-1-4G Pat: Here are some other factors our group thinks you should consider regarding JIT. We think there is some additional information you will need if you are going to be able to make an effective decision. Here is a brief listing and discussion.

Group Experience 16-2
Advanced Manufacturing Support Systems: Balancing Benefits and Risks

A major design consideration for a proposed new HDTV plant is to minimize operational cost. ABZ's management desires a state-of-the-art manufacturing plant. To achieve such a goal, management wants to implement an advanced manufacturing support system. Management includes robotics, computer-aided manufacturing (CAM), and flexible manufacturing systems (FMS) in their definition of advanced manufacturing support systems.

Activity 16-2-1G Joe: Group, I need a brief document that lists and discusses the benefits of the various advanced manufacturing support systems for ABZ's new HDTV facility. I also need information regarding the risks that are apparent in a decision to use one of these advanced manufacturing systems.

Activity 16-2-2G Joe: I have a second assignment for your group. Based upon the information you provided for File 16-2-1G, make recommendations regarding the proper use of an advanced system. Maximizing benefits while reducing or minimizing risks is what I call proper use.

Activity 16-2-3G Pat: Wow! It seems to me that robotics, CAD, and CAM are a threat to unions and to employees at the Mexican plants. For purely ethical reasons, I'm not sure we should suggest the implementation of advanced manufacturing systems. Does ABZ really want to eliminate jobs?

Joe: Hold it! Robotics, CAD, CAM, whatever, will be good for the country, good for ABZ, and good for you. Just sit down and think positive about the impact. In fact, provide a list of five justifications for implementing any advanced manufacturing system at any of our plants.

CHAPTER 17

Project Planning and Control Activities

A project is a group of related activities that are designed to produce a unique one-time product or service or to accomplish a specific set of objectives within a defined time period. Examples of projects are the construction of a dam, the installation of a computer system, the implementation of a cost-reduction program, the launching of a space shuttle, and the remodeling of an office.

A project generally involves several departments in an organization as well as units outside the organization. Employees who may be assigned to the project from these different departments in the organization become members of a team that has its own organization, referred to as a matrix organization. A matrix organization is designed to control all elements of a project and features vertical and horizontal lines of authority. A member of a project team may have two bosses-- the project manager and the department manager. This violates the unity of command principle and the resulting dual loyalty may give rise to conflict between the department and the project.

Simple projects can be planned and controlled with the aid of tools such as a Gantt chart. Large and complex projects require the use of network-based planning and control tools such as PERT (program evaluation and review technique) and CPM (critical path method). In addition to PERT and CPM, there are other similar techniques that were developed for special applications. PERT, CPM, and the other techniques are available for use on mainframe computers, minicomputers, and personal computers.

Managing large and complex projects is a great challenge. Despite the availability of tools such as PERT and CPM, projects are hardly ever completed on time. The actual cost to complete a large project usually exceeds the budget significantly. Again, the human factor is an important key to success.

Listing and Description of Appropriate OM Tools

There are a number of quantitative operations tools available to the operations manager. Among the ones to be discussed in this chapter are the program evaluation and review technique (PERT) and the critical path method (CPM).

Program Evaluation and Review Technique (PERT)

The *program evaluation and review technique* (PERT) was developed for the planning and control of the Polaris missile project. It uses the activity-on-arc approach and is therefore event oriented. An *event* marks the accomplishment of an activity or activities and does not in itself consume time or any other resource. The graphical presentation of the network uses arcs to represent activities and nodes to represent events. The precedence relationships between activities must be defined outside the graph.

PERT is designed to deal with uncertainty. The time estimate for each activity is the mean of the most likely time, the most pessimistic time, and the most optimistic time. The network identifies the critical path which incorporates the minimum slack time at each event along the path. The slack for an event is the difference between the latest allowable achievement date and the earliest expected achievement date. Any delay in the activities along the critical path results in a delay in the completion date of the project. PERT also makes it possible to calculate the probability of completing the project in a certain amount of time.

An extension of PERT, called *PERT-COST*, is used primarily for budgetary control. It can also be used for minimum cost scheduling.

Critical Path Method (CPM)

The name, *critical path method*, could be somewhat misleading since PERT also uses the critical path concept. *CPM* (a network-analysis technique used to schedule and control work on projects for which the time required to complete tasks is known fairly precisely) is quite similar to PERT, but there are some differences. First, CPM uses the activity-on-node convention, that is, activities are represented by nodes and arcs represent precedence relationships. Second, CPM is an activity-oriented network. Third, CPM is deterministic in nature and uses only one set of time estimates.

An extension of CPM, called *CPM-COST*, is used primarily for minimum cost scheduling. It can also be used for budgetary control.

Individual Experience 17-1
Remodeling a Production Area Via Project Planning

The emphasis in competition is shifting away from how companies build their products to how well they serve their customers. ABZ's executives have decided therefore to use the Clarkstown factory to showcase our systems and processes.

Management has determined that the first step should be to actually create within the Clarkstown factory aa showroom featuring ABZ's color television products. Later they hope to configure the entire factory in such a way as to demonstrate the company's superiority in manufacturing, quality, and reliability.

To create the showroom, a 5,000 square foot production area adjacent to the plant's main lobby has been selected for remodeling. The executives want construction of the showroom to take no longer than six weeks. Production activities in the plant are not to be disrupted during the construction period.

Activity 17-1-1 Joe: Pat, the big execs want to create a showroom in our plant to feature ABZ's color television products. There must be display areas for sixteen portable, eight table, thirty-six console, and seven projection models.

A 5,000 square foot production area adjacent to the plant's main lobby has been selected for remodeling. The electronic sub-assembly facility that now occupies the space will be moved to another area in the plant.

Walls will be constructed so that the new showroom area will be separated from the rest of the factory activities. A doorway will have to be opened to the existing lobby of the plant. The showroom will be carpeted and a new false ceiling will be added.

Your first assignment is to prepare a complete list of tasks that have to be completed. Your list must include construction tasks, facility planning tasks, scheduling tasks, floor preparation tasks, and carpeting tasks. Construction tasks should include all remodeling activities including ceilings, walls, and doors. Include in your list any other tasks you feel will be necessary.

Assign the construction tasks to outside contractors since it does not appear that these tasks can be accomplished in-house. Assign the other tasks to ABZ personnel, including janitors, engineers, supervisors, salesmen, and moving and storage personnel. Assign other ABZ support groups if you feel they are necessary.

Activity 17-1-1 (Continued)

Activity 17-1-2 Joe: Pat, your next assignment will be to develop time estimates for each task. Once this is done, you need to develop a graphic representation of your plan. Use a horizontal bar chart to indicate start and finish targets for each task. Show which task or tasks must be completed before another task or other tasks may start.

Remember, the construction activity needs to be accomplished in a six-week time period. Schedule your resources accordingly. Please submit the plan for my approval as soon as possible.

Activity 17-1-3 Joe: Pat, be sure to indicate in your plan that the construction work must be accomplished by outside contractors.
Pat: Do you mean non-union contractors?
Joe: Sure, if they are available.
Pat: That's not ethical and this is why.

Activity 17-1-4 Joe: Pat, are there any additional factors you believe are necessary to know before you start your planning activities? Is there any additional information you need?

Group Exercise 17-1
Planning MRP Implementation with PERT

ABZ's executives have not decided whether to implement an MRP or a JIT system for the Mexico chassis plant. This non-decision will not affect their decision to develop an MRP implementation plan. Management sees this planning-to-plan activity as a good learning experience for its operations specialists. The Mexico plant produces thirty different chassis using twelve different sub-assemblies. It purchases 180 different parts. Twenty different materials are used to fabricate 100 different parts.

Activity 17-1-1G Joe: This group has been organized for the purpose of implementing an MRP system in ABZ's Mexico television chassis plant. You will have access to several information systems specialists during the course of the planning. You will use PERT to plan the MRP implementation.

The first step in your planning will be to develop a list of all the tasks necessary to implement the MRP system in the Mexico plant. At the same time, you must calculate the most pessimistic, most likely, and most optimistic amounts of time it will take to complete each task.

Your list must include decision-making recommendations to be used when multiple options are available. Be explicit. MRP-oriented planning exists at the Mexico plant, but your efforts are to be independent of that information. I want you to reinvent the wheel-- start from scratch.

Activity 17-1-2G Joe: The second step in your planning activity requires you to develop a PERT network for the project. A graphical presentation must be included. Your PERT time frame will be limited to six months, so make sure that the expected project completion time is equal to or shorter than that time frame. Tell me how long you need for this project and then get started!

Activity 17-1-3G Pat: Joe, do you think we should force American culture on these Mexican people?
Joe: No, I don't. Please develop a statement concerning the impact of the American business culture on the ethics and values of the people who work in the Mexico plant. Indicate why you think we should not force our culture on another culture.

Activity 17-1-4G Pat: Joe, why are we doing this?

Joe: Management's logic is that none of ABZ's foreign plants have effective production planning and control systems. Eventually, MRP will be necessary in all foreign plants. This particular assignment is designed as a learning tool. Future implementation of MRP systems will be assigned to this group and you may be responsible for implementing MRP in all our plants.

Now, tell me what additional factors you need to consider. What additional information do I need to pass on to you?

Group Experience 17-2
Planning Standardization Implementation with CPM

Operations managers in the Clarkstown and Mexico plants want to have the operations specialists study the possibility of implementing a program to standardize parts and sub-assemblies. They want this study to involve all ABZ departments as well as units outside. The managers believe that if the same parts were used in more sub-assemblies, inventory and costs would be reduced.

Activity 17-2-1G Joe: Folks, I want you to prepare a graphical presentation of the plan to implement parts and sub-assemblies standardization for existing products. Use a CPM network. Determine the precedence relationships among tasks which will require you to know what task or tasks must be completed before another task can be started. It will not be necessary for you to prepare time estimates for the tasks. Once you complete the graphical presentation, tell me if the preparation of the graph clarified the problem. Also tell me if your work would result in an improved situation should the standardization be implemented.

Activity 17-2-1G (Continued)

Activity 17-2-2G Pat: I am aware that you could use a PERT rather than CPM network. Which network would you recommend for this assignment? Explain.

Activity 17-2-3G Joe: Culturally speaking, do you believe the people in our Mexico chassis plant are up to the challenge of standardization?

Activity 17-2-4G Joe: Tell me what additional factors and what additional information you actually need to complete a CPM or a PERT for the standardization project.

EXHIBIT V.1 Operations Management System

Suppliers • Market • Competitors • Regulators
Associations • Labor Unions • Politics • Technology
Economy • Public Attitudes • Demographics • Prices

GRAND STRATEGY

CORPORATE STRATEGY

BUSINESS STRATEGY

EXTERNAL ENVIRONMENT

STRATEGIC ACTIVITIES

MARKETING • OPERATIONS • FINANCE

Capacity Strategy
Location Strategy
Product Strategy
Process Strategy
Layout Strategy
Human Resources Strategy

FUNCTIONAL ACTIVITIES

Quality Assurance   Maintenance
Material Management
Cost Control   Advanced Manufacturing Support
Project Planning & Control

TACTICAL SUPPORT ACTIVITIES

AGGREGATE PLANNING & MASTER SCHEDULING
INVENTORY CONTROL - INDEPENDENT DEMAND
RESOURCE REQUIREMENTS PLANNING (MRP - CRP)
SHOP FLOOR CONTROL

TACTICAL CORE ACTIVITIES

Operations Management System

SECTION V

TACTICAL CORE ACTIVITIES

The chapters in this section involve you less with planning and more with control. Core operations refer to those tasks that ensure that operations strategies are producing the desired results. Tactical core activities are the most task-oriented of the tactical programming activities, and represent the core of the organization. They permit operations (Chapters 5 through 17) to fit together to build stakeholder value (Chapters 2 through 4).

Chapter 18 focuses on aggregate planning and master scheduling. *Aggregate planning* is a group of activities that determine levels of employment, levels of inventory, and machine output rates for an intermediate time period. Aggregate planning leads to master scheduling activities. If you concentrate on this chapter, you should be able to apply several aggregate planning and master scheduling tools to OM situations.

Inventory control/independent demand is considered in Chapter 19. *Inventory control* activities are aimed at maintaining an inventory level that provides a good balance between the cost of shortages and the cost of excess inventory. The chapter focuses on lot-sizing, order point, safety stock, service level, and simulation techniques. If you read and apply the ideas in this chapter, you should be able to list the steps required to coordinate inventory control with purchasing.

Chapter 20 provides an overview and exercises involving resource requirements planning. If you complete the experiences in this chapter, you should be able to apply materials requirements planning (MRP) and capacity requirements planning (CRP) techniques to organizational resource challenges.

Shop floor control activities are featured in Chapter 21. The information in this chapter will strengthen your effectiveness as an operations specialist by giving you an opportunity to apply sequencing, linear programming, line of balance, and input/output control techniques to shop floor activities.

Chapter 21 completes the conceptual scheme of this book. If you review and apply what you have experienced, you will see an implicit and explicit usefulness of the many OM tools necessary in an operations job situation. You will understand the impact of global/international issues, competition, and ethical and human resource considerations.

CHAPTER 18

Aggregate Planning and Master Scheduling

Aggregate planning is a group of activities that determine levels of employment, levels of inventory, and machine output rates for an intermediate time period. Employment, inventory, and output levels are adjusted to best respond to irregular market demands. Determining employment, inventory, and output levels and their timing is the purpose of an aggregate production plan.

The term aggregate is used because outputs are expressed in unit measures, such as tons of steel or numbers of cars without specifying particular end items, such as car models. A good plan provides a balance between demand and capacity, and several production plans should be evaluated to identify the best one. Aggregate planning links long-term and short-term planning activities.

Aggregate planning decisions affect not only operations, but also marketing, finance, and other strategic activities of the organization. When evaluating different production plans, all segments of the organization must be considered. For example, the fact that the plan determines employment levels requires that the plan incorporate ethical and cultural considerations.

Aggregate planning leads to master scheduling activities. The master production schedule (MPS) is a formal plan that breaks down the aggregate plan into quantities of specific end items or models that will be produced in specific time periods.

The MPS links aggregate planning to short-term production planning by generating capacity and material requirements. Thus, it also links the aggregate plan to material requirements planning (MRP) and capacity requirement planning (CRP) systems.

Listing and Description of Appropriate OM Tools

There are a number of quantitative operations tools available to the operations manager. Among the ones to be discussed in this chapter are aggregate planning--trial and error, aggregate planning--mathematical models, rough-cut capacity planning, and master scheduling.

Aggregate Planning--Trial and Error

The most common method of generating a satisfactory aggregate production plan is the *trial-and-error method*. The aggregate plan specifies levels of employment, levels of inventory, and levels of machine output. Different plans are formulated based on the different strategies. One plan might focus on changes in employment levels to offset fluctuating demand which might result in massive hiring or firing. Another plan might focus on changes in inventory levels. A third plan, a mixed strategy, might focus on changing both employment and inventory levels. Using charts and graphs, the best strategy can be identified, that is, the strategy that is determined to be the least costly to implement. When additional factors, including non-monetary ones, are considered, a different plan may be chosen.

Aggregate Planning--Mathematical Models

Numerous mathematical models may be used to solve aggregate planning problems. These models help minimize the uncertainties of the basic trial-and-error approach, but although they are often recommended, these mathematical models are rarely used. Among the recommended mathematical models are the *linear decision rule method, goal programming, linear programming,* the *management coefficients method, parametric production planning,* and *computer search.*

Linear programming is the most frequently used mathematical model. It can allocate limited resources to two or more competing products so that profit is maximized, and can also provide aggregate scheduling alternatives. Linear programming may be used to present alternatives graphically by using a computation method such as Simplex. A special application of the transportation method of linear programming has been helpful in solving aggregate scheduling challenges.

Rough-Cut Capacity Planning

Rough-cut capacity planning is an aggregate planning tool that can be used to evaluate a trial aggregate plan or a trial MPS by focusing on production work loads. Rough-cut capacity planning produces department load reports or load profiles. When load profiles are determined to be unacceptable, load leveling alternatives are studied. Load leveling may be attempted by revising the aggregate plan or the MPS. If load leveling does not occur within current available capacity, capacity levels must be changed. Capacity changes may be accomplished by adding a shift, subcontracting, hiring more employees, transferring work from one department to another, or working overtime.

Master Scheduling

Master scheduling activities result in a master schedule referred to as the *master production schedule (MPS)*. The MPS focuses on the number of end items that can be produced in a specific time period. The MPS depends on forecasts which are helpful when made-to-stock items are to be manufactured, and customer orders, which are helpful when made-to-order items are to be manufactured.

The MPS generates the amounts and need dates for the manufacture of specific end products. Rough-cut capacity planning reviews the MPS to make sure that there are no obvious capacity constraints that would require the schedule to be changed, since changes in the MPS could affect delivery dates, customer service, and customer relations. An efficient master schedule results in a balance between required and available capacity. A good master schedule is one that promotes efficiency without sacrificing customer relations and that has the confidence of personnel throughout the organization.

Individual Experience 18-1
Aggregate Plan in the Traffic Department

Jon Helberg, traffic manager at ABZ's Clarkstown plant, is developing next year's shipping plan which targets finished goods for ABZ's customers and distribution centers. Jon's plan is based on statistics derived from past customer orders, past distribution center orders, and a forecast. His plan requires knowledge about destination mileage and weights of television sets.

Using this information, Jon has estimated the aggregate quarterly demand for next year at 6,000, 8,000, 10,000, and 5,000 ton-miles. The different sources of trucks available and their maximum capacities and costs are:

Source	Maximum Capacity (Ton-Miles per Quarter)	Cost (Per Ton-Mile)
ABZ Trucks and Drivers		
Straight time	5,000	.30
Overtime	2,500	.35
Leased Trucks and ABZ Drivers	3,000	.45
Trucking Company		
(Including Drivers)	4,000	.50

Activity 18-1-1 Jon Helberg: Pat, take this shipping information and find an optimal aggregate plan. First, formulate the data into a linear programming problem. Next, use any available computer software to help you find an optimal aggregate plan.

Activity 18-1-2 Todd Madrid (union steward): Hello, Jon. Todd Madrid here. I guess you heard that your people in the front office promised to try to reduce the maximum quarterly shipping capacity for that independent trucking company. You know I get concerned when your outside contract threatens union jobs. So how hard did you try?

Jon: Todd, what is this loss-of-job stuff? Don't I always place your union's needs at the top? Just today, I am expecting some planning information from one of our operations specialists. First, he determined the White Trucking share at 4,000 ton-miles per quarter. Next, at top brass's suggestion, he set the White Trucking share by reducing their maximum quarterly capacity by 50 percent. As soon as I get the new optimal plan figures, I will get back to you.

Jon: Hello, Pat. I have your calculations regarding the optimal aggregate shipping plan. Did I also tell you to recalculate the data by reducing the maximum quarterly capacity allocated to the White Trucking company by 50 percent? If I didn't tell you to do that, I'm telling you now. Please do the recalculation and determine a new optimal aggregate plan. When that is done, compare the costs of both plans.

Activity 18-1-3 Pat: Jon, I recalculated the aggregate plan. Here are the figures. Tell me, should Todd Madrid be happy or should he be hollering "unethical, unethical, anti-union, anti-union"?

Activity 18-1-4 Jon: Pat, I have not shown the planning information to Todd. Before I do, I want to know if you think I have all the information I need on the subject. Are there any factors I haven't considered?

268 CHAPTER 18

Group Experience 18-1
The Trial-and-Error Method of Aggregate Planning

Calvin Ying, the assembly manager, at the ABZ's Melrose Park assembly plant, is preparing an aggregate production plan for the first six months of next year. His line produces sixteen models of portable color television sets to-stock (forecast) and to-order. The labor needed to assemble the different models is quite similar, which allows Calvin's planning to be performed in terms of a pseudo-product. A pseudo-product is a fictitious product that represents the average characteristics of all the 16 models. Calvin has provided a group of operations specialist with the following information:

Month	Total Demand (All Models, (Forecast Plus Orders)	No. Working Days
January	15,000	20
February	12,000	19
March	10,000	22
April	12,000	21
May	14,000	22
June	18,000	22

Cost Item	(Average) Cost
Materials	$87/set
Inventory carrying cost	3/set/month
Stockout	30/set
Hiring	150/employee
Layoff	200/employee
Labor (.75 hours/set x $16/hour straight time)	12/set
Overtime (.75 hours/set x $24/ hour overtime)	18/set

Calvin Ying projected the beginning inventory for January 1 of next year at 3000 sets.

Activity 18-1-1G Calvin: Thank you for coming to see me. I need you to assist me by considering two different production strategies. My first strategy targets production at the exact monthly total demand. I used an eight-hour day and I varied the size of the crew. The second strategy targeted monthly production at an average six-month total demand. The crew size remained constant. According to my calculations, inventory will vary and stockouts might occur. Now, will you please compare the cost of the two plans?

Activity 18-1-1G (Continued)

Activity 18-1-2G Calvin: Oh yes, I also would like you to formulate at least one more strategy and calculate its cost. Then, please tell me which of the three strategies represents the least cost.

Activity 18-1-3G Joe: Hold it! I understand that Calvin Ying asked you to do some trial-and-error aggregate planning. He was pleased, but I want you to tell me if there were additional factors he should have incorporated into the final decision-making process. Tell me what additional information he needed.

Group Experience 18-2
Rough-Cut Capacity Planning

A team of operations specialists at the Clarkstown plant has prepared a master production schedule (MPS). The schedule is attached. The schedule is for two product groups (portable television sets and table television sets) that are assembled on the main Clarkstown plant assembly line. The total weekly demand for each group represents the sum of demands for all models in the group. The data is based on known orders and forecasts.

Master Production Schedule (MPS)						
Week	1	2	3	4	5	6
Portable sets						
Total Demand	1,000	2,000	3,000	5,000	6,000	7,000
Beginning Inventory	8,000	7,000	5,000	8,000	9,000	9,000
Required Production	-0-	-0-	6,000	6,000	6,000	6,000
Ending Inventory	7,000	5,000	8,000	9,000	9,000	8,000
Table sets						
Total Demand	3,000	2,000	4,000	3,000	2,000	4,000
Beginning Inventory	4,000	6,000	4,000	5,000	7,000	5,000
Required Production	5,000	-0-	5,000	5,000	-0-	5,000
Ending Inventory	6,000	4,000	5,000	7,000	5,000	4,000

Activity 18-2-1G Joe: Group, based on the attached data and additional data I am going to give you, I need you to calculate the weekly assembly hours required to produce the MPS for both the portable and table television groups. These hours are sometimes referred to as loads.

The Clarkstown plant assembly line produces at a much higher speed than the Melrose Park plant assembly line. A portable set requires .01 hours of assembly capacity and a table unit requires .025 hours of assembly capacity. The available weekly capacity for the assembly line is 160 hours.

Now for the kicker: Please compare the loads to the available capacity and detect underloads and overloads.

Activity 18-2-1G (Continued)

Activity 18-2-2G Joe: You did a great job, group. Now revise the MPS. Your goal is to minimize underloads and overloads. Use the same production lot sizes. Recalculate the weekly loads and compare them to available capacity. Tell me, does the revised MPS meet your goal? Please explain.

Activity 18-2-3G Joe: Now group, tell me what additional factors I should incorporate into the preparation and revision of the MPS. Also tell me what additional information is needed for any revision.

CHAPTER 19

Inventory Control/Independent Demand Activities

A merchant had twenty items on the shelf when the store was opened at 8:00 a.m. At 9:00 a.m., a customer bought five of the items. At 11:30 a.m., another customer bought three of the items. At 2:00 p.m., another customer purchased two of the items.

At 4:55 p.m., a stock clerk noted that ten items had been sold. He went to the stock room and retrieved ten items and noted that there were only thirty of these items remaining in stock. He checked the reorder stock card and noticed that the last order of these items was for fifty items. He also noted that the store sells an average of twenty of these items a week. He further noted that the manufacturer requires ten working days to deliver fifty items. He immediately sent a fax order to the manufacturer for fifty items.

Later, he was notified that the item was out of stock and that the order would be delayed for thirty days. By the end of the week, twenty items had been sold, which represented an average week. On Tuesday of the next week, the merchant's best customer bought fifteen items and told the merchant that he would need twenty additional items on each of the two following Mondays. The customer had been purchasing an average of ten items per week. The merchant told the customer that he would not be able provide the last twenty items on the order.

Later that day, the customer called the merchant to tell him that he did not need the forty additional items. In fact, he stated that he would not need any additional items because he had found a new merchant with a similar product for the same price. He told the merchant that the new supplier guarantees any orders of fifty items on two days' notice.

The items represented 50 percent of the merchant's business and had a markup of 60 percent. The merchant had an inventory control problem. He could not satisfy a customer's demand for the product.

Effective inventory control reduces the risk of product shortage and reduces the threat of losing current and potential customers. An *inventory* is held so that vendors can make sure the customers' demand for a product can be met by what is on the shelf, what is in the stock room, what is on order, and/or what is being manufactured.

Shortages can occur for a number of reasons. A supplier can be late with a shipment. Items in inventory can be defective, requiring that they be returned to the vendor or manufacturer for replacement. Shortages can occur when a manufacturing machine is down and causes an interruption in delivery activities, or when there is a sudden surge in demand.

At the other end of the inventory continuum is excessive inventory, which disrupts the cash flow of a company and requires additional space and special handling. Excessive inventory of one product may also limit the inventory of a profitable product.

Inventory control activities are intended to maintain an inventory level that provides a good balance between the cost of shortages and the cost of excess inventory. Inventory control helps a manager determine when to order an item and how much to order.

Independent demand—demand from outside the organization for a finished good, a replacement part, or a sub-assembly—is calculated on the basis of demand forecasts and customer orders. Dependent demand is directly related to the demand for another item. The demand for the parts and sub-assemblies that are used to produce a finished good is an example of a dependent demand.

A *material requirements planning (MPR) system* determines the dependent demand for parts and sub-assemblies based on the demand for the finished good and the bill of materials for that good.

Inventory control activities for independent demand are more complex than those for dependent demand. They too involve the use of forecasts and customer orders, but they also include analytical models for lot sizing, order point, safety stock, and service level. Inventory control activities are linked with purchasing activities to ensure that the right materials at the right cost are obtained from vendors.

Listing and Description of Appropriate OM Tools

There are a number of quantitative operations tools available to the operations manager. Among the ones to be discussed in this chapter are lot-sizing techniques; order point, safety stock, and service level techniques; and simulation.

Lot-Sizing Techniques

One of the two questions that must be answered when establishing an inventory control system is how much to order. *Lot-sizing techniques* are used to determine the most economical quantity to be ordered. Each of the different lot-sizing techniques is tailored to a different set of operation conditions.

There are two types of orders: orders to outside vendors (purchase order) and orders to the production department (shop order). For purchase orders, the most economical quantity to purchase is called EOQ, or economic order quantity. The most economical quantity to produce is called EPL, or economic production lot. The most economical order quantity is one that minimizes the annual total of two costs: order costs and carrying costs. The fixed cost that is associated with placing a purchase order or a shop order is the order cost. The variable cost of carrying inventory is the carrying cost. Carrying costs depend on the size of the inventory.

Order Point, Safety Stock, and Service Level

Management must determine when to place an order. Another way of stating this is, *"At what point is an order placed?"* This point is called the *reorder point*. Once the quantity of an item in stock gets down to a specified level--the reorder point--a purchase or a shop order is placed. The quantity in stock on the day of the order is supposed to last until the new order arrives. Due to variability in consumption and delivery times, stockouts can occur. A stockout is costly because it disrupts production, reduces sales, and often results in the loss of customers.

The *service level* is the percentage of orders in which a stockout does not occur. To reduce the risk of a stockout, managers use the *safety stock* which allows a manager to adjust the reorder point and the service level upward, but which results in higher inventory carrying cost. An optimal policy tries to minimize both the total stockout cost and the inventory carrying cost.

Simulation

Simulation is the process of experimenting with a model of a real system or of an activity. Managers use simulation to analyze system behavior under different conditions. Simulation is a problem-solving tool that can be applied to many different situations. In inventory control, simulation can be used in situations where appropriate analytical solutions are not available. A simulation can be used to formulate inventory policy by showing management when the reorder point will occur and how many units of an item will need to be ordered. Simulation can also be used to evaluate different inventory policies according to a specific criterion so that the best policy can be selected.

Individual Experience 19-1
Taking Advantage of Quantity Discounts

ABZ Electronics purchases 50,000 cast handles for one of its television consoles. The price/volume schedule followed is:

Number of Units Purchased per Order	Acquisition Cost per Handle
1-4,999	$3.05
5,000-9,999	2.90
10,000+	2.70

There is a $200 per order setup charge. The annual carrying cost per unit is 25 percent of the acquisition cost.

Activity 19-1-1 Joe: Pat, based on the attached information, how many handles should ABZ Electronics purchase in each order? Show me your calculations.

Activity 19-1-2 Joe: Pat, by the end of the year the vendor for the handles used on our television consoles will become a JIT vendor and begin delivering each order in weekly lots of 2,000 units. ABZ uses the handles at a constant rate of 1,000 units per week, 50 weeks per year. Because of the implementation of JIT, the vendor wants to negotiate a price rise of $.15 per handle for each price level. My question is, is ABZ better off financially under the new or the old arrangement? Please explain.

Activity 19-1-3 Joe: Pat, what additional factors should I incorporate into the final decision concerning the $.15 per handle price increase? What additional information will I need if I were to encounter a possible conflict in negotiations?

Group Experience 19-1
Safety Stock: A Key to Good Customer Service

ABZ's regional warehouse in Los Angeles is experiencing stockouts of the popular 19-inch portable television set, D1910B. Management would like to formulate a better safety-stock policy. Management analyzed the Los Angeles warehouse records for a two-year period and it was determined that the mean (EDDLT) demand for model D1910B while waiting for a shipment from the Clarkstown plant was 754.6 sets. The standard deviation was 142.8 sets. (The demand while waiting for a shipment is normally distributed.)

Activity 19-1-1G   Joe: Group, this morning I had a telephone conversation with Michael P. Bradley, warehouse manager in Los Angeles, concerning stockouts for the popular 19-inch portable television set, D1910B. Management determined that the mean (EDDLT) demand for model D1910B while waiting for a shipment from the Clarkstown plant was 754.6 sets. The standard deviation was 142.8 sets.

Given this information, tell me how much safety stock of model D1910B should be carried if the risk of stockout is kept to 10 percent? What will be the order point for D1910B?

Activity 19-1-2G Joe: Bradley feels that a stockout risk of 10 percent is too high. He believes such a stockout risk will result in a significant loss of sales and/or a loss of customers (retail stores). If the stockout risk is kept to 5 five percent, calculate the percentage increase in carrying costs that ABZ should expect.

Activity 19-1-3G Joe: Is there some other operations tool that we could use to help reduce stockout risks? What about JIT? Do you have any suggestions?

Group Experience 19-2
Simulating Different Inventory Policies for Maintenance Parts

The maintenance department at the Clarkstown plant is experiencing shortages in a popular standard hydraulic pump used on most of the injection molding machines. When a shortage occurs, Federal Express is sometimes used to ship pumps to us from our vendor in Wisconsin, but this stop-gap measure is expensive and has not eliminated machine downtime.

Maintenance department records reveal the following facts:

Daily Demand for Hydraulic Pumps	Frequency (Days)
1	36
2	72
3	144
4	90
5	18
	360

The purchasing department consulted its records for the last forty pump orders and provided the following information (Federal Express shipments are not included):

Purchasing Lead Time (Days)	Frequency
2	8
3	20
4	12
(Orders)	40

Activity 19-2-1G Joe: Group, review the attached data and introductory material. We need to provide some advice and data for the Clarkstown plant management based on the data at hand.

The situation is this: Currently, the order point for the pump is four units and the order quantity is eight units. You need to develop a "30-day Monte Carlo simulation" and calculate the average daily ending inventory and the average daily number of pumps that were needed but not in stock. To improve your accuracy, if you have a computer program for this simulation, simulate 100 days rather than 30.

Use two-digit random numbers from any source.

Activity 19-2-1G (Continued)

Activity 19-2-2G Joe: Now group, consider a new inventory policy for the pump. Make your order point five units and make the order quantity six units. Then prepare another "30-day Monte Carlo simulation" making the appropriate calculations to determine if your proposed policy will improve the stockout situation. To improve accuracy, if you have a computer program for this simulation, simulate 100 days rather than 30.

CHAPTER **20**

Resource Requirements Planning Activities

Resource requirements planning (RRP) activities are used to determine the quantities and timing of all the resources needed in the short term to execute the master production schedule (MPS). The resource list includes human resources, purchased parts and raw materials, produced parts and sub-assemblies, production equipment capacity, and financial resources.

In the short term, management has very little control over the availability of resources, overtime can be used to increase the availability of labor, but adding a new assembly line is not possible. Resource requirements cannot substantially exceed the levels of the readily available resources.

Effective RRP systems are based on inputs from all functional areas. For example, the marketing department must provide information on short-term forecasts and customer orders (via MPS), accounting personnel must provide cash availability information, and the human resource department needs must provide information about the availability of employees.

Resource requirements planning results in the development of production schedules and resource requirements schedules. An end-item production schedule, which is based on quantities and delivery dates requested by the customers may be used by marketing when reporting to customers. The human resources department relies on an employee requirements schedule when hiring and laying off employees.

An RRP system uses aggregate plan, inventory status, product structure, shop routing, and work center status information, all of which should be part of the management information system.

Listing and Description of Appropriate OM Tools

There are a number of quantitative operations tools available to the operations manager. Among the ones to be discussed in this chapter are materials requirements planning (MRP) and capacity requirements planning (CRP).

Materials Requirements Planning (MRP)

Managers use an *MRP system* to determine quantity and timing in purchasing and producing dependent-demand inventory items. This information is of short-term value and is used to execute the master production schedule (MPS).

An MRP system uses aggregate plan, MPS, inventory status, and product structure information. The types and quantities of end items called for in the MPS and the product structure files are used to generate gross requirements for all dependent-demand items. The demand for parts and sub-assembly items, which are used to produce end items, depends on the demand for the end items.

Dependent-demand items are either purchased or produced. An MRP compares gross requirements with the inventory on hand and on order to arrive at net requirements. The capacity requirements planning (CRP) system is then compared with the MRP to check for adequate capacity. If capacity is not adequate, capacity changes are made so that the MPS can be executed.

The net requirement quantities for purchased and produced items can be reviewed using lot-sizing techniques and safety-stock requirements to determine the actual quantities to be purchased. These quantities cannot be smaller than the net requirements quantities. At this stage, purchase orders to vendors and shop orders to production are issued. Shop orders include orders for the parts and sub-assemblies called for in the MRP and orders for end items specified by the MPS. Vendor and production delivery times and assembly time must be considered when determining when to issue the orders.

Capacity Requirements Planning (CRP)

CRP systems determine the human resources and equipment capacity needed in the short term to execute the MPS based on shop routing, work-center status, and released shop-order information from the MRP. Work-center status files include the status of human resources and equipment capacity.

Capacity requirements planning is used in conjunction with materials requirements planning to perform short-term capacity adjustments when capacity requirements do not match available capacity. CRP also checks the overall capacity utilization generated by MRP to arrive at a tentative production plan. If capacity use is shown to be below an acceptable level or if capacity cannot be increased to the required level, the MPS must be revised. In the short term, capacity can be increased by having employees work overtime, adding an additional shift, subcontracting, or producing parts on alternative machines.

CRP produces capacity adjustment notices and workload reports. Workload reports are used for short-term capacity control, which is part of shop floor control.

Individual Experience 20-1
Adding Safety Stocks to the Materials
Requirements Planning (MRP) System

ABZ domestic plants in Missouri and Illinois are using a state-of-the-art MRP system, but the implementation of MRP has not eliminated stockouts of purchased parts at the Melrose Park or the Clarkstown plant. The result is that production of sub-assemblies and finished goods is disrupted and production must be rescheduled. Another result is that two warehouses are overstocked with low-margin and slow-selling color television sets, while some orders, often for high-margin and fast-selling color television sets, cannot be filled.

An investigation of the situation revealed that the safety-stock option of MRP was not adopted when MRP was implemented. While the stockouts are not excessive, various ABZ operations managers feel that the MRP safety-stock option should now be adopted to reduce production disruptions to minimum.

Activity 20-1-1 Mac Bosse (Operations Manager): I want you to do a special project for my colleagues and me. We have recommended that the safety-stock option be added to our existing MRP system. The proposal will be considered by ABZ executives in the near future. It has come to our attention that the safety-stock option will be opposed by at least the accounting and finance people. They believe that such a change will result in higher levels of inventories. I want you to help us overcome this opposition.

What we need is a detailed explanation of why safety stocks should be used and why they cannot be automatically ruled out when using an MRP system. Please supply us with this explanation and some additional tips to help us in our negotiations with ABZ executives. Okay?

Activity 20-1-2 Mac: Pat, regarding the assignment I gave you this morning. My colleagues asked me to have you prepare for the implementation of the safety-stock option. Their thinking is that we should be ready to implement the recommendation as soon as approval is given. Please provide such a plan. Your plan should include at least two different methods of introducing safety stocks into the existing MRP system. Got the idea?

Activity 20-1-3 Mac: Pat, now that you have completed your assignment, can you suggest any additional factors I should incorporate into the final decision-making process? Is there some additional information I will need?

Group Experience 20-1
Using the Materials Requirements
Planning (MRP) Data Base for Special Projects

ABZ domestic plants in Missouri and Illinois are using a state-of-the-art MRP system, but the implementation of MRP has not eliminated stockouts of purchased parts at the Melrose Park or the Clarkstown plant. The result is that production of sub-assemblies and finished goods is disrupted and production must be rescheduled.

The operations managers in the Missouri and Illinois plants know that an in-house study of MRP recommends the introduction of safety stocks into the MRP system. They endorse the idea of safety stocks, but they want to go at least one step further and have the operations specialists study the possibility of implementing a program to standardize parts and sub-assemblies. They believe that if the same parts were used in more sub-assemblies, inventory would be reduced. They feel this would help them sell the safety-stock concept to top management.

Activity 20-1-1G Mac: Hello, group. Hey, do I have a deal for you. I want you to prepare a detailed plan for a company-wide standardizing of parts and sub-assemblies of existing products. I want you to use information from the MRP data base. Please identify the information that will be needed. Indicate where in the data base the information is located. The deal is that I am going to assign an information system specialist to your group for this project. In addition, I'm going to allow you to recommend what other types of personnel should be included on the implementation team. Okay?

Activity 20-1-2G Mac: Now that you people have prepared a detailed plan for standardizing parts and sub-assemblies, I want you to prepare a detailed procedure for standardizing products in the design stage. Be as specific as you can in terms of information needed and where the information is located in the MRP data base.

One other request: Since standardization will result in benefits other than those derived from inventory reduction, prepare a list of those benefits. Got the idea?

Activity 20-1-3G Pat: Mac, standardization is great. It may save money. But do you believe saving money is in the best interests of the people in Clarkstown? Here is what I think!

Activity 20-1-4G Mac: Good. Okay, you raised an issue that others may want to discuss. Maybe there is other information I will need to defend our position. Tell me what additional factors I should incorporate into the final decision to implement standardization. Tell me what additional information I will need.

Group Experience 20-2
Materials Requirements Planning (MRP) or Just-In-Time (JIT)?

ABZ Electronics
"Quality With A View!"

M E M O R A N D U M

From: Joe Yehudai

To: Mac Bosse

RE: MRP/JIT Options

Mac, here is some background on a situation that is being debated at the executive level.

ABZ has made an effort to reduce production-line setup times at its Mexico chassis plant (see Files 16-1, 2, 3, and 4). The reduction of setup times will solve some of ABZ's operations challenges, but it will not eliminate what the Clarkstown plant managers feel is a stress situation. Stress, they say, is living out of the back of a truck and this is what they say they are doing. Their assembly production schedule depends on whether the truck with needed parts arrives on time. When it does not, production schedules have to be changed. This results in a warehouse overstocked with low-margin and slow selling color television sets, or a warehouse unable to fill orders for high-margin and fast selling color television sets.

Managers believe the culprit to be a lack of planning and scheduling. Shipments to Clarkstown are often quite late and the quantities are often smaller than anticipated. The Mexico plant does not use an MRP system, it relies on an old manual system. ABZ's management wants to consider two options: first, whether to implement a JIT system and second, whether to implement of an MRP system.

The Mexico plant fabricates parts, sub-assembles television sets, and assembles black and white television sets. Fabricated parts and sub-assembled television sets are then shipped to other ABZ assembly plants including the one in Clarkstown.

The Mexico plant purchases parts for assembly and materials used in fabrication from outside vendors.

Mac, could you get your operations specialists to develop the information and accompanying strategies? Call me if you need additional information.

Activity 20-2-1G Mac: I have distributed to you Joe Yehudai's memo. You are aware of the situation. First, please get together and make a recommendation as to what option should be chosen for the Mexican plant. Base your recommendation on a thorough analysis of the situation and your knowledge of the OM tools. Okay?

Activity 20-2-2G Mac: After you have accomplished the first assignment, suppose that MRP where to be chosen regardless of your recommendation. Tell me whether your group would recommend an independent MRP system for the Mexico plant or an MRP subsystem of ABZ's domestic plants.

Activity 20-2-3G Pat: Mac, MRP and JIT are great operations tools. They may save money. However, do you believe saving money is in the best interests of the people in Mexico? Here is what we think!

Activity 20-2-4G Mac: Okay, Pat. You raised an issue that others may want to discuss. Maybe there is other information I will need concerning a recommendation. You people tell me what additional factors I should incorporate into the final decision-making process. Tell me what additional information I will need.

CHAPTER 21

Shop Floor Control Activities

Shop floor control activities require a continuous daily effort. Their purpose is to ensure that production is carried out in the quantities and timing specified by a plan.

Shop floor control--sometimes called production activity control--includes priority control and capacity control activities. A shop floor control system is based on data from an MRP system and a CRP system. A shop floor control system also uses other data base information relating to routing, work centers, parts, sub-assemblies, and finished goods.

Priority control starts with the assignment of a *shop order*. The order is assigned to the first work center and the first machine where it can be processed. The processed item is then routed to the next work center and the next machine, where it continues to be processed in accordance with the routing information. Sometimes orders must be routed through alternative routes because the preferred routes are overloaded.

Priority control also determines the sequence or arrangement in which shop orders will be processed. Multiple orders require a detailed schedule. In addition, priority control activities can be used to keep track of the progress of orders, to monitor late and critical orders, to revise schedules in response to changes in priorities or performance.

Capacity control activities ensure that labor and machine capacity are used according to plan by employing such tools as line of balance (LOB) and input/output control.

Capacity problems cannot be corrected by using priority control techniques. Expediting an order to overcome a capacity problem will only treat a symptom of ineffective shop control. Expediting an order in such a case will delay other orders without solving the capacity problem.

Listing and Description of Appropriate OM Tools

There are a number of quantitative operations tools available to the operations manager. Among the tools to be discussed in this chapter are sequencing, linear programming, line of balance, and input/output control.

Sequencing

Processing a list of shop orders effectively and efficiently is a function of sequencing. *Sequencing* is based on priority rules established by management. A number of different rules can be implemented in the sequencing process, which may require different production sequences.

Among the list of simple sequencing rules available to operations managers are first-come, first-served (FCFS); shortest processing time; critical ratio; and Johnson's rule. It is impossible to determine in advance the precise sequence rule for a given situation. Several sequencing rules may be used simultaneously, resulting in several different sequence alternatives. These sequence alternatives can then be evaluated on the basis of average flow time, average job lateness, or other criteria to arrive at the best sequence alternative. The evaluation criteria that a manager uses depends on the importance and priority of the organization's functional objectives. A given situation may dictate that management improve customer service before cash flow is improved or vice versa.

Linear Programming

Linear programming is a mathematical technique that can be used when shop control variables are linear. Linear programming can be used to identify an optimal solution to a shop floor control challenge--a solution that minimizes total cost or total time or maximizes total efficiency-- and enable managers to assign orders or jobs to machines on the basis of these performance, time, and cost requirements. Linear programming may be used with Simplex, a computation methodology. Linear programming cannot be depicted graphically because assignment problems involve more than two variables. A modified method of linear programming known as the assignment method of linear programming, will be used to solve the ABZ challenge that will be described.

Line of Balance (LOB)

Line of balance (LOB) is a charting and computational technique that can be used to monitor the progress of parts and sub-assemblies and compare it with delivery date requirements. LOB is used when management's main objective is meet established delivery schedules. CRP may be used in place of LOB techniques.

Input/Output Control

Input/output control is a technique that operations managers can use to identify capacity problems by analyzing input/output reports and then take corrective action. For each work center, an input/output control report identifies the planned and actual input-labor hours, the planned and actual output-labor hours, and the corresponding deviations. A manager might find, for example, low output of a particular work center is being caused by problems with an upstream work center or by internal problems. When cumulative deviations exceed specific levels, corrective action must be taken, in the form of overtime, subcontracting, or revision of the MPS.

Individual Experience 21-1
Minimizing Total Processing Time

All of ABZ's wooden-console television sets are equipped with cast handles. The handles vary in size and color depending on the model being assembled. These handles are purchased from an outside JIT vendor. The handles must be tumbled and plated before they can be attached. Tumbling and plating is done on-site in the Clarkstown plant.

The department responsible for tumbling and plating employs a production scheduler who schedules a number of projects during a given day. To achieve a high degree of efficiency, the production scheduler is responsible for properly sequencing the handle lots (lots vary in size) according to the final assembly schedule and for coordinating the handle tumbling and plating activities with other ABZ tumbling and plating activities.

There are five lots of handles awaiting the tumbling and plating sequence. Dawn Dias (Production Scheduler IV) used past experience to estimate the tumbling and plating time that it will take to process Lots 1001, 1002, 1003, 1004, and 1005. Dawn's estimates for the tumbling and plating of handles that are now needed by the assembly department are shown in Exhibit 21.1.

EXHIBIT 21.1
Tumbling and Plating Estimates
Console Handles

Lot	Tumbling (Hours)	Plating (Hours)
1001	4.9	3.9
1002	5.3	2.1
1003	2.7	2.9
1004	3.6	4.6
1005	3.1	3.5

306

Activity 21-1-1 Dawn Dias (Production Scheduler IV): Mike, we have several lots of television handles that need to be tumbled and plated for various wooden cabinet models that must be assembled and shipped within the next two weeks.

Mike Morano (Production Supervisor): How long is each operation going to take?

Dawn Dias: Based on our past experience, Exhibit 21.1 shows my estimates.

Mike: Great. What I want you to do is use Johnson's rule to sequence the lots. Determine the optimal sequence. Then tell me what the minimum flow time is to complete the five lots.

Activity 21-1-2 Mike: Dawn, yesterday you used Johnson's rule to sequence those five lots of handles that needed to be tumbled and plated. The information was great. We also need to consider doing the work according to sequence in which the lots arrived (1001, 1002, 1003, 1004, and 1005). Now I need to know the minimum flow time it will take to complete the tumbling and plating in this sequence. Also, tell me in how many different sequences the five lots could be processed.

Dawn: No problem.

Activity 21-1-3 Dawn: Mike, now that I know the sequence in which the handles arrived, I'm wondering if there are any ethical or cultural factors that you should consider in your sequence decision?

Mike: Let me explain.

Activity 21-1-4 Mike: Dawn, now that we have looked at Johnson's rule of optimal sequencing, the first-come, first-served (FCFS) sequencing, and the ethical or cultural sequencing considerations, tell me what additional factors we should incorporate into a long-range strategy that will minimize processing time. Is there additional information we will need if we are to minimize the processing time?

Dawn: Here is what I think we ought to consider in a long-range processing strategy.

Dawn: This is the additional information we will need to consider if we are to adopt a long-range strategy that will minimize processing time.

Group Experience 21-1
Selecting the Right Sequencing Rule

ABZ Electronics continuously produces television picture tubes. There are three reasons for such production. First, the tubes are used in the production of ABZ's own television sets. Second, the tubes are used by competitors who prefer to subcontract for various components of their own sets. Third, the tubes are used as replacement parts.

A production scheduler is responsible for sequencing the different jobs. Unless the scheduler is instructed differently, ABZ jobs and customers' jobs are treated the same. Information regarding seven jobs follows. These seven jobs are listed in first-come, first-served (FCFS) order.

EXHIBIT 21.2
FCFS Processing Times

Job	Estimated Processing Time (Hours)	Time to Promised Completion (Hours)
A	22	44
B	48	19
C	33	55
D	41	50
E	17	15
F	29	33
G	36	22

The production scheduler has access to ad hoc groups of operations specialists who perform a variety of planning activities that may benefit production scheduling. Production Scheduler IV Dawn Dias has contacted a group of operations specialists, via her supervisors, to ask that they perform some production scheduling calculations.

Activity 21-1-1G Dawn Dias (Production Scheduler IV): Please sequence the jobs according to the shortest processing time rule. Next, sequence the jobs according to the earliest due-date rule and the critical ratio rule.

Activity 21-1-1G (Continued)

Activity 21-1-2G Dawn: Now that you have sequenced the jobs on the basis of first-come, first-served, shortest processing time, earliest due date, and critical ratio , I would appreciate it if you would evaluate and rank the four sequences according to the following criteria: average flow time, average number of jobs in the system, and average job lateness.

Tell me what sequencing rule you would recommend in each of the following situations: The company wants to (1) improve customer relations, or (2) improve cash flow, or (3) improve internal operations control. Explain.

Activity 21-1-3G Dawn: Are there any ethical and cultural factors that I should consider before I make my sequencing decision? Explain.

Activity 21-1-4G Dawn: Are there any additional factors I should incorporate into my sequencing decision? What additional information do you believe I will need in order to make the best sequencing decision? Explain.

Group Experience 21-2
Using the Best Machine for the Job

The foreman in the injection molding department complained to the operations control manager about a scheduling problem that he believes has something to do with matching jobs and machines. The foreman realizes that most jobs can run on several different machines. What he doesn't understand is why certain jobs are not run on machines that would minimize processing time.

Operations specialists were asked to study the possibility of better machine use. They were told to make only those recommendations that would not jeopardize other scheduling objectives, e.g., on-time completion. To simplify the analysis, the operations specialists first studied five small parts that could be produced on any one of five machines. They used a study of past performance that contained the run time in hours (including setup times) for equal-size lots of each of the five parts on each of the five machines.

			Machine		
Part	1	2	3	4	5
A	30	55	45	32	47
B	44	22	26	40	33
C	21	29	24	38	31
D	37	26	38	24	32
E	41	39	36	34	40

Activity 21-2-1G Sidny Faber: Thank you for seeing me about my scheduling concerns. What have you done?

Pat: We used the assignment method of linear programming to determine which part should be assigned to which machine in order to minimize the total processing time. Here are our results.

Activity 21-2-2G Sidny: Okay, what are some of the potential benefits of this approach? Explain.

Activity 21-2-3G Sidny: If I implement your recommendation, will I get heat from management, the union, my supervisors, or the workers? Why? Explain.

Activity 21-2-4G Sidny: Are there additional factors I should incorporate into a final decision? Explain.

SECTION VI

EPILOGUE

As an operations specialist, you have moved from a passive to a crucial role at ABZ. This real-life corporate scenario and sixteen OM tool-related chapters have been designed to allow you to understand, formulate, apply, control, and implement operations management concepts and processes as an active participant in operations management activities.

Now you should be ready for a new evaluation of ABZ's operations. This is accomplished through an exit interview in Chapter 22. This final phase of learning allows you to determine if you are ready for the multinational business challenges of the future.

CHAPTER 22

An Exit Interview

The future holds tremendous opportunities and challenges for operations specialists. Operations managers convert raw materials and components into goods and services that consumers purchase. An effective operations manager must:

1. Recognize the vital importance of manufacturing and service;
2. Understand how operations management provides and supports the firm's strategic and competitive advantage;
3. Know how to make decisions regarding capacity, location, products, processes, layout, and human resources;
4. Understand how aggregate planning, master scheduling, inventory control, resource requirements planning, and shop floor control affect service and manufacturing operations;
5. Establish an attitude of action and quality;
6. Establish effective operations planning and control systems so the company can satisfy customer needs at minimal cost;
7. Understand the impact of ethics, values, and culture on suppliers, competitors, regulators, associations, labor unions, politics, technology, economics, public attitudes, demographics, and prices;
8. Know how operations fit together to build stakeholder value; and

9.   Understand the factors--quality, production cost, product
        availability, dependability, and flexibility--that form the
        basis for an operations strategy.

As an ABZ operations specialist, you moved from a passive to a crucial role. You were given the opportunity to understand, formulate, apply, control, and implement operations management concepts and processes. You were a participant in operations management.

Now you must move on to another level of learning: you must prepare for an exit interview. The exit interview, conducted when an employee leaves an organization, is one of the most valuable interviews that can be conducted. In many instances, it indicates what is right and what is wrong with an organization. The information obtained in the exit interview could identify and control the reasons for employee separations by pinpointing strengths and weaknesses in the organization.

ABZ's management wants to know what ABZ should be doing if it is to survive as the United States' only world-class producer of television sets. You have been given the opportunity to help salvage the company by applying appropriate operations management techniques and activities. Now it is time for you to give management the feedback it deserves.

Experience 22-1
SWOT Analysis of ABZ

Review *Experiencing Operations Management,* the information you may have gained from the suggested readings, and other information concerning the consumer electronics industry. Prepare for your exit interview by completing activities 22-1-1 through 22-1-4. Appropriate space is provided so that you may list answers and other information prior to issuing an official response to your instructor.

Activity 22-1-1 Discuss your position on the strengths and weaknesses of ABZ's tactical support activities, and the opportunities and threats posed by those activities. Consider ABZ's position in the consumer electronics industry.

Activity 22-1-1 (Continued)

Activity 22-1-2 Among the six functional strategies implemented at ABZ, list and discuss the three that you feel would be most important if ABZ is to survive as the United States' only world-class producer of television sets.

Activity 22-1-3 List and discuss four or five strategies that ABZ could implement that would result in an increase of market share in the consumer electronics industry.

Activity 22-1-4 ABZ believes that a strong ethical corporate culture is a vital key to survival and profitability in a highly competitive era. ABZ believes in fundamental honesty and adherence to U.S. law; product safety and quality; health and safety in the workplace; avoiding conflicts of interest; fairness in selling and marketing practices; financial reporting; maintaining good relationships with suppliers; fairness in pricing, billing, and contracting; prohibiting payments to obtain business; protecting the environment; and respecting intellectual property and proprietary information.

What are the strengths and weaknesses of ABZ's actual ethical culture? Respond on the basis of your experiences with ABZ.

Strengths.

Activity 22-1-4 (Continued)

Weaknesses.

Experience 22-2
Strategy Analysis of ABZ

Review *Experiencing Operations Management*, the information you may have gained from the suggested readings, and other information concerning the consumer electronics industry. Prepare for your exit interview by completing activities 22-2-1 through 22-2-7. Appropriate space is provided so that you may list answers and other information prior to issuing an official response to your instructor.

Activity 22-2-1 Does price drive ABZ's business strategy in the consumer electronics market? Explain.

Activity 22-2-2 Does competition drive ABZ's business strategy in the consumer electronics market? Explain.

Activity 22-2-3 Does market share drive ABZ's business strategy in the consumer electronics market? Explain.

Activity 22-2-4 Do profits drive ABZ's business strategy in the consumer electronics market? Explain.

Activity 22-2-5 Does survival drive ABZ's business strategy in the consumer electronics market? Explain.

Activity 22-2-6 Do tactical support activities and tactical core activities drive ABZ's business strategy in the consumer electronics market? Explain.

Activity 22-2-7 Is there something other than what was listed in activities 22-2-1 through 22-2-6 that drives ABZ's business strategy in the consumer electronics market? Explain.

References and Suggested Readings

Chapter 1
Introduction to Operations Management

Chase, Richard B., and Nicholas J. Aquilano, *Production and Operations Management: A Life Cycle Approach*, 5th ed. (Homewood, IL: Irwin, 1989): Chapter 1, "Introduction and Overview," pp. 4-25; Chapter 2, "Productivity and Competitiveness," pp. 26-45; Chapter 18, "Revising Operations Strategy," pp. 840-868.

Dilworth, James B., *Production and Operations Management: Manufacturing and Nonmanufacturing*, 4th ed. (New York: Random House, 1989): Chapter 1, "Zeroing In On Operations," pp. 3-20; Chapter 18, "A Glance at the Big Picture," pp. 731-735.

Electronic Industries Association, Advanced Television Committee, *Consumer Electronics, HDTV and the Competitiveness of the U.S. Economy*. Report submitted to the House Telecommunications and Finance Subcommittee, February 1, 1989, pp. 1-66.

French, Wendell, *The Personnel Management Process*, 6th ed. (Dallas: Houghton Mifflin, 1987).

Gaither, Norman, *Production and Operations Management: A Problem-Solving and Decision-Making Approach*, 4th ed. (Chicago: Dryden, 1990): Chapter 1, "Production and Operations Management (POM): An Introduction," pp. 2-29.

Krajewski, Lee J., and Larry P. Ritzman, *Operations Management: Strategy; and Analysis*, (Reading, MA: Addison-Wesley, 1987): Chapter 1, "Introduction," pp. 1-28.

Monks, Joseph G., *Operations Management: Theory and Problems*, 4th ed. (New York: McGraw-Hill, 1989): Chapter 1, "Operations and Productivity Concepts," pp. 5-31; Chapter 16, "A Strategy for Future Operations," pp. 667-684.

Robert R. Nathan Associates, Inc., *Television Manufacturing in the United States: Economic Contributions — Past, Present, and Future*. Prepared for the Electronic Industries Association, February 1989, pp. 1-79.

Port, Otis, "Smart Factories: America's Turn?" *BusinessWeek* (May 8, 1989): 142-148.

Stevenson, William J., *Production/Operations Management*, 3d ed. (Homewood, IL: Irwin, 1990): Chapter 1, "Production and Operations Management," pp. 4-32.

Chapter 2
Welcome to ABZ's New Employee Orientation

Barnett, John, *Poughkeepsie Journal* (February 2, 1988): 3.

Bartimo, Jim, "A Bumper Crop From Tandy," *San Jose Mercury News* (August 16, 1987): 2.

Bednarski, P. I., "Tariffs Don't Help Us Enough, Zenith Chief Tells Meeting," *Chicago Sun Times* (April 29, 1987): A3.

Bukeley, William M., "Clone-Computer Business Is Booming," *Wall Street Journal* (October 7, 1988): C2.

"Compaq Corporation," *Compact Disclosure* (computer disk, 1989).

"The Corporate Elite," *BusinessWeek* (October 23, 1987): 337.

Crontner Group, "The Last Strikes To Be The First In A Booming Market," *Fortune* (August 1, 1988): 39.

Dinnen, S. P., "Zenith Will Close 1 Of 2 Evansville Plants," *Indianapolis Star* (December 17, 1986): A1.

Dodson, Paul, "St. Joseph Not Too Far From Silicon Valley," *South Bend Tribune* (May 3, 1988): 2.

Dorsey, James M., "Virginia Firm Sinks Toshiba In Bid Battle," *Washington (D.C.) Post* (August 12, 1987): D16.

Forbes, Jim, "Zenith Fine-Chip Work Station Said To Deliver Up To 15 MIPS," *PC Week* (August 28, 1988): 217.

"The Fortune 500 Largest U.S. Industrial Corporations," *Fortune* (Vol. 117, No. 9): 17.

Frank, Allan Dodds, "Why Is This Man Smiling?" *Forbes* (March 10, 1986): 40.

Greenhouse, Steven, "Zenith to Sell PC Subsidiary," *New York Times* (October 1, 1989): D1, D2.

Holden, Ted, "The Americans are Hitting High-Tech Homers In Europe," *BusinessWeek* (April 11, 1988): 117.

Holton, Lisa, "Cutbacks At Zenith To Trim At Least 650 Jobs," *Chicago Sun Times* (September 22, 1987): D13.

Holton, Lisa, "Zenith Chief Fields Rumors, Makes Pitch To Ignore Them," *Chicago Sun Times* (May 2, 1988): D2.

Holton, Lisa, "Zenith In Consumer Electronics Talks," *Chicago Sun Times* (June 2, 1988): D1.

"International Business Machines," *Compact Disclosure* (computer disk, 1988).

Knoedelseder, William, "Sony To Expand Its VCR Format To Include VHS," *Los Angeles Times* (January 12, 1988): C1.

Levine, Jonathan B., "Sony's Back In Computers," *BusinessWeek* (February 8, 1988): 64.

Moore, Patricia, "Sharks Menacing Zenith, But Future Still Holds Promise," *Chicago Sun Times* (August 30, 1987): D1.

Moore, Patricia, "Zenith Exec Niched Way To The Top," *Chicago Sun Times* (September 14, 1987): D1.

Palmer, Jay, "Brightening Picture; for Zenith's Fortunes, The Nadir is Past," *Barrons* (March 20, 1989): 13-40.

Potts, Mark, "Zenith Survives TV Wars," *Washington (D.C.) Post* (August 23, 1987): D1.

"Sanyo Corporation," *Compact Disclosure* (computer disk, 1988).

"Sanyo Corporation," *Value Line* (1987).

Scheier, Robert L., "Vendors: PC Trade In Is Risky," *PC Week* (July 11, 1988): 6.

Scheier, Robert L., "Zenith Makes Defensive Moves, But Claims There's No Takeover On Horizon," *PC Week* (August 28, 1988): 217.

Seto, Benjamin, "Sony 'Admits' VHS Has Defeated Beta Format," *Los Angeles Times* (January 12, 1988): C1.

Slutsker, Gary, "Zenith's Bright Side And Its Dark Side," *Forbes* (May 2, 1988): 112-113.

"Sony Corporation," *Compact Disclosure* (computer disk, 1988).

"Sony Corporation," *Value Line* (1987).

Stavro, Barry, "No Jinx," *Forbes* (November 19, 1984): 345.

"Tandy Corporation," *Compact Disclosure* (computer disk, 1988).

"Tandy Corporation," *Value Line* (1987).

Therrien, Lois, "Why Jerry Pearlman Gave Up His Brainchild," *BusinessWeek* (October 16, 1989): 35.

Therrien, Lois, "Zenith Is Doing Quite Well, Thank You--In Computers," *BusinessWeek* (July 11, 1988): 80.

Therrien, Lois, "Zenith Is Sticking Its Neck Out in a Cutthroat Market," *BusinessWeek* (August 17, 1987): 72-73.

Therrien, Lois, "Zenith's Jerry Pearlman Sure Is Persistent," *BusinessWeek* (February 27, 1989): 41.

"The Top 1000," *BusinessWeek* (April 15, 1988): 244.

"The Undervalued 200," *BusinessWeek* (April 15, 1988): 94.

Wiegner, Kathleen K., "Last Chance?" *Forbes* (May 30, 1988): 58.

"Zenith Chairman Backs Imported Board Tariffs," *Electronic News* (September 7, 1987): 1-2.

Zenith Electronics Corporation, *Annual Report* (December 31, 1984-December 31,1988).

"Zenith Electronics Corporation," *Compact Disclosure* (computer disk, 1989).

Zenith Electronics Corporation, *The Company Story* (no date).

Zenith Electronics Company, *Proxy Statement* (April 26, 1988).

Zenith Electronics Company, *SEC 10K Report* (December 31, 1987).

"Zenith Electronics Corporation," *Standard and Poors* (March 28, 1988).

"Zenith Electronics Corporation," *Value Line* (1978-1988).

Zenith Electronics Corporation, *The Zenith Story: A History from 1918 to 1954* (Glenview, IL: Zenith Electronics Corporation, 1988)

Zenith Radio Corporation, *Annual Report* (December 31, 1978-December 31, 1983).

"Zenith Sticks with TVs, Sells Computer Line," *Arizona Daily Sun* (October 2, 1989): 4.

"Zenith to Increase Color TV Prices," *New York Times* (December 28, 1988): D 4.

"Zenith's Return to Roots May Be Plunge into Problems," *Wall Street Journal* (October 5, 1989): A10.

Chapter 3
More ABZ Orientation

Barnett, John, *Poughkeepsie Journal* (February 2, 1988): 3.

Bartimo, Jim, "A Bumper Crop From Tandy," *San Jose Mercury News* (August 16, 1987): 2.

Bednarski, P. I., "Tariffs Don't Help Us Enough, Zenith Chief Tells Meeting," *Chicago Sun Times* (April 29, 1987): A3.

Bukeley, William M., "Clone-Computer Business Is Booming," *Wall Street Journal* (October 7, 1988): C2.

"Compaq Corporation," *Compact Disclosure* (computer disk, 1989).

"The Corporate Elite," *BusinessWeek* (October 23, 1987): 337.

Crontner Group, "The Last Strikes To Be The First In A Booming Market," *Fortune* (August 1, 1988): 39.

Dinnen, S. P., "Zenith Will Close 1 Of 2 Evansville Plants," *Indianapolis Star* (December 17, 1986): A1.

Dodson, Paul, "St. Joseph Not Too Far From Silicon Valley," *South Bend Tribune* (May 3, 1988): 2.

Dorsey, James M., "Virginia Firm Sinks Toshiba In Bid Battle," *Washington (D.C.) Post* (August 12, 1987): D16.

Forbes, Jim, "Zenith Fine-Chip Work Station Said To Deliver Up To 15 MIPS," *PC Week* (August 28, 1988): 217.

"The Fortune 500 Largest U.S. Industrial Corporations." *Fortune* (Vol. 117, No. 9): 17.

Frank, Allan Dodds, "Why Is This Man Smiling?" *Forbes* (March 10, 1986): 40.

Holden, Ted, "The Americans are Hitting High-Tech Homers In Europe," *BusinessWeek* (April 11, 1988): 117.

Holton, Lisa, "Cutbacks At Zenith To Trim At Least 650 Jobs," *Chicago Sun Times* (September 22, 1987): D13.

Holton, Lisa, "Zenith Chief Fields Rumors, Makes Pitch To Ignore Them," *Chicago Sun Times* (May 2, 1988): D2.

Holton, Lisa, "Zenith In Consumer Electronics Talks," *Chicago Sun Times* (June 2, 1988): D1.

"International Business Machines," *Compact Disclosure* (computer disk, 1988).

Knoedelseder, William, "Sony To Expand Its VCR Format To Include VHS," *Los Angeles Times* (January 12, 1988): C1.

Lehrer, C. Merill, "Has the Orient Totally Conquered U.S. Electronics? Seven Companies Say No," *USA Today* (January 7, 1989): 19.

Levine, Jonathan B., "Sony's Back In Computers," *BusinessWeek* (February 8, 1988): 64.

Moore, Patricia, "Sharks Menacing Zenith, But Future Still Holds Promise," *Chicago Sun Times* (August 30, 1987): D1.

Moore, Patricia, "Zenith Exec Niched Way To The Top," *Chicago Sun Times* (September 14, 1987): D1.

Potts, Mark, "Zenith Survives TV Wars," *Washington (D.C.) Post* (August 23, 1987): D1.

"Sanyo Corporation," *Compact Disclosure* (computer disk, 1988).

"Sanyo Corporation," *Value Line* (1987).

Scheier, Robert L., "Vendors: PC Trade In Is Risky," *PC Week* (July 11, 1988): 6.

Scheier, Robert L., "Zenith Makes Defensive Moves, But Claims There's No Takeover On Horizon," *PC Week* (August 28, 1988): 217.

Seto, Benjamin, "Sony 'Admits' VHS Has Defeated Beta Format," *Los Angeles Times* (January 12, 1988): C1.

"Share of U.S. Color TV Market by Model Year," *Television Digest With Consumer Electronics* (July 25, 1988): 15.

Slutsker, Gary, "Zenith's Bright Side And Its Dark Side," *Forbes* (May 2, 1988): 112-113.

"Sony Corporation," *Compact Disclosure* (computer disk, 1988).

"Sony Corporation," *Value Line* (1987).

Stavro, Barry, "No Jinx," *Forbes* (November 19, 1984): 345.

"Tandy Corporation," *Compact Disclosure* (computer disk, 1988).

"Tandy Corporation," *Value Line* (1987).

Teinowitz, Ira, "Zenith Seeks Image Change: Return to Network TV in Bid for Baby-Boomers," *Advertising Age* (September 4, 1989): 26.

"Television Digest Camcorders Market-Share Survey," *Television Digest with Consumer Electronics* (April 3, 1989): 12.

"Television Digest VCR Market-Share Survey," *Television Digest with Consumer Electronics* (April 3, 1989): 11.

Therrien, Lois, "Zenith Is Doing Quite Well, Thank You--In Computers," *BusinessWeek* (July 11, 1988): 80.

"The Top 1000," *BusinessWeek* (April 15, 1988): 244.

"The Undervalued 200," *BusinessWeek* (April 15, 1988): 94.

Wiegner, Kathleen K., "Last Chance?" *Forbes* (May 30, 1988): 58.

"Zenith Chairman Backs Imported Board Tariffs," *Electronic News* (September 7, 1987): 1-2.

Zenith Electronics Corporation, *Annual Report* (December 31, 1984-December 31, 1988).

"Zenith Electronics Corporation," *Compact Disclosure* (computer disk, 1989).

Zenith Electronics Corporation, *The Company Story* (no date).

Zenith Electronics Company, *Proxy Statement* (April 26, 1988).

Zenith Electronics Company, *SEC 10K Report* December 31, 1987).

"Zenith Electronics Corporation," *Standard and Poors* (March 28, 1988).

"Zenith Electronics Corporation," *Value Line* (1978-1988).

Zenith Radio Corporation, *Annual Report* (December 31, 1978-December 31, 1983).

"Zenith's Return to Roots May Be Plunge into Problems," *Wall Street Journal* (October 5, 1989): A10.

Chapter 4
ABZ and the International Consumer Electronics Union

Agreement Between Zenith Electronics Corporation Springfield Division and International Brotherhood of Electrical Workers, AFL-CIO, and Local Union No. 1453 of the International Brotherhood of Electrical Workers, AFL-CIO, 1987-1992. (Springfield, MO: Zenith Electronics Corporation, 1987).

Battle, Donald L., "Buy American Crusade Struggles On," *U.S. News and World Report* (January 27, 1986): 52.

Edwards, Robert, "Springfieldians Start Own Buy-American Effort," *The Daily News* (February 25, 1986): D2, D4.

Hendricks, Mike, "Last U.S. TV Maker Hangs On," *Kansas City Star* (August 21, 1988): F1, F8-F9.

Hillkirk, John, "Zenith Tries to Keep From Fading Out," *USA Today* (December 9, 1987): B1-B2.

Mahnken, Don, and Patricia Fennewald, "Japanese Ties to be Explained," *Springfield Leader and Press* (May 20, 1986): A1-A2.

Mahnken, Don, "Springfield Unions Cheer Closings Bill," *Springfield News-Leader* (August 3, 1988): A8, A16.

Mahnken, Don, "2,200 May Vote Soon at Zenith," *Springfield News-Leader* (March 18, 1987): B1.

Mahnken, Don, "Union: Pay Cut Saved Zenith," *Springfield News-Leader* (March 24, 1988): B1, B4.

Mahnken, Don, "Zenith Labor Pact Seen As Setting a Precedent," *Springfield News-Leader* (March 24, 1987): 1.

Mahnken, Don, "Zenith: Recall Affects 300 Jobs," *Springfield News-Leader* (April 22, 1987): A1, A11.

Ryan, Elisabeth, "Zenith Shifting 200 Jobs to U.S. TV Plant," *Manufacturing Week* (April 20, 1987): 5.

Whall, Louise, "200 Zenith Workers to Lose Jobs," *Springfield News-Leader* (September 30, 1987): A1.

Whall, Louise, "Zenith Eyes Future," *Springfield Leader and Press* (June 5, 1989): E1.

Ward, Sam, "Imports Invade TV Market," *USA Today* (December 9, 1987): 1.

Your Zenith Employee Benefits: For the Hourly Employees of Zenith Electronics Corporation, Springfield Division, International Brotherhood of Electrical Workers, Local 1453 (Springfield, MO: Zenith Electronics Corporation, June, 1985): A1-G5.

"Zenith Contract A Working Model," *Springfield News-Leader* (March 24, 1987): C1.

Zenith Profit-Sharing Retirement Plan: A Description for Hourly Employees (Chicago: Zenith Electronics Corporation, February, 1988)

Chapter 5
Functional Management Activities

Dilworth (1989), Chapter 2, "Operations Strategy," pp. 49-66.

Gaither (1990), Chapter 2, "Operations Strategy," pp. 30-71.

Higgins, James M., and Julian W. Vincze, *Strategic Management*, 4th ed. (Chicago: Dryden, 1989): "SWOT," pp. 63, 64, 66, 80, 130.

Johnson, H. Thomas and Robert S. Kaplan, *Relevance Lost: The Rise and Fall of Management Accounting*. (Boston: Harvard Business School Press, 1987): pp. 243-263.

Krajewski (1987): Chapter 1, "Introduction," pp. 1-28.

Chapter 6
Capacity Strategy Activities

Chase (1989), pp. 270-285.

Gaither (1990), pp. 310-324.

Krajewski (1987), pp. 249-270.

Monks (1989), pp. 70-79, 91-93.

Stevenson (1990), pp. 305-321.

Financial Investment Evaluation Methods
Chase (1989), pp. 870-886.

Gaither (1990), pp. C1-C24.

Krajewski (1987), pp. A1-A11.

Monks (1989), pp. 80-90, 93-98.

Stevenson (1990), pp. 329-340.

Waiting Lines

Chase (1989), pp. 120-155.

Dilworth (1989), pp. 416-429.

Gaither (1990), pp. D1-D18.

Krajewski (1987), pp. B1-B23.

Monks (1989), pp. 545-550, 567-568.

Stevenson (1990), pp. 740-772.

Decision Trees

Chase (1989), pp. 282-285.

Dilworth (1989), pp. 81-83.

Gaither (1990), pp. 321-324.

Monks (1989), pp. 54-56, 62-63.

Stevenson (1990), pp. 56-59.

Payoff Tables

Dilworth (1989), pp. 79-80.

Gaither (1990), pp. 438-440.

Krajewski (1987), pp. 474-476.

Stevenson (1990), pp. 52.

Forecasting Methods

Chase (1989), pp. 214-258.

Dilworth (1989), pp. 89-134.

Gaither (1990), pp. 72-114.

Krajewski (1987), pp. 71-112.

Monks (1989), pp. 261-299.

Stevenson (1990), pp. 126-175.

Break-Even Analysis

Chase (1989), pp. 64-66.

Dilworth (1989), pp. 559-561.

Gaither (1990), pp. 158-161.

Krajewski (1987), pp. 41-43.

Monks (1989), pp. 43-47, 57-59.

Stevenson (1990), pp. 317-320.

Make-Or-Buy Analysis

Chase (1989), pp. 885-886.

Dilworth (1989), pp. 223-224.

Gaither (1990), pp. 595-596, C20-C22.

Krajewski (1987), pp. 129-130.

Monks (1989), pp. 363-365, 378-380.

Stevenson (1990), pp. 296-297, 570.

Chapter 7
Location Strategy Activities

Beauchamp, Tom L., and Norman E. Bowie, *Ethical Theory and Business*, 3d ed. (Englewood Cliffs, NJ: Prentice Hall, 1988): Chapter 2, "Corporate Responsibility," pp. 56-111.

Chase (1989), pp. 285-294.

Dilworth (1989), pp. 549-568.

Gaither (1990), pp. 324-343.

Krajewski (1987), pp. 285-313.

Monks (1989), pp. 104-122.

Stevenson (1990), pp. 228-243.

Forecasting

Chase (1989), pp. 214-258.

Dilworth (1989), pp. 89-134.

Gaither (1990), pp. 72-114.

Krajewski (1987), pp. 71-112.

Monks (1989), pp. 261-299.

Stevenson (1990), pp. 126-175.

Linear Programming

Chase (1989), pp.286-287, 308-346.

Dilworth (1989), pp. 169-172, 185-208, 563-564.

Gaither (1990), pp. E1-E52, 337-339, 602-605.

Krajewski (1987), C1-C37.

Monks (1989), pp. 117-121, 139-143, 166-175.

Stevenson (1990), pp. 75-112, 90-103.

Center of Gravity Method

Chase (1989), pp. 289-291.

Gaither (1990), pp. 333-334.

Krajewski (1987), pp. 299-305.

Factor Rating

Chase (1989), pp. 287-288.

Dilworth (1989), pp. 561-562.

Gaither (1990), pp. 325-332, 340-343.

Krajewski (1987), pp. 41, 298-299.

Monks (1989), pp. 121-122.

Stevenson (1990), pp. 341-342.

Cost Comparisons

Chase (1989), pp. 287-288.

Gaither (1990), pp. 335-337.

Break-Even Analysis

Chase (1989), pp. 64-66.

Dilworth (1989), pp. 559-561.

Gaither (1990), pp. 158-161.

Krajewski (1987), pp. 41-43.

Monks (1989), pp. 115-117, 137-138.

Stevenson (1990), pp. 239-41.

Chapter 8
Product Strategy Activities

Chase (1989), pp. 48-56.

Dilworth (1989), pp. 62-65.

Gaither (1990), pp. 52-60.

Krajewski (1987), pp. 29-65.

Monks (1989), pp. 158-175, 188-196.

Stevenson (1990), pp. 196-216.

Linear Programming

Chase (1989), pp. 308-326.

Dilworth (1989), pp. 169-172, 185-196.

Gaither (1990), pp. E1-E26.

Krajewski (1987), C1-C22.

Monks (1989), pp. 166-175, 188-196.

Stevenson (1990), pp. 77-103.

Break-Even Analysis

Chase (1989), pp. 64-66.

Dilworth (1989), pp. 559-561.

Gaither (1990), pp. 158-161.

Krajewski (1987), pp. 41-43.

Monks (1989), pp. 43-47, 57-59.

Stevenson (1990), pp. 317-320.

Decision Trees

Chase (1989), pp. 282-285.

Dilworth (1989), pp. 81-83.

Gaither (1990), pp. 321-324.

Monks (1989), pp. 54-56, 62-63.

Stevenson (1990), pp. 56-59.

Payoff Tables

Dilworth (1989), pp. 79-80.

Gaither (1990), pp. 438-440.

Krajewski (1987), pp. 474-476.

Stevenson (1990), pp. 52.

Make-Or-Buy Analysis

Chase (1989), pp. 885-886.

Dilworth (1989), 223-224.

Gaither (1990), pp. 595-596, C20-C22.

Krajewski (1987), pp. 129-130.

Monks (1989), pp. 363-365, 378-380.

Stevenson (1990), pp. 296-297, 570.

Chapter 9
Process Strategy Activities

Chase (1989), pp. 56-70.

Gaither (1990), pp. 132-176.

Krajewski (1987), pp. 119-147.

Monks (1989), pp. 175-187, 196-202.

Financial Investment Evaluation Methods

Chase (1989), pp. 61-62, 870-886.

Gaither (1990), pp. C1-C24.

Krajewski (1987), pp. A1-A11.

Monks (1989), pp. 80-90, 93-98.

Stevenson (1990), pp. 329-340.

Break-Even Analysis

Chase (1989), pp. 64-66.

Dilworth (1989), pp. 559-561.

Gaither (1990), pp. 158-161.

Krajewski (1987), pp. 41-43, 125-126.

Monks (1989), pp. 43-47, 57-59, 182-183.

Stevenson (1990), pp. 317-320.

Payoff Tables

Dilworth (1989), pp. 79-80.

Gaither (1990), pp. 438-440.

Krajewski (1987), pp. 474-476.

Stevenson (1990), pp. 52.

Decision Trees

Chase (1989), pp. 282-285.

Dilworth (1989), pp. 81-83.

Gaither (1990), pp. 321-324.

Monks (1989), pp. 54-56, 62-63.

Stevenson (1990), pp. 56-59.

Process Planning Charts

Chase (1989), pp. 67-69.

Gaither (1990), pp. 161-164.

Krajewski (1987), pp. 135-139, 140-141.

Monks (1989), pp. 178-180.

Chapter 10
Layout Strategy Activities

Chase (1989), pp. 356-379.

Dilworth (1989), pp. 577-620.

Gaither (1990), pp. 224-258.

Krajewski (1987), pp. 321-359.

Monks (1989), pp. 122-135, 143-147.

Stevenson (1990), pp. 346-376.

Process Layout Analysis Techniques

Chase (1989), pp. 359-364.

Dilworth (1989), pp. 603-609.

Gaither (1990), pp. 239-245.

Krajewski (1987), pp. 330-336.

Monks (1989), pp. 129-131, 143-144.

Stevenson (1990), pp. 351-353, 368-376.

Systematic Layout Planning

Chase (1989), pp. 364-366.

Dilworth (1989), pp. 609-610.

Gaither (1990), pp. 243-244.

Monks (1989), pp. 132.

Stevenson (1990), pp. 370-375.

Assembly Line Balancing Heuristics

Chase (1989), pp. 369-376.

Dilworth (1989), pp. 598-602, 619-620.

Gaither (1990), pp. 248-257.

Krajewski (1987), pp. 348-355.

Monks (1989), pp. 132-135, 144-147.

Stevenson (1990), pp. 357-367.

Waiting Lines

Chase (1989), pp. 120-155.

Dilworth (1989), pp. 416-429.

Gaither (1990), pp. D1-D18.

Krajewski (1987), pp. B1-B23.

Monks (1989), pp. 545-550, 567-568.

Stevenson (1990), pp. 740-772.

Chapter 11
Human Resource Strategy Activities

Chase (1989), pp. 428-462.

Dilworth (1989), pp. 659-685, 695-725.

French, Wendell, *The Personnel Management Process*, 6th ed. (Dallas: Houghton Mifflin, 1987), pp. 3-14.

Gaither (1990), pp. 624-672.

Keough, J. ed., *Corporate Ethics: A Prime Business Asset*. (New York: Business Roundtable, February, 1988)

Monks (1989), pp. 212-243, 244-248.

Scarpello, Vida Gulbinas, and James Ledvinka, *Personnel/Human Resource Management: Environments and Functions*. (Boston: PWS-Kent, 1988), pp. 3-15.

Stevenson (1990), pp. 392-436.

Work Methods Analysis

Chase (1989), pp. 441-448.

Dilworth (1989), pp. 676-685, 695-700.

Gaither (1990), pp. 640-650.

Krajewski (1987), pp. 134-145.

Monks (1989), pp. 225-228.

Stevenson (1990), pp. 400-408.

Work Measurement Methods

Chase (1989), pp. 446, 449-461.

Dilworth (1989), pp. 701-716.

Gaither (1990), pp. 650-663.

Krajewski (1987), pp. 213-230.

Monks (1989), pp. 228-239, 244-248.

Stevenson (1990), pp. 415-432.

Behavioral Job Design Methods

Chase (1989), pp. 432-441.

Dilworth (1989), pp. 674-676.

Gaither (1990), pp. 636-640.

Krajewski (1987), pp. 148-155.

Monks (1989), pp. 213-225.

Stevenson (1990), pp. 396-400.

Compensation Methods

Chase (1989), pp. 461-462.

Dilworth (1989), pp. 716-725.

Gaither (1990), pp. 652-653.

Krajewski (1987), pp. 157-160.

Monks (1989), pp. 239-243.

Stevenson (1990), pp. 432-435.

Learning Curves

Chase (1989), pp. 516-537.

Dilworth (1989), pp. 361-364.

Gaither (1990), pp. 663-670.

Krajewski (1987), pp. 230-240.

Monks (1989), pp. 543-545, 566-567.

Stevenson (1990), pp. 449-459.

Linear Programming

Chase (1989), pp. 308-326, 336-339.

Dilworth (1989), pp. 169-172, 185-196.

Gaither (1990), pp. E1-E26, E38-E41.

Krajewski (1987), p. C1-C22, C36.

Monks, (1989), pp. 166-175, 188-196, 502-503, 519-520.

Stevenson (1990), pp. 77-103, 659-664.

Chapter 12
Quality Assurance Activities

Chase (1989), pp. 162-196.

Deming, W. Edwards, *Out of the Crisis*. (Cambridge, MA.: MIT Press, 1986).

Dilworth (1989), pp. 503-541.

Gaither (1990), pp. 684-728.

Krajewski (1987), pp. 689-716, 721-748.

Monks (1989), pp. 578-622.

Ouchi, William, *Theory Z: How American Business Can Meet the Japanese Challenge*. (Reading, MA.: Addison-Wesley, 1981).

Stevenson (1990), pp. 804-857.

Acceptance Sampling

Chase (1989), pp. 172-180.

Dilworth (1989), pp. 527-535.

Gaither (1990), pp. 714-722.

Krajewski (1987), pp. 723-735.

Monks (1989), pp. 592-607, 618-621.

Stevenson (1990), pp. 829-838.

Process Control

Chase (1989), pp. 180-191.

Dilworth (1989), pp. 516-527, 540-541.

Gaither (1990), pp. 705-713.

Krajewski (1987), pp. 735-748.

Monks (1989), pp. 607-616, 621-622.

Stevenson (1990), pp. 838-855.

Chapter 13
Maintenance Activities

Dilworth (1989), pp. 491-499.

Gaither (1990), pp. 786-813.

Krajewski (1987), pp. 270-278.

Monks (1989), pp. 629-647, 655-660.

Simulation

Chase (1989), pp. 386-417.

Dilworth (1989), pp. 435-447.

Gaither (1990), pp. D9-D18.

Krajewski (1987), pp. B23-B33.

Monks (1989), pp. 183-187, 198-199, 636-639.

Stevenson (1990), pp. 779-794.

Waiting Lines

Chase (1989), pp. 120-155.

Dilworth (1989), pp. 416-429.

Gaither (1990), pp. D1-D18, 796.

Krajewski (1987), pp. B1-B23.

Monks (1989), pp. 545-550, 567-568, 640-641, 655-657.

Stevenson (1990), pp. 740-772.

Financial Investment Evaluation Methods

Chase (1989), pp. 61-62, 870-886.

Gaither (1990), pp. C1-C24.

Krajewski (1987), pp. A1-A11, 277-278.

Monks (1989), pp. 80-90, 93-98.

Stevenson (1990), pp. 329-340.

Preventive Maintenance Versus Breakdown Policy

Dilworth (1989), pp. 496-498.

Gaither (1990), pp. 802-805.

Krajewski (1987), pp. 271, 275-276.

Monks (1989), pp. 639-640, 657-659.

Payoff Tables

Dilworth (1989), pp. 79-80.

Gaither (1990), pp. 438-440, 796-798, 802-804.

Krajewski (1987), pp. 474-476.

Stevenson (1990), pp. 52.

Chapter 14
Cost Control Activities

Horngren, Charles T., and George Foster, *Cost Accounting: A Managerial Emphasis*, 6th ed. (Englewood Cliffs, NJ: Prentice-Hall, 1989), pp. 1-11, 20-36, 714-732, 909-924.

Monks (1989), pp. 647-654.

Rayburn, L. Gayle, *Principles of Cost Accounting*, (Homewood, IL: Irwin, 1989), pp. 85-91, 371-375.

Cost Standards

Horngren and Foster (1989), pp. 138-166, 179, 188-193, 197, 808, 811-938.

Monks (1989), pp. 651-654.

Rayburn (1989), pp. 27-35, 371-376.

Cost-Variance Analysis

Horngren, Charles T. and George Foster, *Cost Accounting: A Managerial Emphasis*. 6th ed. (Englewood Cliffs, N.J.: Prentice-Hall, 1989), pp. 183-189, 201-202, 268-270, 274-281, 799-822.

Monks (1989), pp. 654.

Rayburn, L. Gayle, *Principles of Cost Accounting*. (Homewood,IL: Irwin, 1989), pp. 315-319.

Value Analysis

Chase (1989), pp. 711-712.

Dilworth (1989), pp. 223.

Gaither (1990), pp. 592.

Monks (1989), pp. 164.

Stevenson (1990), pp. 569-570.

Standardization

Dilworth (1989), pp. 65.

Stevenson (1990), pp. 202-204.

Learning Curves

Chase (1989), pp. 516-537.

Dilworth (1989), pp. 361-364.

Gaither (1990), pp. 667-670.

Krajewski (1987), pp. 230-240.

Monks (1989), pp. 543-545, 566-567.

Stevenson (1990), pp. 449-459.

Chapter 15
Materials Management Activities

Chase (1989), pp. 702-724.

Dilworth (1989), pp. 213-241.

Gaither (1990), pp. 582-611.

Krajewski (1987), pp. 369-402.

Monks (1989), pp. 356-377.

Stevenson (1990), pp. 565-576.

Vendor Selection Systems

Chase (1989), pp. 709-710.

Gaither (1990), pp. 588.

Monks (1989), pp. 361-362.

Stevenson (1990), pp. 571-572.

Marginal Analysis (Single-Period Inventory)

Dilworth (1989), pp. 227-229, 239-241.

Gaither (1990), pp. 446-450.

Monks (1989), pp. 400-402.

Stevenson (1990), pp. 540-545, 548-549.

Distribution Requirements Planning (DRP)

Chase (1989), pp. 720-721.

Dilworth (1989), pp. 306-308.

Gaither (1990), pp. 602-603.

Krajewski (1987), pp. 553-554.

Payoff Tables

Dilworth (1989), pp. 79-80.

Gaither (1990), pp. 438-440.

Krajewski (1987), pp. 474-476.

Stevenson (1990), pp. 52.

Make-Or-Buy Analysis

Chase (1989), pp. 885-886.

Dilworth (1989), pp. 223-224.

Gaither (1990), pp. 595-596, C20-C22.

Krajewski (1987), pp. 129-130.

Monks (1989), pp. 363-365, 378-380.

Stevenson (1990), pp. 296-297, 570.

Linear Programming

Chase (1989), pp. 286-287, 308-346.

Dilworth (1989), pp. 169-172, 185-208, 563-564.

Gaither (1990), pp. E1-E52, 337-339, 602-605.

Krajewski (1987), pp. C1-C37.

Monks (1989), pp. 117-121, 139-143, 166-175.

Stevenson (1990), pp. 75-112, 90-103.

Chapter 16
Advanced Manufacturing Support Activities

Computer-Aided Design (CAD) and Computer-Aided Manufacturing (CAM)
Chase (1989), pp. 55-56, 64, 78-82.

Dilworth (1989), pp. 633-637.

Gaither (1990), p. 15.

Krajewski (1987), pp. 202-203, 241.

Monks (1989), pp. 164-165.

Stevenson (1990), pp. 205-207, 299.

Flexible Manufacturing Systems
Chase (1989), p. 64.

Dilworth (1989), pp. 637-640.

Gaither (1990), p. 15.

Krajewski (1987), pp. 197-200.

Monks (1989), pp. 128-129, 177.

Stevenson (1990), pp. 303-304, 357.

Manufacturing Resource Planning (MRPII)
Chase (1989), pp. 647-656.

Dilworth (1989), pp. 289-290.

Gaither (1990), p. 498-499.

Krajewski (1987), p. 543.

Monks (1989), pp. 435-436, 541.

Stevenson (1990), pp. 607-609, 838-840.

Just-In-Time (JIT) Production System
Chase (1989), pp. 711-714, 734-769.

Dilworth (1989), pp. 223, 238.

Gaither (1990), pp. 520-534.

Krajewski (1987), pp. 572-584.

Monks (1989), pp. 416-417.

Stevenson (1990), pp. 622-646.

Financial Investment Evaluation Methods
Chase (1989), pp. 870-886.

Gaither (1990), pp. C1-C24.

Krajewski (1987), pp. A1-A11.

Monks (1989), pp. 80-90, 93-98.

Stevenson (1990), pp. 329-340.

Cost Benefit Analysis
Gaither (1990), pp. 53-55.

Chapter 17
Project Planning and Control Activities

Chase (1989), pp. 472-505.

Dilworth (1989), pp. 453-483.

Gaither (1990), pp. 740-772.

Krajewski (1987), pp. 639-678.

Monks (1989), pp. 550-565, 568-571.

Stevenson (1990), pp. 694-723.

Program Evaluation and Review Technique (PERT)
Chase (1989), pp. 483-490, 501-505.

Dilworth (1989), pp. 460-475, 481-483.

Gaither (1990), pp. 761-771.

Krajewski (1987), pp. 646-659, 677-678.

Monks (1989), pp. 558-565, 568-571.

Stevenson (1990), pp. 699-700.

Critical Path Method (CPM)
Chase (1989), pp. 490-497, 501-505.

Dilworth (1989), pp. 460-469.

Gaither (1990), pp. 750-760, 765-766, 770-771.

Krajewski (1987), pp. 659-673, 677-678.

Monks (1989), pp. 554-558, 562-565.

Stevenson (1990), pp. 700-710, 716-722.

Chapter 18
Aggregate Planning and Master Scheduling

Chase (1989), pp. 544-570, 624-631.

Dilworth (1989), pp. 145-176.

Gaither (1990), pp. 360-393.

Krajewski (1987), pp. 489-517.

Monks (1989), pp. 309-347.

Stevenson (1990), pp. 464-489.

Aggregate Planning--Trial and Error
Chase (1989), pp. 554-560.

Dilworth (1989), pp. 156-162.

Gaither (1990), pp. 369-377.

Monks, (1989), pp. 317-322.

Stevenson (1990), pp. 445-451, 487-488.

Aggregate Planning--Mathematical Models

Chase (1989), pp. 286-287, 308-346, 567-570.

Dilworth (1989), pp. 162-166, 169-171, 185-208, 563-564.

Gaither (1990), pp. E1-E41, 337-339, 378-381.

Krajewski (1987), pp. C1-C37.

Monks (1989), pp. 117-121, 139-143, 166-170, 322-330.

Stevenson (1990), pp. 75-112, 241, 251-281, 482-489.

Rough-Cut Capacity Planning

Chase (1989), pp. 548, 657-658.

Dilworth (1989), pp. 152-155.

Gaither (1990), pp. 383, 386-388.

Krajewski (1987), pp. 505-509.

Monks (1989), p. 460.

Master Scheduling

Chase (1989), p. 548.

Dilworth (1989), p. 152.

Gaither (1990), pp. 382-393.

Krajewski (1987), pp. 489-517.

Monks (1989), pp. 330-340, 346-347.

Stevenson (1990), pp. 584-586.

Chapter 19
Inventory Control/Independent Demand Activities

Chase (1989), pp. 576-611.

Dilworth (1989), pp. 247-281.

Gaither (1990), pp. 406-458.

Krajewski (1987), pp. 447-480.

Monks (1989), pp. 366-374, 381-385, 391-427.

Stevenson (1990), pp. 496-489.

Lot-Sizing Techniques

Chase (1989), pp. 584-600.

Dilworth (1989), pp. 252-265, 280-281.

Gaither (1990), pp. 418-430, 444-446.

Krajewski (1987), pp. 450-456, 465-471.

Monks (1989), pp. 367-374, 381-385.

Stevenson (1990), pp. 507-524, 537-545.

Order Point, Safety Stock, and Service Level

Chase (1989), pp. 587-597.

Dilworth (1989), pp. 265-277.

Gaither (1990), pp. 430-444.

Krajewski (1987), pp. 456-466.

Monks (1989), pp. 394-414, 420-427.

Stevenson (1990), pp. 525-531, 533-537.

Simulation

Chase (1989), pp. 386-417.

Dilworth (1989), pp. 435-447.

Gaither (1990), pp. D9-D18.

Krajewski (1987), pp. B23-B33, 469-470.

Monks (1989), pp. 183-187, 198-199, 636-639.

Stevenson (1990), pp. 779-795.

Chapter 20
Resource Requirements Planning Activities

Chase (1989), pp. 622-662.

Dilworth (1989), pp. 287-322.

Gaither (1990), pp. 472-506.

Krajewski (1987), pp. 525-554.

Monks (1989), pp. 434-473.

Stevenson (1990), pp. 580-610.

Materials Requirements Planning (MRP)

Chase (1989), pp. 622-645, 653-662.

Dilworth (1989), pp. 288-304, 308-313, 316-322.

Gaither (1990), pp. 478-501.

Krajewski (1987), pp. 529-545, 548-554.

Monks (1989), pp. 437-458, 465-473.

Stevenson (1990), pp. 580-610.

Capacity Requirements Planning (CRP)

Chase (1989), pp. 645-647.

Dilworth (1989), pp. 313-316.

Gaither (1990), pp. 501-505.

Krajewski (1987), pp. 545-548.

Monks (1989), pp. 458-464, 473.

Stevenson (1990), pp. 604-606.

Chapter 21
Shop Floor Control Activities

Chase (1989), pp. 672-693.

Dilworth (1989), pp.331-361, 365-366.

Gaither (1990), pp. 518-567.

Krajewski (1987), pp. 547-548, 608-627.

Monks (1989), pp. 484-521.

Stevenson (1990), pp. 650-675.

Sequencing

Chase (1989), pp. 678-683.

Dilworth (1989), pp. 348-352.

Gaither (1990), pp. 540-549.

Krajewski (1987), pp. 612-620.

Monks (1989), pp. 497-501, 518-519.

Stevenson (1990), pp. 664-672.

Linear Programming

Chase (1989), pp. 308-326, 336-339.

Dilworth (1989), pp. 169-172, 185-196.

Gaither (1990), pp. E1-E26, E38-E41, 549.

Krajewski (1987), pp. C1-C22, C36.

Monks (1989), pp. 166-175, 188-196, 502-503, 519-520.

Stevenson (1990), pp. 75-112, 90-103.

Line of Balance (LOB)

Gaither (1990), pp. 554-557.

Monks (1989), pp. 514-515.

Input/Output Control

Chase (1989), pp. 685-686.

Dilworth (1989), pp. 354-357.

Gaither (1990), pp. 537-538.

Krajewski (1987), pp. 547-548.

Monks (1989), pp. 515-516, 520-521.

INDEX

A

AACSB v
AFL-CIO 339
AI (artificial intelligence) 8
acceptance sampling 167,
170-179, 347, 357
accounting v-vi, 35, 281, 289,
340, 349
achievement 1, 3-4, 7, 14, 25,
29, 45-46, 48-49, 62, 148, 151-
152, 170, 205, 209, 225, 238,
242, 305
acquisition 17, 48, 280
aggregate 5, 49, 250, 260,
264-265, 266, 268, 271,
289-290, 323, 353
aggregate planning 49, 259,
261, 263, 323
    computer search 262
    goal programming 262
    linear programming 85, 96,
    154, 211, 262, 304, 342, 343,
    347, 350, 355
    management coefficients
    method 262
    parametric production
    planning 262
aggregate planning--
    mathematical models 262,
    353
aggregate planning--trial and
    error 262, 352
alpha 172-175
alternatives 62-63, 81, 197,
262, 304
Anderson, R. 15
antidumping 29, 31, 33, 36
antitrust 29, 31, 33

Apple 26
Aquilano, N. 335-355
artificial intelligence 8
Asian 7-8
assembly 30, 32, 35, 39-40, 42,
46, 66, 83-85, 96, 107, 112,
115, 130-131, 137, 143, 146,
156, 170-172, 174, 177-178,
197, 209, 226, 228, 235, 248,
252, 268, 272, 278, 288-289,
294-295, 303-304, 346
assembly chart 113
assembly line balancing
    heuristics 130, 345
automation 7-8, 112-114, 120-
121, 126, 155, 225
    levels 2, 7-8

B

balancing 5, 61, 250-261, 263,
278, 303-304, 356
Baldwin, C. 118
Barnett, J. 336, 337
Bartimo, J. 336, 337
Battle, D. 339
Beauchamp, T. 342
Bednarski, P. 336, 338
behavioral job design methods
153, 346
Bosse, M. 198-200, 291, 296, 302
Bowie, N. 342
Bradley, M. 283-284, 292-302
breakdown 61, 349
breakdown policy 179-193, 349
break-even analysis 63, 80, 96,
112, 341, 343-344
budgets 22, 153, 196, 201-205,
241-242

Bukeley, W. 336, 338
business strategies 4, 29, 30, 31-
37, 48, 59, 330-333

C

CAD (computer-aided design)
5, 226, 240, 351
CAE (computer-aided
    engineering) 226
CAM (computer-aided
    manufacturing) 226, 238,
    240, 351
CIM (computer-integrated
    manufacturing) 225-226
    computer aided design 5,
    226, 240, 351
    computer aided
    manufacturing 226, 238,
    240, 351
    cost-benefit analysis 227,
    352
    financial investment
    evaluation methods 62, 112,
    181, 227, 340, 344, 348
    flexible manufacturing
    systems 236, 238, 243, 351
    just-in-time production
    system 5, 170, 227-228, 234-
    237, 248, 281, 285-286, 290,
    298, 301, 303, 306, 310
    manufacturing resource
    planning (MRPII) 5,226-227,
    351, 355
CPM (critical path method) 5,
168, 241-242, 252. 254, 256,
352
CPM-COST CRP (apacity
CRP (capacity requirements

planning) 5, 49, 227, 259, 261, 290, 303-304, 355
camcorders 10, 27, 339
capacity requirements planning (See CRP)
capacity strategy 45, 61
carrying out 4
center of gravity method 80, 342
Champion Way 150
Champion Way in Action 150
charting 5, 46, 112-113, 130, 152-153, 171, 177-178, 241, 245, 304, 345
Chase, R. 125, 335-355
Chihuahua 16
Code of Conduct 149
coefficients 262
Colortrak 29
Compact Disclosure 13, 336-338
Compaq 26-27, 336, 338, 342, 344
compensation methods 153, 347
components 4-5, 13, 16, 46, 48, 52, 54, 96, 129, 196
computer-aided design (See CAD)
computer-aided engineering (See CAE)
computer-aided manufacturing systems (See CAM)
computer graphics 220
computer-integrated manufacturing systems (See CIM)
computer search 262
continuous 16, 110, 149, 194, 208-209, 226, 302
continuous process 111
Corporate Ethics: A Prime Business Asset 148-149, 152
corporate planning 48
corporate strategies 4, 29-36, 48
cost comparisons 80, 343
cost control 167
cost-benefit analysis 227, 352
cost standards 196, 349
cost-variance analysis 196, 349
Credo of Johnson and Johnson 149
critical path method (See CPM)
Crontner Group 336, 338

D

DRP (distribution requirements planning) 210, 215, 224-226, 228, 360
decision-tree analysis 112
decision trees 5, 46, 63, 96, 112, 341,344
decoders 30-34
Deming, W. 347
Dias, D. 305-310, 312-314
Dilworth, J. 335-355
Dinnen, S. 336, 338
distribution 5, 9, 17, 19, 22, 35-37, 41, 45, 78, 80, 168, 209-210, 216, 219, 221, 263
distribution requirements planning 210, 350
Dodson, P. 336, 338
Dorsey, J. 336-338
Dustman, J. 15, 50, 158-161

E

EOQ (economic order quality) 279
Edwards, R. 339
efficiency 47
effectiveness 47
Emerson 17
end 4
ethics vi, 8, 45-46, 51, 148-152, 342
evaluation 5, 45-46, 62-63, 112, 149, 167, 180-181, 210, 212, 226-227, 241-242, 261-262, 279, 304
events 4, 6,
excess capacity 61
experiential vi, 1, 2
exponential smoothing 63, 79
external environment 7, 48, 79, 168

F

FCFS (first-come, first-served) 304, 309-315
FMS (flexible manufacturing systems) 236, 238, 243, 351
Faber, S. 316-319
factor rating 80, 342
Fennewald, P. 339
financial investment evaluation methods 62, 112, 181, 227, 340, 344, 348
financial resources 47
first-come, first-served (FCFS) 304, 309-310
Fisher 17
Fitch, C. 81
flexible manufacturing systems (See FMS)
flow 4
Forbes, J. 336, 338
forecasting 5, 25, 45, 62-63, 79, 278, 289
forecasting methods 63, 341-342
Foster, G. 349
Frank, A. 336, 338
French, W. 4, 24, 335, 346
functional activities 5
functional management 47
functional strategies 4, 48, 49

G

GNP (Gross National Product) 3
Gaither, N. 335-355
Gantt chart 241
Gardner L. 201, 203-208
global vi, 2, 8, 13, 18, 22, 25-26, 152, 198, 201, 205, 225, 260
goal 4, 7
goal programming 262
Goldstar 23
grand strategies 4, 30-36, 48
Grape, G. 15, 23, 25-37,
graphics, computer 226
Gray, J. 81
Greenhouse, S. 336

H

HDTV 9, 28, 335
Hall, D. 81
Heerding, D. 81
Heerding, M. 81
Helberg, J. 264-267
Hendricks, M. 339
heuristic methods 130
Higgins, J. 340
High-Definition Television (See HDTV)
Hillkirk, J. 339
Hitachi 34, 81
Holden, T. 336, 338
Holton, L. 336, 338
Horngren, C. 349
human resource strategy 47, 147-166, 346
    Champion Way 150
    Champion Way in Action 150
    Corporate Ethics: A Prime Business Asset 148-149, 152
    Code of Conduct 149
    job design 148
    job enlargement 153
    job enrichment 153
    job rotation 153
    manpower planning 147
    productivity 147-148, 150, 224
    profit sharing 154
    time-based compensation method 153
    time study 153
    work measurement methods 148, 153, 346
    work methods analysis 148, 152, 346
    work sampling 153
    worker-machine chart 152
Hutchens, C. 18

I

IBM 27, 32-33, 41, 336, 338
input/output control 5, 305, 355
inputs 5, 87, 160, 215, 265, 294, 308-310
insufficient capacity 61
integrated systems 8, 168, 225
Intel 14, 41
Inteq 17
interrelated 4
inventory control 259, 323
    economic order quality 279
    lot-sizing techniques 279, 353
    order point, safety stock, and service level 279, 354
    simulation 1-2, 8, 176-177, 180, 271-272, 279-280, 348, 354

J

JIT (just-in-time production system) 5, 170, 227-228, 234-237 248, 281, 285-286, 290, 298, 301, 303, 306, 310
JVC 81

Japan 7-8, 18-19, 28-30. 40, 43, 63, 234, 340, 348
job design 148
job enlargement 153
job enrichment 153
job rotation 153
job-shop process 111
Johnson, H. 340
Johnson rule 303, 305-306, 308
Juarez 24, 70, 83
just-in-time production system (See JIT)

K

kanban 227
Kaplan, R. 340
Kemper, D. 216-218
Kemper, R. 17-19, 50-51, 82, 158
Keough, J. 148-152 (See *Corporate Ethics: A Prime Business Asset*)
Knoedelseder, W. 336, 338
Korea 9-10, 23, 87
Kotobuki 81
Krajewski, L. 335-355

L

LOB (line of balance) 303-304, 355
layout strategy 46, 129
learning curves 153, 197, 347, 349
Ledvinka, J. 346
Lehrer, C.M. 338
levels of automation 2, 7-8
Levine, J. 336, 338
line of balance (LOB) 303-304, 355
linear decision rule method 262
linear programming 85, 96, 154, 211, 262, 304, 342, 343, 347, 350, 355
linear regression 63, 79
Lloyds 17
location strategy 45, 78
lot-sizing techniques 279, 353
learning curves 153, 197, 347, 349

M

MPS (master production scheduling) 261-263, 272-275, 289-290, 305
MRP (materials requirements planning) 5, 49, 210, 227, 248-249, 251, 259, 261, 264, 290-292, 294-301, 303, 355
MRPII (manufacturing resource planning) 5, 226-227, 351, 355
Madrid, T. 40-43, 49, 157, 265-267
Magana, L. 81
Magnavox 9, 81
Mahnken, D. 339-340
maintenance strategies 167
make-or-buy 5, 45, 62-63, 96-97, 102, 210-211, 342, 344, 351

management 3
management coefficients method 262
manpower planning 147
manufacturing resource planning (MRPII) (See MRPII)
marginal analysis (single-period inventory) 210, 344
Marion, Indiana 78
Martinez, P. 81
master production scheduling (See MPS)
Matamoros 16, 70
materials 4, 111, 152, 205, 210-212, 225-227, 259, 278, 289-291, 298, 305, 355
materials requirements planning (See MRP)
matrix 241
Matushita 70, 81
maxi 61
McAuliffe, M. 18
measurement 25, 46, 48, 62, 148, 151-153, 195-196, 346
Mexico 9, 16-18, 28-29, 32-35, 40, 70, 90, 228, 248-255, 300-301, 304-306, 335,
microcom 16-17, 29-30, 32-33, 35
microcomputers 10, 25-26, 30-31, 33, 35, 40
Mintzberg, H. 14
mission 7, 10, 13, 14-16, 39, 41-42
Mitsubishi 23, 34
models 2, 3, 5, 7, 13, 62, 131, 180, 262, 267, 304-305, 340, 357
analytical model 278
mathematical model 262, 353
OM model 6
queuing model 180
simulation model 279
waiting-line models 131, 180
Monks, J. 335-355
Monte Carlo simulation 180-184, 286-287
Moore, P. 336, 338
Morano, M. 306-309
motion study techniques 148
multi-activity chart 153
multinational vi, 321 (See also global)

N

NAD 81
NEC 23, 81
Nathan, R. 335
natural resources 47

O

objectives 7
Olufsen 81
operational planning 48
operational strategy 49
operations 3
operations budget 196
operations control 4
operations strategy 48
opportunities 15, 22, 55, 77, 95,

110-111, 323-324
optimal aggregate plan 264-265
optimal capacity strategy 61
optimal inventory control 210
optimal preventative maintenance policy 181
optimal product mix 96, 106, 279, 303, 305, 308
optimal shipping schedule 211
optimal sequencing 306, 309
optimal solution 304
order point, safety stock, and service level 279, 354
organizing vi, 3, 47
Ouchi, W. 347
output 5, 48, 61, 148, 153, 171, 180, 210, 259-262, 303-304, 355
output-based compensation 153
overcapacity 61-62
overhead 180, 195-196, 202
overloads 272, 274
overstocked 291
overtime 262-263, 268, 289-290, 305

P

PERT (program review and evaluation technique) 4-5, 168, 241-242, 248, 252, 254-256, 352
PERT-COST 242
Palmer, J. 336
Panasonic 81
parametric production planning 262
payoff tables 62, 97, 112, 181, 211, 341, 343-344, 349, 350
personnel 46, 147, 151, 335, 346
human resource strategy 47, 147-166, 346
pF capacitor 174
Philco 9, 22, 81
Philips 63, 81
planning v, 3, 5, 8
functional 4-5, 47 48, 49
operational 48-49
strategic 48
tactical programming 49
Poe, J. 212-215
policies 7
Potts, M. 7, 335, 338
predetermined time standards 153
preventative maintenance 181, 348
procedures vi, 2, 4, 7, 15
process 4
process chart 113, 153
process control 171, 348
process layout analysis techniques 130, 345
process planning charts 113, 345
process strategy 46, 111
product 4
product choice 112
product strategy 45, 95
production and operations management 3
program evaluation and review technique (See PERT)

programming 5
  linear 85, 96, 154, 211, 262,
    304, 342, 343, 347, 350, 355
  optimal aggregate plan 264-
    265
  optimal inventory control
    210
  optimal preventative
    maintenance policy 181
  optimal shipping schedule
    211
  optimal sequencing 306, 309
  optimal solution 304
programs 5
  tactical 49
purpose 4, 8

Q

quality 3, 5
quality assurance 49, 167, 169,
  178, 347
quality circles 170
Quasar 9
queuing model 179

R

RCA 9, 17, 22, 29-30, 33, 81
RRP (resource requirements
  planning) 289, 294
Rayburn, L. 349
regression, linear 63, 79
rejects 169, 171-172, 178
reliability 29-33, 169, 226-227,
  243
reorder point 279
repetitive process 105
resources v-vi, 2, 5, 7-8, 15, 288-
  289, 322
resource requirements
  planning (See RRP)
Ritzman, L. 335-355
robotics 7, 124-128
Rodriguez, J. 81
rough-cut capacity planning
  262, 353
rule 4, 130, 262, 291, 304-305,
  307-309, 310, 312
  Johnson's 304, 306-307, 309
  linear decision 262
  simple-rule heuristic method
    130
Ryan, E. 340

S

SWOT 25, 329, 347
  opportunities 22, 94, 110-111,
    322-323
  strengths 15, 19, 22-23, 54,
    95, 112, 324, 328
  threats 22, 55, 95, 111, 324
  weaknesses 15, 19, 22-23, 54,
    74, 112, 324, 328-329
safety stock 219, 259, 278, 283-
  288, 354
Samsung 23, 81
Sansui 81
Sanyo 17, 28-29, 81, 104, 336,
  338
Scarpello, V. 346
schedule 4, 41, 147, 170, 192-

193, 211, 242, 261, 263, 272,
  280, 288-290, 302-305
scheduler 305-306, 310
Scheier, R. 336-338
Schlumberger 36
sequencing 210, 260, 304, 309,
  311-314, 355
  first-come, first-served
    (FCFS) 304, 309-310
Seto, B. 337-338
Sherman Antitrust, 33
shop floor control activities
  260, 297, 317
Simplex 5, 80, 85, 96, 106, 154,
  211, 262, 304
simulation 1-2, 8, 176-177, 180,
  271-272, 279-280, 348, 354
  Monte Carlo simulation 180,
    183-184, 286-287
single-period inventory 210
Slutsker, G. 337-338
Sony 28, 104, 109, 210, 337-338,
  345
spotter 81
standardization 96, 167, 196-
  197, 252-256, 294, 297
standard 5, 29, 41-42, 47-48,
  148-149, 167, 170, 196, 349
  work measurement 148, 153,
    346
statistical process control 171
statistics v
Stevenson, W. 335-355
stockouts 268, 279, 283-288, 291,
  294
strategic plans 48
strategies 4,-7, 12-15, 17, 23, 25,
  29-37, 47-49, 51, 94, 166,
  168, 258, 261, 267, 269,
  325-326
  business strategies 4, 29, 30,
    31-37, 48, 59, 330-333
  corporate strategies 4, 29-36,
    48
  functional strategies 4, 48, 49
  grand strategies 4, 30-36, 48
  maintenance 63
strategy 4
strategy system 48
strengths 15, 19, 22-23, 54, 95,
  112, 324, 328
suppliers 7-9, 13, 29, 97, 149,
  211, 227, 236, 277-278, 323,
  328
Sylvania 81
"System 3" 29-30
system 4
systematic layout planning 130,
  345

T

tactical core activities 49
tactical core operations 5
tactical programming 49
tactical support operations 5,
  332
Taiwan 23, 35, 38-39, 46
Tandy 26, 337-338
targets 7, 25, 61, 74, 129, 170,
  263, 268
task 49, 61, 88, 147, 152-154,
  167, 197, 211-212, 245, 248,
  252, 259

Tatung 81
techniques 5
technology 7
  learning curves 153, 197,
    347, 349
  lot-sizing techniques 279,
    353
Teinowitz, I. 339
Teknika 81
Therrien, L. 337, 339
Thompson 81
threats 22, 55, 95, 111, 324
tier distribution system 29, 33
Tijuana 70
time-based compensation
  method 153
time study 153
Toshiba 23, 70, 81, 342, 344
transportation 209-210, 261
transportation method of
  linear programming 80
Trinitron 28

U

uncertainty 227, 242
undercapacity 61
underloads 272-274

V

VCR 16, 33-34, 39, 342, 345
VHS 342-343, 345
value analysis 180, 196, 205, 349
  actual values 195
  standard values 195
vendor selection systems 210,
  350
Vincze, J. 340

W

waiting line models 131, 180
waiting lines 56, 62, 129-131,
  180, 346, 348
Walkman 28
Ward, S. 340
weaknesses 15, 19, 22-23, 54, 74,
  94, 112, 324, 328-329
Whall, L. 340
Wiegner, K. 337, 339
work measurement methods
  148, 153, 346
work methods analysis 148,
  152, 346
work sampling 153
worker-machine chart 152
Wright, C. 81
Wunsch, M. 18
Wysk, R. 18

Y

Yamaha 81
Ying, Calvin 268-271

Z

Zenith 10, 210, 337, 339-340